BY *DAVE SCOTT* WITH *LIZ BARRETT*

DAVE SCOTT'S

TRIATHLON TRAINING

A FIRESIDE BOOK PUBLISHED BY SIMON & SCHUSTER

NEW YORK   LONDON   TORONTO   SYDNEY   TOKYO   SINGAPORE

Unless otherwise indicated, the photographs in this book are
copyrighted in the name of Dave Epperson, and are used by permission.

Rockefeller Center
1230 Avenue of the Americas
New York, New York 10020

FIRESIDE and colophon are registered trademarks of Simon & Schuster, Inc.

Designed by Bonni Leon

Manufactured in the United States of America

20

Library of Congress Cataloging in Publication Data

Scott, Dave.
    Dave Scott's triathlon training.

    "A Fireside book."
    Includes index.
    1. Triathlon—Training.   I. Barrett, Liz.   II. Title.
III. Title: Triathlon training.
    GV1060.7.S38   1986   796.4′07   86-9996
    ISBN: 0-671-60473-2

CONTENTS

Foreword by Liz Barrett   9

1   In the Beginning:
An Introduction to Triathlons   13

2   Physiology for Triathletes   21

3   Swimming   30

4   Cycling   54

5   Running   75

6   A Plan for All Seasons:
Year-Round Triathlon Training
Program   88

7   Weight Training and Stretching   136

8   Dave Scott's Racing Secrets   182

9   You Are What You Eat:
A Champion's Diet   208

10   Hindsight   229

Appendix A: Dave Scott's Triathlon
Record   235

Appendix B: Where to Swim   237

Appendix C: Triathlon Clubs and
Organizations   238

Index   247

ACKNOWLEDGMENTS

This book is about perseverance, a quality Webster's New 20th-Century dictionary defines as "the ability to steadfastly pursue any design or course once begun." It takes a great deal of perseverance to train and compete in triathlons—but I never imagined how much it would take to write a book about it!

A few days before my wedding, I sat in my kitchen at 4:00 in the morning, dictating hundreds of pages of notes about vitamins and minerals into a tape recorder. Those solitary all-night sessions could have made me feel alone, but there were a few other people who persevered right along with me—all the way to the end.

My wife Anna was patient and supportive throughout the project, even during the most hectic stages of pre-wedding plans. My parents—Verne and Dorothy—provided not only moral support, but research and information as well. My sisters Jane and Patti, and my brother-in-law Rick Baier, cheered me up and prodded me along.

Linda Allen sat endlessly at my typewriter, transcribing dozens of tapes that eventually became a manuscript. David Epperson's photographs reflect his synthesis of artistic talent and technical expertise. Bud Light and Centurion provided material assistance.

Pat Feeney is my faithful friend and mechanic, whose attention to details lightened my load considerably. And my friend Mike Norton started this whole thing by talking me into doing the Ironman the very first time, and nudging me along ever since.

Finally, I thank Liz Barrett for countless patient hours through many crises, near-misses, and extended deadlines. Our mutual sense of humor carried us both through this enormous endurance event.

"Don't give up on me—I haven't even put on my running shoes yet!"

FOREWORD

The first time I saw Dave Scott, it was through a broken blood vessel in my eye. The injury had occurred as I rode across the Ironman Triathlon's infernal 112-mile bicycle course in a cramped press vehicle; I was tired, thirsty, and sunburned. It was extremely difficult to imagine why anyone would voluntarily pedal across that lava oven for five or six hours. We had passed about a hundred cyclists on their way out to the turnaround point at the tiny town of Hawi when we finally caught our first glance of Dave—going the opposite direction. He was more than 20 minutes ahead of his closest competitor in a field that featured the best triathletes in the world. Unlike myself, he looked fresh, relaxed, and determined.

A California fitness magazine had flown me to Hawaii's Kona Coast to cover the October 1982 spectacle, but there was really no story to tell. Dave Scott made his second Ironman victory look easy. He simply jumped into the water, swam faster than everyone else, then biked faster than everyone else and ran faster than everyone else—all day long. No one ever got close enough to him to even fantasize about catching up. He swam 2.4 miles, cycled 112, and ran a marathon in nine hours, eight minutes, 32 seconds. To me, and to many of his competitors, it seemed that the triathlon world was divided into two groups: Dave Scott and everybody else.

Two weeks later, I ran into him again at a race in Malibu Beach, California. The Pacific Ocean registered a bone-chilling 56 degrees and the previous night's rain had flooded part of the bike course; Dave was glad he would be sitting that race out. As other triathletes came over to say hello or congratulate him on his second Ironman victory, Dave smiled and cracked jokes and wished them luck. Few of them had any idea that he had already been up for nearly four hours setting up course markers and trying to figure out how to get the water off the road so the race would be safe for competitors.

His eyes were bloodshot when the starting gun went off—he was obviously tired—but when Dean Harper came staggering onto the beach, dazed from hypothermia, Dave rushed to his side to help him. I followed them to Dean's bike, where the race director warned Dave that Dean would be disqualified if he received any further assistance. That was the first time I heard Dave shout.

"That's ridiculous!" he said. "The guy's freezing. If you're not going to let anybody help him, get him a doctor!"

I stood back, scribbling furiously in my reporter's notepad. It was going to be a long day. A constant drizzle discouraged spectators, and I knew I would have given up and gone home if my job hadn't depended on it. But Dave stayed there all day, through the rain and the countless flub-ups, cheering on the few triathletes who survived the cold swim and finished the race.

A year later, after a long season flawed by personal problems and an extended slump, triathlon's "Mr. October" beat the odds—and all of his skeptical opponents—to win a third Ironman crown. He had been smothered with media attention for 12 months; the press didn't seem to know or care whether any other triathlons or triathletes existed. When Dave crossed the 1983 Ironman finish line utterly exhausted—and just 33 seconds ahead of second-place Scott Tinley—reporters had a field day. They were so busy snapping photographs of the winner that they barely noticed the guy right behind him.

But Dave didn't overlook Tinley's magnificent performance. At the awards dinner, when the spotlight was reserved for him, he told the crowd that it had been Tinley's superb race that had pushed him to his own victory. Dave's modesty wasn't false; to this day he claims he doesn't know how he ever won that race. Just to compete at that time in his life had been a huge emotional drain, but he had found the energy to share his limelight with the man who almost took it away from him.

By that time, I had become a shameless admirer. I had tried rooting for various underdogs and I had many friends in the sport, but there was something very special about Dave Scott, something beyond athletic prowess. Like everyone else who competed against him or wrote magazine articles about him, I tried many times to figure out what made him tick, what made him so different from his peers. I understood that he had training down to a science, and I knew that he could concentrate like a Zen monk, so I could see how he won races. But what was it about him that was so extraordinary?

Reporters had been asking that question for months after Dave's third Ironman victory in 1983. A few days before the 1984 race, I asked Rick Gaffney, one of the press coordinators, what he thought about the "invincible Ironman."

"I really couldn't tell you anything you don't already know," he said, as we drove along Alii Drive in a rental car. "But I will say this much: I've dealt with thousands of athletes here, and we've had a few winners. But Dave Scott is more than a winner; he's a true champion."

I thought about that for the next few days. There had been a lot of pre-race speculation that Dave would be no match for younger, hungrier athletes such as Mark Allen, who had won every race he entered during the season. Dave wouldn't participate in the guessing game. He just said that Mark was a fine athlete and that it would be a long day.

On race morning, Dave had his share of problems, including a several-minute fumble with cycling gloves that was resolved by riding the 112 miles bare-handed. Mark Allen practically flew his bike over the course, widening his lead over Dave by more than 11 minutes with about 30 miles to go. Reporters were already calling it Mark's race. At that point, our press vehicle pulled up beside Dave. He later told us we looked absolutely forlorn, but at the time, he simply peered into the car and tried to cheer us up.

"Don't give up on me," he smiled. "I haven't even put on my running shoes yet."

I sat back in my seat and savored a deep sigh of relief. I had no way of knowing that he would win the race by a huge margin, but I was absolutely certain he would have his best race possible. Right then I knew why Dave Scott is such a champion: I have seen him finish first and I have seen him come in ninth, but I have never seen him *lose*.

If that attitude can be learned, this book is definitely the place to start. Working with him to share his knowledge has been a rare pleasure.

Liz Barrett
Walnut Creek, California

TRIATHLON TRAINING

1 IN THE BEGINNING: AN INTRODUCTION TO TRIATHLONS

When I competed in my first triathlon in 1975, I never dreamed I would still be at it more than 10 years later. My family and I had driven 60 miles so my sister could compete in a race in San Francisco. I didn't know the first thing about triathlons, but I knew that cycling was the first event in that particular race. I had agreed to ride along with Patti so that she could draft me. I didn't really know what drafting was, but I figured if she kept her front wheel right behind my rear wheel she would be in my slipstream and it would allow her to pedal a little easier.

I was out there in tennis shoes and shorts with my old 10-speed Raleigh; I have never believed that an outfit makes an athlete. When

I have refined my training and racing techniques since my first Ironman Triathlon (1980). Courtesy of Scott Enterprises.

I saw a group of skinny-looking guys in slick, black tights and cleated cycling shoes, I thought, "Who are these peacocks kidding? They look ridiculous; I bet they can't even work out."

Once the race started, though, I was right out there in the midst of all the shiny shorts and cleated shoes, pedaling like mad. I guess I got caught up in the competition, because it seemed like no time until I realized I had dropped Patti altogether, and I was in third position by the end of the bike race.

I don't know how all those peacocks felt, but my legs were killing me. I had never planned on doing the run, because my knee was injured and sore, but when I saw my father cheering me on from the side of the road, I decided to keep on going.

I was going totally on instinct—I had no specific triathlon training—but I wanted to see what I could do. I figured I could lumber through the 4-mile run and I knew I could handle the swim, so I took off running in my sneakers. I have to admit that a few people passed me, despite my objection to their fancy outfits, and I was down to 10th place by the time I jumped into the freezing-cold bay. I was four or five minutes behind the leader, a modern pentathlete from the national team. Needless to say, I didn't win the race, but I narrowed the gap between us down to about 30 seconds, and finished the race in second place.

I had never competed in cycling and running before (I was a competitive swimmer) and I had no idea how well I could do in triathlons—but I was itching to find out. Triathlons were a rare commodity in those days, so I competed in as many run/swim biathlons as I could find.

Three years later—September 1978—I was in Hawaii for the Waikiki Rough Water Swim, a 2.4-mile race in the warm, blue Pacific Ocean. Swimming in open water was particularly pleasurable for me, not just because of the beauty of the tropics, but because I could beat swimmers who used to pass me in the pool. Some of them had just gotten out of shape, I suppose, but I also suspect that I may have been better suited to a mile in the ocean than a 1,650-yard race in a pool. I like the challenge of racing in a natural environment; I like swimming where there's no pace clock, no flip turns, and no lane lines.

I especially liked the race in Hawaii; the water was warm and I felt confident. At the pre-race meeting, a tall, lanky, rather unathletic-looking man approached me with a grin on his face. He was promoting a race he had finished the previous January—the Ironman Triathlon.

It was a 2.4-mile swim in Waikiki, a 112-mile bicycle race around Oahu, and a marathon run. Twelve men had done it that first time. I guess he figured I might be game for it because I had won the Waikiki swim in 1976 and 1977.

"You'd be a good candidate for this, Dave," he said, handing me a printed announcement. "What do you think?"

What I thought was that only somebody from the nut farm would do something like that.

"That's quite a workout," I said with a straight face. My honest reaction was utter disbelief. Even though I had done the swim, I couldn't envision the other two events. It might be possible for me to cycle 112 miles, I thought, but run a marathon? That was out of the question.

Then he told me they did all three events in one day. That did it. I decided this guy was some kind of lunatic. I just couldn't believe he had done that race. It turned out that he was John Collins, the Navy commander who had invented the race with some of his buddies after a few too many beers. I knew no one would have dreamed it up sober.

As soon as I got back to California, I threw his advertisement away. But his event stuck in my mind. Here was a race that wasn't a race—it was one long workout. The winner that year had done it in around 11 hours, and the longest I had ever sustained a workout was about 5.

From the age of 13 I had taken pride in being a "workout king"; I hadn't been born with the natural ability to swim, but I wanted to be the best at it, anyway, so I swam until it hurt then went back for more. As an adult, I was working 55 hours a week as a Masters swim coach, swimming 7,000 yards a day, lifting weights one or two hours every day, and running 30 to 35 miles a week. I honestly believed I could outpersevere anyone. But this Ironman Triathlon seemed ludicrous, even to me.

How did that guy do it? I kept asking myself. I wondered what it would take for me to get in shape to do it.

Finally it came down to my ego. If someone else could do it, I could do it. My friend Mike Norton—a runner who shared my obsession with perseverence—persisted in discussing the race with me, going over clippings from *Sports Illustrated* that gave inspirational little details such as finishers' split times.

"Look, I know you've never run a marathon," he told me after the February 1979 Ironman, "but Tom Warren [the winner that year] ran it in three hours and fifty-one minutes; I know you can do it a lot faster than that."

In June, with just over six months before the 1980 race, I finally made a commitment to compete in the Ironman.

I didn't change my swim training, but I knew I'd have to really work on cycling and running. I started riding as far as the dam at Lake Berryessa, a grand total of 43 miles round-trip. (A couple of years later, I would be riding twice that distance as a matter of daily routine.)

I ran my first marathon in September, and I kept waiting to "hit the wall" like all the running magazines said I would. But it never happened; maybe all my cross-training had paid off better than I expected. I felt fresher at mile 20 than I had all day, and I took an almost perverse pleasure in picking off other runners one by one. I finished in 2 hours and 45 minutes, 33d place.

At the end of October, I decided to try a simulated Ironman to find out how I would react to that level of fatigue. First I swam 5,000 yards in the pool, then I rode about 110 miles—fast. My legs were on fire, throbbing and burning inside. I had never felt that kind of aching before. I couldn't even walk without pain, but I knew I would have to make that same transition in Hawaii, so I figured I better know what to expect.

I discovered that fatigue doesn't affect just your body, it tends to wreak a little havoc with your temperament as well. I barked orders at my family and snarled as I put on my running shoes.

I guess it doesn't pay to alienate your pit crew, because I ran at least eight miles without water before I realized that my friends had apparently found better things to do than stand out in the blazing heat to hand me drinks. By the time I had run 10 miles, I was getting light-headed and angry. The test had become real. I really didn't know if I could even get back to town, if I could finish this stupid training exercise.

Six more miles down the road, I saw my parents drive up with water for me. I drank a little and yelled a lot and eventually started feeling better. For the last couple of miles, I actually started feeling light on my feet. I was back in town, I knew the end was near, but most of all I knew that it was no longer a matter of trying to finish the Ironman, it had become a question of how fast I could do it. Suddenly I didn't care how tired I was, I felt strong.

That mental strength became one of my most reliable resources. Being mentally and emotionally prepared for a race is as important as being physically in shape. Though I wouldn't recommend a simulated Ironman as a required training exercise, it is good to incorporate mini-triathlons into your training, increasing the distances and decreasing the transition times as you progress. I learned some extremely valuable lessons during my simulated Ironman. I found out what to expect—from my body, my mind, my vocal cords—when I pushed myself to the limit demanded by the race I would be running.

One of the weaknesses many triathletes have is that they have never put out maximum physical and mental efforts in training, so when they do it in a race, they lose control of themselves. They become victims of their own lack of preparation, much like an actor who gives a performance without a dress rehearsal.

The most important thing you can learn about training for a triathlon is to simulate race conditions as closely as possible. No one wants to crawl across a finish line or be carted off a course on a stretcher; train yourself in advance to deal with the discomfort and fatigue you'll experience when you race. This book will teach you how to do that.

There is a difference between being fatigued and losing control. When I crossed the Ironman finish line in 1983, with my head tilting back and my knees about to curl up under me, I was so exhausted I couldn't even lift my hand to wave to the crowd without throwing myself off balance. But I remember telling myself, Forget the crowd pleasers, put your hand back down and just finish the race. I still had enough control to make that critical choice.

* * *

From the time I crossed my first Ironman finish line in 1980, I wanted to find out the upper limit of my ability. At that race, I watched second-place Chuck Newman come in an hour behind me. He looked like he was ready—and practically willing—to roll over and die. The television crew zoomed in, focusing on Newman's eyes as they rolled back in his head.

"Do you think you'll do [the Ironman] again?" they asked him. He reeled backward, and struggled to gain enough composure to answer.

"No way in Hell," he said. I felt just the opposite. I was ready to do it all over again—I wanted to try to perfect my performance.

In this brand-new sport, however, there were no training formulae; you had to figure it out for yourself. There were no clinics, no coaches, no books. It took several years—and thousands of training miles—to develop an efficient, scientifically sound training program that produces the best possible results for the least possible effort.

I started with the basic belief that there are no shortcuts, no magic secrets to athletic performance. You can buy a thousand self-hypnosis cassettes and take a million milligrams of

I nearly collapsed from exhaustion at the 1983 Ironman—*after* I crossed the finish line.

energy-producing herbs, but none of it will ever make up for a lack of physical preparation. It seemed obvious to me that the first step in improving my triathlon performance was to develop a keen understanding of the raw material I was working with—my own body.

I had studied exercise physiology in college, so I already had an idea that my muscle fiber balance was naturally better suited to long, sustained activity than to short bursts. I knew that I had more red (aerobic/endurance) than white (anaerobic/speed) fibers. Eventually I learned how to specifically "train" my rarer white fibers to "breathe" better so that I could do faster work for a longer period of time without tiring.

You can learn that too. You can train your body to adapt to any distance, but first you have to know what your genetic tendencies are. Chapter 2, "Physiology For Triathletes," will discuss your heart, your energy systems, your muscle fiber balance, and how all of it is affected by triathlon training.

Chapter 6, "A Year-Round Triathlon Training Plan," will show you how to train properly. How far should you be going? How should you determine the intensity of your workouts? How often should you swim, cycle, and run? Too many people lose momentum because they can't answer those kinds of questions— they don't know *how* to improve.

I know from my years as a Masters swim coach that a comprehensive training program starts with a technique period, during which you work on your skills. But every phase of improvement during training goes hand in hand. As your endurance and strength increase, your technique changes a little bit. If you devote all your time to technique in the beginning, your efficiency will improve very slowly. But if you incorporate other training, such as interval work and distance training, you will be much stronger and your technique will automatically come around.

One of the most important things to understand about triathlon training and technique is that you are dealing with one sport which is made up of three interrelated components; you are not dealing with three separate sports. Your considerations must be different from those of a swimmer, runner, or cyclist who doesn't have to save any energy for two more events. That's why my triathlon technique is specially adapted for maximum efficiency over the entire race. In Chapters 3, 4, and 5 ("Swimming," "Cycling," and "Running"), you will learn the fine points of technique for the three sports as it applies specifically to triathlon training and racing.

I *always* think about technique when I train as well as when I race. Reporters continually ask me what I think about during a long, hard race. If there are psychological tricks that somehow distract a triathlete from weariness and discomfort, I don't use them. I think about one thing: *what I am doing*. I think about the way I am holding my head, the sound of my feet hitting the ground, any clues that might help me maintain (or regain) winning form. I also think about the people I see around me, especially if one of them passes me!

Don't underestimate the value of a psychological edge; it can really help you in a race. But the best psychological advantage you can have is the knowledge that you are physically prepared for any obstacles you might encounter. In Chapter 8, "Dave Scott's Racing Secrets," we'll talk about some methods of using your physical preparedness to psych out your opponents.

There is something else that can't go unsaid: You can be the greatest textbook athlete in the world, but if you don't have a total program, you're still going to be limited. You need to build your strength and flexibility with weight training and stretching (Chapter 6), and you need to eat right (Chapter 9). Every individual has his or her own tastes—and maybe allergies—but I can offer what I consider to be an optimum diet for health as well as for triathlete performance. I know it works for me, and most importantly, I know *why* it works.

Every aspect of triathlon training has to be

I always think about technique when I train and race.

customized and adapted to each individual. You can't be a copycat, keying off of other people, or you'll never learn your own cues. The same is true for racing. I never look over my shoulder. I know as soon as I start basing my performance on what someone else is doing, I have lost my own race.

Every athlete develops his or her own strategy and tactics, but I think I can offer some tips from my experience to help you form your own game plan. After all of the miles I have put in on the road and in the pool, I finally have the chance to share my "secrets."

2 PHYSIOLOGY FOR TRIATHLETES

Think back, for a moment, to your school days. The contrast between typical physics students and physical education students would have led the average observer to believe that the two disciplines were worlds apart. But now an entire area of science—*biomechanics*—deals specifically with the physics of the human body in motion. And virtually every successful athletic technique is based—knowingly or not—on a scientific or natural law.

Let's look at Newton's most famous law of physics: For every action there is an equal and opposite reaction. One of the ways this law is manifested in the human body is that there are actually sets of muscles which are *antagonistic*—every time one contracts, it causes the

A sound training program starts with all the vital information. Here, a triathlete takes a lab test to determine his maximum oxygen uptake during exercise (VO$_2$ max).

other to stretch. In his book *Sportscience* (Simon & Schuster, 1984), physicist Peter J. Brancazio uses your *triceps* (the large muscle on the back of your upper arm) and your *biceps* (on the front) as an example of this law.

Here's how it works: Hold a 10-pound dumbbell in your hand and lift it by bending your arm at the elbow—a *curl*. Since your triceps and biceps are actually attached to opposite sides of your lower arm near your elbow, your biceps stretches as your triceps contracts to extend (straighten) your lower arm. Likewise, your triceps stretches when your biceps contracts to flex (bend) your arm.

But there's more than Newton's law to the science of being a triathlete. You need to know how the human body functions—how blood is circulated throughout your body, how oxygen

is transported to your muscles, how food turns into energy, how your muscles generate force, how your heart works.

To be the best triathlete you can be, you have to become your own scientist. When I first started competing as a triathlete, I had no idea how to develop an ideal training program, nor did my peers. Those of us who studied about our bodies, tried new approaches to training, and changed our diets to turn our daily bread into fuel went on to excel in the sport and to reach heights of human endurance that were once thought impossible. Those who clung to old ideas and shunned the concept of total fitness—total health—were left behind.

Don't skim over this chapter just because it seems complicated or technical at first. As you progress, it will make more sense to you and you will apply it to your daily training efforts. If you want to enjoy competing in triathlons with the least discomfort and the greatest efficiency, you need to know the inside of your body like the back of your hand. That includes discovering whether you have more fast-twitch than slow-twitch muscle fibers, taking and recording your resting pulse (and knowing what that means to you in terms of performance), determining your maximum oxygen intake, and learning how to increase it.

So do as the very best triathletes do—become an expert about yourself!

THE HEART OF THE MATTER

Let's talk about "resting pulse." The theory is that the more fit you are, the bigger and stronger your heart is, and the more blood it can pump on each beat. And if it can pump more each beat, it obviously needs to beat fewer times in order to serve its purpose. One popular notion is that the slower your heart beats, the more fit you must be.

Maybe yes and maybe no. Consider my own example. The average resting pulse for a 25-year-old male is about 65 to 70 beats per minute; when I was around that age, mine was 46. I was in college at the time, dozing off in the back of the class, so I'm not sure if the timing of the measurement was exactly scientific.

Many factors enter into any physiological measurement; you have to understand your own genetic makeup before you compare yourself to someone else. Knowing that my resting pulse was 20 beats slower than the statistical average at age 25 wasn't as important to me as knowing that it dropped down 10 more beats (to 36) after several years of triathlon training.

As a triathlete, you must be concerned with subjective measurements—how long it takes your heart to return to its own normal pulse after strenuous exercise, for instance. The most basic measurement you'll need is your *heart rate,* or pulse. Always take your pulse first thing in the morning, before you get out of bed. (We'll talk about monitoring your heart rate during exercise in Chapter 6.)

Your pulse can be felt over any sizeable artery in your head, neck, or limbs. The most common way of measuring your pulse is by placing your thumb firmly over the artery in your wrist. However, many people have trouble finding it there; it is often easier to feel it on the artery just below your jaw (on the side of your neck). Where you take it doesn't matter.

Once you have found your pulse, you need to count the number of times it beats per minute. With your thumb on your pulsating artery, set your stopwatch at zero (or wait until the second hand of your watch or clock is at 12). Then count the number of beats for 15 seconds. Multiply that by 4 (4 × 15 seconds = 60 seconds, or 1 minute) to get your heart rate. If you counted 16 beats, your heart rate is 64 (16 × 4 = 64). Average adult heart rates at rest (or moderate physical activity) vary from 60 to 80; as you become more aerobically fit, your heart functions will improve and your resting pulse may slow down considerably.

To figure your *maximum heart rate,* subtract your age from 220. For example, if you are 28 years old, your maximum heart rate is 192 (220 − 28 = 192). You will use that figure as a guideline when you monitor your exertion in training. (See Chapter 6.)

Stroke volume is the amount of blood that is pumped with each beat. It is measured in milliliters, with the statistical average between 70 and 100 milliliters per beat at rest. (This measurement must be taken in a lab.) As you do more aerobic training, your stroke volume should increase. That's where slow resting pulse comes in as a factor in cardiovascular fitness—if your stroke volume goes up, your heart doesn't have to work as hard.

Cardiac output is the amount of blood pumped per minute. That probably won't change much with training. Your heart has to pump a certain amount of blood, and if the stroke volume increases and the heart rate decreases proportionately, the cardiac output is still the same.

The exact measurement is figured by multiplying your stroke volume (milliliters per beat) by heart rate (beats per minute). For example, if your stroke volume is 85 milliliters per heartbeat and your heart rate is 64 beats per minute, your cardiac output is 5,440 milliliters per minute ($85 \times 64 = 5,440$).

How much blood your heart needs to pump depends on your body size, your level of fitness, your sex, your age, and other health factors.

But what does blood have to do with your ability to perform as a triathlete? Your ability to endure prolonged periods of aerobic exercise depends to a great extent upon the amount of oxygen that can be delivered—via your blood—to your muscle tissues.

THE OXYGEN DELIVERY ROUTE

When you take a breath, the oxygen you inhale is transported to your tissues through a sequence of physiological responses:

1 The air is ventilated (moves in, then out) through your lungs.
2 The oxygen is diffused from your lungs to your blood.
3 Your blood "picks up" the oxygen (this depends upon the amount of hemoglobin in your blood).
4 Your heart pumps the oxygenated blood.
5 The blood is carried through your arteries, arterioles, and capillaries to your muscles.
6 The fiber cells in your muscles accept and use the oxygen (this depends upon the innate ability of the fiber to assimilate oxygen, and upon the number of *mitochondria*—microscopic structures within the cell—present in the fiber).

Aerobic training can actually increase the amount of hemoglobin present in your blood, the amount of mitochondria in your cells, and the density of capillaries in your tissue. Those physiological changes will increase the amount of oxygen that is carried to your working muscles—you will be able to swim, cycle, and run longer and more efficiently. An accompanying increase in your stroke volume will compound your improvement.

You can see why expanding your aerobic capacity is a key factor in becoming an efficient, competitive endurance athlete. As you train according to my year-round program, you will also develop the ability to recover rapidly and to elevate your VO_2 max (maximum oxygen intake) and anaerobic threshold (see page 109). All of these attributes—combined with your own desire to win—will accelerate your success as a triathlete.

HOW DO MUSCLES WORK?

How does a muscle exert force? We are concerned mostly with the *skeletal* muscles, those that are responsible for body movement. The muscles that move your torso and limbs usually extend from one bone to another, ending in *tendons* (strong, cordlike tissues) that attach to the bones. When a muscle contracts—shortens—it basically pulls the tendon, which pulls the bone and moves the limb, as in the biceps curl mentioned earlier.

But what causes a muscle to contract? You probably don't usually think about it; you just bend your arm or lift your foot, for instance. Yet a person whose spinal cord has been sufficiently damaged can't do that, even though he may have the same muscles as you.

Your spinal cord is the high-voltage wire that powers your muscles. If electrical impulses from your brain can't get through to your muscle fibers, the muscles won't contract, and your leg or arm simply won't move. To understand the way your muscles are electrically "charged," Brancazio explains, you have to start with the basic unit: the *muscle fiber*.

Each muscle fiber is a rod-shaped cell a few millionths of an inch in diameter and several inches long. Skeletal muscles are made up of many bundles of fibers, lined up next to each other. An electrical impulse generated from the spinal cord travels along a *motor neuron* to the muscle. At that point (the *neuromuscular junction*) the impulse hits the muscle fiber and causes it to *twitch*—contract and relax for just a moment—like a tiny shock.

A single twitch is very short in duration, anywhere from five hundredths to one half of a second. But a rapid series of "shocks" can merge a great number of twitches into one long, sustained twitch—a perceptible muscle contraction. One nerve impulse can charge hundreds of fibers at once, shocking them into simultaneous twitches.

Once the muscle has been charged, tiny receptors called *muscle spindles* send the nerve impulse back on its way to the spinal cord. It's a form of feedback from the muscle fibers to the nervous system: "We got that one, now send us some more." Impulses have to reach the muscle fibers, then get back to the spinal cord to send out more impulses.

During periods of prolonged physical activity, such as a triathlon, your motor neurons are constantly active, carrying impulses back and forth from your spinal cord to your muscle fibers. Neuromuscular fatigue is a critical factor in any endurance activity; to properly prepare for a race, you must train your nerves as well as your muscles. This is done primarily by simulating the exact muscle movements of swimming, cycling, and running in your weight training program (see Chapter 7) and by simulating exact race conditions in all of your training (see Chapter 6).

FAST-TWITCH VERSUS SLOW-TWITCH MUSCLE FIBERS

You've probably heard more than one conversation about fast-twitch and slow-twitch muscle fibers. The general consensus is usually that good endurance athletes have more slow-twitch fibers, whereas sprinters have a predominance of fast-twitch fibers. Though that statement is oversimplified, it is not entirely false.

Every body has both types of fibers in varying proportions. While the very best sprinters may have a one-sided ratio of fast- to slow-twitch fibers, the most dramatic predominance is found in certain muscles within each individual's body. Muscles that are designed primarily to move a large mass, such as your leg, usually have many more slow-twitch fibers than a muscle designed merely to flutter an eyelash, which is made up of predominantly fast-twitch fibers.

That's because a fast-twitch fiber responds more quickly to the electrical charge. It contracts sharply, producing a quick burst of force, but then it tires out just as quickly. It has little or no oxygen supply to draw from, because it holds very little *hemoglobin* (the substance in your blood that gives it the reddish color). So if all a muscle has to do is flick your eyelid for a split second, a fast-twitch fiber is perfect.

Slow-twitch fibers, on the other hand, don't fire up as quickly or as forcefully, but their contractions can last a long, long time. They are rich in hemoglobin and highly *oxidative*, which means that they can take on and use oxygen freely. That plentiful oxygen supply makes these slow-twitch fibers particularly well-suited to do the work that takes a steady flow of energy over a longer period of time, like moving your legs for a 10-mile run—or any distance in a triathlon.

Yet lab tests in which parts of the muscle are removed and examined have revealed that many of the world's top sprinters have as much as 90 percent "white" (fast-twitch) fiber, even in their quadriceps.

The best way to figure out your muscle fiber breakdown without a muscle biopsy is to look back on the activities in which you excelled as a youngster. If you loved baseball and football and sprint races—and you did them well—you probably have a high percentage of fast-twitch fibers. If you were more inclined toward long hikes or soccer games, you may be endowed with mostly slow-twitch fibers.

Either way, you can still be successful as a triathlete. The key is to know what you have to work with, then take advantage of your strengths.

WHEN IS A FAST-TWITCH NOT A FAST-TWITCH?

A crucial—but surprisingly little-known fact about fast-twitch muscle fibers is that not all of them are alike. Some of them can actually be trained to function more like the slow-twitch fibers, taking on more oxygen and operating for longer periods of time without fatigue.

Because a triathlon calls for a combination of endurance and speed—especially in the shorter races—your body uses the different types of fibers throughout the race. At the start of the swim, for example, you have to be fairly explosive to get out quickly. If you haven't trained your anaerobic white fibers (Type B) for that type of activity, the demands placed on them will be more than they can readily withstand; you will exhaust those fibers and recruit the next source of energy—lactic acid. (See page 27.) All of a sudden your arms and legs will feel heavy and stiff.

Later you might be riding your bike over a series of rolling hills. On the first few, your legs start burning, and by the time you get to the top of the last one, you wonder if you'll be able to even finish the race. But when the course flattens out, you start feeling great again. Why does this happen?

On the flat ground, you were working at a steady pace, using those slow-twitch fibers that had been trained to keep on chugging along. But on the hills, your effort wasn't as static, and you had to use not just your red slow-twitch fibers, but your oxidative (Type A) white ones as well.

Many exercise physiologists believe that fast-twitch fibers produce lactic acid and slow-twitch expedite the removal of it. An aerobically fit triathlete tends to accumulate less lactic acid in his or her muscle tissues because (1) it is resynthesized rapidly for use as a fuel, and (2) the excess is removed relatively quickly from his or her working muscle tissues.

You can further control lactic acid accumulation by (1) working at a pace that is appropriate to your ability and level of training, and (2) incorporating *anaerobic threshold* training into your program, so that you train your Type A (oxidative) white fibers to function more efficiently. My year-round training program includes this type of training. (More about lactic acid on page 98.)

HOW YOUR BODY PRODUCES (AND USES) FUEL

In a car, gasoline is poured into the tank, where it goes through the fuel system to be processed so that it can power the engine to make the wheels turn. In your body, food goes into your digestive system, and is processed into fuel to power your vital functions, including making your muscle fibers contract. During exercise, your body calls upon three systems for energy:

1 *ATP-CP* (5 to 30 seconds at maximum effort).
2 *ATP-lactic acid* (30 seconds to 2 minutes at 85% to 95% effort.
3 *ATP-aerobic* (2 minutes to 20 hours at 60% to 85% effort). Within this system, both the lipolytic (fat metabolism) and glycolytic (carbohydrate metabolism) processes are used.

Adenosine triphosphate—ATP—is a chemical stored in muscle cells which allows the fibers to contract. When the muscles are used, ATP is depleted and must be replenished.

ATP-CP

During the first burst of energy, which uses only anaerobic fast-twitch fibers (Type B), one of the ATP phosphates is depleted; adenosine triphosphate (ATP) is broken down to adenosine diphosphate (ADP). When ADP combines with creatine phosphate (CP), which is also stored in the muscles, it resynthesizes ATP. No additional oxygen is required for this high-energy ATP-CP system—it is anaerobic.

But the sudden burst, as we have learned, is short-lived. After about 30 seconds, CP stores are depleted and another source of ATP replenishment is required.

You may have experienced this transition climbing flights of stairs. You can start off fast, but after a couple of flights, your heart starts pounding and your legs feel heavy. Your anaerobic (ATP-CP) energy is depleted; that heavy feeling is lactic acid which has been produced to yield more ATP in your muscles.

If you want to start a triathlon with a surge of power—to sprint away from the thrashing mob at a mass swim start, for instance—you'll have to train your anaerobic systems to sustain that burst of energy without producing excess lactic acid, which can cause muscle cramps. It will also require that your muscles immediately begin to use a great deal of glycogen; glycogen depletion causes muscular fatigue and failure—you literally run out of gas.

ATP-LACTIC ACID

Your anaerobic system doesn't totally shut down before the aerobic system is activated. There is a carryover period between all of your body's energy systems, in which one winds down and the next builds up. When your CP stores start to run low, the *glycogen* stored in your muscles begins to break down for use as a fuel, a process called *anaerobic glycolysis.*

The word "glycogen" comes from the Greek word *glykys* (sweet) and suffix *genes* (producing). Glycogen is a starchlike substance pro-

duced when the food you eat is converted into sugar in your bloodstream.

When glycogen breaks down, lactic acid is formed as a waste product. During this interim (30 seconds to 2 minutes), you are at an *anaerobic threshold:* Your anaerobic energy is almost depleted but your aerobic energy system has not yet been activated. Your anaerobic threshold is the point at which lactic acid first begins to form and diffuse into your bloodstream.

A long run from the water to your bike will use your ATP-lactic acid energy system.

Once lactic acid has begun to form in your muscle tissues, it has to somehow be removed or it will build up and inhibit muscular contraction—your muscles will become stiff and sore. To be removed, lactic acid must merge with oxygen carried by the mitochondria in your muscle cells, after which it moves into your bloodstream. Then (1) some of it is neutralized by alkaline blood "buffers," (2) some of it is resynthesized, and (3) a small percentage of it is eventually excreted through urine.

The more oxidative the muscle fiber, the more readily lactic acid will be removed. Thus, if your Type A (oxidative) white fibers are able to take on more oxygen, you will be able to exercise for a longer period of time at your anaerobic threshold, and will have an easier time recovering from the extra effort. I think one of my strongest advantages in competition has been my ability to recover very rapidly; I may not get up the hills faster than anyone else, but I get over them sooner.

The ATP-lactic acid system is called into play intermittently throughout a triathlon, because the changes in the course terrain and in types of activity require differing levels of effort (and energy output). During a two-hour triathlon, you will probably use your ATP-lactic acid system 8 to 15 times, for up to two minutes each time. At that rate, you could deplete as much as 90 percent of your glycogen stores. It is obviously to your advantage to be able to operate for as long as possible without crossing your anaerobic threshold.

ATP-AEROBIC

As a triathlete, you will use the aerobic energy system more than any other. You can expend physical energy for up to 20 or 30 hours—if you have trained properly—at about 60 to 85 percent of your maximum heart rate. And because oxygen is abundant, lactic acid does not build up in your muscle tissues, so you have less stiffness, less soreness, and less fatigue.

If you exceed 85 percent of your maximum heart rate, however, you will push yourself back over your anaerobic threshold to the ATP-lactic acid or ATP-anaerobic systems—you'll be working too hard. If you start breathing faster or with greater difficulty, slow down. You should be able to say at least three or four words out loud without hyperventilating.

Simply speaking, aerobic exercise is that in which oxygen is the chief resynthesizing agent in the process of replenishing the ATP in your muscle cells. The primary source of fuel for aerobic exercise is glycogen, but free fatty acids can also be used. During prolonged periods of exercise, such as a long triathlon, fat tissue is broken down into *glycerol*—a carbohydrate—and free fatty acids, then mobilized into the bloodstream. Glycerol is eventually converted to glycogen.

Your *lipolytic*—fat-burning—system works more efficiently when you are in shape, just as fuel burns more efficiently in an engine that is tuned-up. Part of the reason is that you develop more mitochondria when you are aerobically fit, so you have more available oxygen for the process.

If you weigh around 160 pounds, you probably have 3,500 to 3,800 usable calories of glycogen stored in your muscles and liver, which you might deplete in the first three hours of a triathlon if you're working fairly hard. But your tissues and bloodstream store about 50,000 calories of free fatty acids—a virtually unlimited source of energy. Most aerobically fit athletes will begin to burn fatty acids within the first 20 minutes of sustained activity. It pays to be fit enough to use fat for fuel!

BENEFITS OF AEROBIC EXERCISE

1 Increases stroke volume.
2 Increases maximum cardiac output.
3 Increases ability to store and conserve glycogen.

Riding up long, moderate hills is primarily aerobic, but will also use some of your fast-twitch/A (oxidative) muscle fibers.

4 Increases number and density of capillaries.
5 Increases number and density of mitochondria.
6 Increases ability to use free fatty acids as fuel.
7 Increases ability to remove lactic acid from muscle tissue.

LIMITATIONS DURING AEROBIC EXERCISE

Though the ATP-aerobic energy system allows you to exercise for a long time, there are still a few factors that figure into your ability to keep on going endlessly. These are (1) your individual glycogen stores and ability to use free fatty acids, (2) neuromuscular fatigue, (3) muscular-skeletal fatigue, (4) dehydration, (5) lack of sleep, (6) lack of concentration, and (7) your overall psychological and emotional preparedness.

In Chapters 3, 4 and 5, you will learn the most efficient swimming, cycling, and running techniques for triathlon competition. Using those techniques, Chapter 6 outlines a year-round training program that will prepare you—physically and psychologically—for the demands of endurance racing. Chapter 7 offers a weight-training and stretching program that will minimize neuromuscular fatigue, and Chapter 8 advises you how to specifically prepare for a race (including a few tricks of the trade). Finally, Chapter 9 presents a dietary approach that will provide you with the best possible fuel.

3 SWIMMING

'll never forget the first time I saw myself on "television." My college swimming coach had videotaped my crawl stroke, and I was shocked at what I saw. My overarm recovery was totally asymmetrical; my right arm was high in the air and my left arm was flat and swung out wide. My hand slapped the water, stirring up a frothy mass of bubbles. For years I had neglected proper stroke mechanics, except for the underwater phase. I knew that the real power of the stroke was generated underwater; what my arms did above water seemed totally unimportant.

Suddenly I was faced with the unavoidable truth: My stroke was not a pretty sight. De-

It all starts here—in the water.

spite my rationalizations to the contrary, every phase of stroke mechanics is an indispensible factor in effective swimming. My failure to recognize that had held back my performance.

As a triathlete, you can save yourself a lot of wasted time and energy by learning how to swim properly from the start. Some of the information in this chapter might seem prohibitively technical to beginning swimmers, but don't let it scare you. When you get in the water and follow the instructions, you'll see for yourself that little details such as the way your wrist is flexed make a big difference in how efficiently you can swim.

WHY THE FREESTYLE STROKE?

The freestyle, or crawl, stroke is best for triathlons because (1) it is the fastest competitive stroke, (2) it keeps your body in a streamlined position (at least it should!), (3) it makes it easier to see the obstacles and course markings in open water, and (4) the recovery phase of the stroke provides a slight resting phase in each arm cycle.

The streamlined effect occurs because your body rolls from side to side—you rotate your shoulders—every time your hand enters the water. That rolling motion essentially reduces your surface area and thus your frontal resistance in the water. With the breast and butterfly strokes, on the other hand, your shoulders are flat; the backstroke also limits your shoulder rotation more than the freestyle stroke, so that your frontal resistance is greater.

Being streamlined in the water means that the flow you're creating in the water—the *laminar flow*—isn't disrupted. A physics teacher would explain it like this: Water moves around your body in uniform layers of differing speeds. If the shape of an object moving through the water—your body, in this case—were to change abruptly, the layers of water would separate and create turbulence (commonly called the *wake*).

If you were moving along smoothly and suddenly you dropped your knee, the water would hit your thigh (you would feel the pressure on the front of your leg), and you would slow down. That would happen because the water pressure in front of your leg would have become greater than the pressure behind it. In physics, that effect is called *form drag*. Keeping your body as sleek and straight as possible, and rotating your shoulders, minimizes drag and lateral sway (feet fishtailing, etc.), which in turn lessens frontal resistance to the water.

BASIC FREESTYLE STROKE TECHNIQUE

The freestyle stroke is made up of six basic phases: (1) the *entry*, when your hand goes into the water; (2) the *catch*, when you bend your wrist slightly to actually catch the water; (3) a slight *downward press;* (4) the *pull,* a sort of sculling motion through the water, in which you bend your elbow and bring your hand toward the midline of your body, gradually accelerating your arm; (5) the *finish,* an outward press during which you straighten your arm and eventually hyperextend your wrist; and finally (6) the *recovery,* when you lift your hand and arm back out of the water to set up your next stroke.

It may sound as though the stroke is a series of separate motions, but each phase is actually a consecutive part of one overall motion. We'll discuss the phases individually in order to define the ideal way to move your hands and arms through the water, but keep in mind that the idea is to develop a rhythmic, fluid stroke.

Triathletes who started out as cyclists or runners often swim as though their arms were windmill blades, using the "rapid-fire" approach. With outstretched arms, they try to forcefully grab, pull, then push the water from the point of entry to the bottom of their hips, digging a sort of trough on either side of their bodies. To try to swim faster, they simply turn the "windmill blades" faster.

At one time, this rapid-arm straight-line turnover was thought to be the most effective style of freestyle racing. That straight-arm pull is not the best method for triathletes, however. Your hand may initially grab a firm hold of the water, but as your arm accelerates, the water will begin to move faster in front of your hand, causing a wave in front and a sort of vacuum behind—a trough. Your hand will slip through that trough with very little forward motion for your effort.

World-class triathletes weave their hands through the water in a reverse S-shaped pattern, rather than pulling their arms straight through the water. The point where each hand comes out of the water (for the recovery) is only a short distance—maybe 10 inches—from the previous point of entry. They put their hands into the water and pull themselves up to that point as though they were grabbing rungs on a ladder and pulling themselves up to each successive rung.

You can check your own stroke by having a friend watch you from the side of the pool, to see where your hands enter and exit the water. If there is more than 10 or 12 inches' difference, your hands are probably slipping, rather than pulling, through the water. You probably have too much stroke turnover—too many straight-arm pulls in rapid succession—which will cause undue fatigue in addition to producing poor results.

As a triathlete, you should learn to think in terms of *distance per stroke,* getting the most out of every arm turnover. Faster turnovers will not get you to the finish line faster—moving farther on each stroke will.

ENTRY: WHERE YOUR HAND GOES INTO THE WATER

Your stroke starts when your hand first enters the water. Your right hand should be in line with your right shoulder, or slightly toward your right ear. It should be turned outward (30 to 60 degrees off the water surface) so that your slightly down-turned thumb initiates the entry. Your elbow should be flexed at 130 to 160 degrees. If you over-reach in front—lining up your right hand with your left ear, for example—your body will sway or fishtail.

A good way to fully understand the over-reaching problem is to stand in front of a mirror and simulate an overhead over-reach (as described above). Watch how your hips sway. The same thing happens in the water.

Ideally, you should feel as though your body could slide through a tube just about the width of your shoulders. Pretend you are swimming in a very narrow pool, just barely wider than your shoulders, and any time your arms or legs move out of that lane, your hands, hips, or feet will hit the side. Obviously, that would slow you down and waste a lot of effort—not to mention scrape up your skin.

If you do not have a swimming background, your upper-back and shoulder muscles are probably inflexible. You may need to use a slightly wider entry—your right hand might come into the water just outside your right shoulder, for example—but try to keep as close to shoulder width as possible. In any case, you should work on increasing your upper-body flexibility; try the stretching exercises in Chapter 7. Also, have a friend watch you when you swim and tell you if your entry is too far off.

When your hand enters the water, try to cut a nice, clean hole with your whole arm. Imagine that the water is Jell-O, and you have to reach through it to pick up a spoon on the bottom of the pool without disturbing the gelatin; your hand leads the way and your arm must follow directly behind it.

It is extremely important that you maintain that trajectory with your arm in order to catch the water for the pull—power—phase of your stroke. Proper elbow flexion (the angle at which your elbow is bent) and hand tilt will allow you to make that clean slice into the water with a minimum of air bubbles.

Most beginning swimmers enter the water with their arms straight. That allows them to press down longer, which elevates their heads above water for a longer breath. That is a bad practice for several reasons: (1) It slows you

Your hand should be turned outward (30–60 degrees) before it enters the water.

Your elbow should be flexed at 130–160 degrees.

Try not to overreach.

down, (2) it causes your head and shoulders to bob (a waste of energy), (3) it increases frontal resistance, and (4) it often causes shoulder pains. Often, the straight-arm entry is precipitated by tight *deltoids* (shoulder muscles) that cause your elbows to drop and your hands to enter the water too close to your shoulders.

To check how you're doing, try this drill: Every third complete stroke, lift up your head and turn it forward so you can look at your arm as your hand enters the water. Check your hand tilt, elbow flexion, and angle of entry.

AFTER THE ENTRY, BEFORE THE CATCH: ROTATE YOUR SHOULDERS

Once your arm is into the water and extended in front of you, your upper body should reach its maximum rotation—your shoulders should have rotated about 40 to 60 degrees (slightly less during a head-up stroke—see page 198.) Your shoulders should be rotated forward, as well as side to side. Imagine someone is on the bottom of the pool, grabbing your shoulders and pulling them forward with each successive recovery. This rolling motion decreases your frontal resistance in the water and alleviates shoulder muscle stress. It incorporates your *latissimus dorsi* (a large, fanlike muscle that starts in your spine and attaches to a bone in your upper arm), which is the prime muscle used to initiate the catch and in the first phase of the pull.

Make sure you don't shrug your shoulders when you rotate them. If your arm is properly extended when you roll, this should not become a problem.

Rotate your shoulders forward, as well as to the side.

DRILLS TO CORRECT ENTRY PROBLEMS

As a swim coach, I found that in order to actually effect a change in body orientation, you need to drastically overcompensate for your error. Going through the full range of motion increases your neuromuscular sensations and spatial awareness.

1   *Problem:* You slap the water on your entry.

Remedy: Go to the extreme—pitch your hand so that the back of it enters the water first. That is not the proper pitch, and will feel extremely awkward, I guarantee. Then on each successive stroke (for the next 10 strokes) gradually rotate your hand so that it eventually returns to your "slapping" position. If you repeat this drill many times, you will eventually find the proper hand tilt, where your hand slips quietly into the water with no resistance and no bubbles.

2   *Problem:* You drop your elbow on your entry.

Remedy: Exaggerate your entry angle and elbow flexion. Put your hand in the water just beyond your shoulder, with your elbow sharply bent and high above the water. Then slowly lengthen your spot of entry until you finally complete a full arm extension above water.

Repeating these drills will help you find the ideal arm position during recovery and the best angle of entry. You should not slap the water with your arm or splash water to the side. Your arm should feel relaxed as you place your hand into the entry spot; don't unduly tense your muscles.

To correct a dropped elbow, exaggerate your entry angle and elbow flexion.

CATCH

After you have completed your entry and extended your arm in front of you, you are ready for the catch phase of your stroke. Catch the water as you would grab a rung on a ladder beneath you. Reach out and hook your hand over the rung—like a horizontal bar—and pull yourself up to it.

Bend your wrist slightly (about 20 to 30 degrees) to initiate the motion. To get that wrist flexion right, pretend that the water is sand, and that you have to pull your body forward without elevating your torso or lifting your head off the ground. You have to grab the sand by flexing your wrist and digging in. Don't push the sand back—you won't get anywhere—pull yourself up to that little hole you've dug. It all depends on flexing your wrist and getting a firm hold on that sand.

Your wrist should be flexed and turned outward for a more powerful catch. This is particularly effective for triathletes with heavily muscled backs and shoulders.

DOWNWARD PRESS

Once you catch the water, press downward and go on with the rest of your stroke. This is a very quick motion for competitive sprint swimmers, whose radical wrist flexion (almost 90 degrees) allows a very high elbow. A sprint stroke provides no rest period after the catch, however, and requires very strong deltoids.

An efficient triathlon stroke involves a longer, slower catch phase, with wrists bent at a much more moderate angle. Taking advantage of the brief rest phase after the catch is critical in triathlon competition.

Don't press down with the heel of your hand. Your wrist was slightly flexed during the catch, and you should maintain that angle throughout the downward press. (You may feel some tension in your deltoids because the power in the downward press is generated by your shoulder.)

Your arm reaches the deepest point in the stroke at the bottom of the downward press—about 12 to 18 inches for most people. You should gradually straighten your forearm and wrist for the inward pull.

PULL

From the bottom of your downward press, gradually allow your wrist to straighten out as you start to pull your hand in a sculling motion toward your shoulder and then your chin. You're aiming for an imaginary midline drawn from your head to your toes.

At that point, your hand should line up with your forearm. If you try to keep your wrist flexed as it was for the catch and press, or if you hyperextend it and let it bend back the other way, you're going to look like a gorilla walking around. Let your wrist loosely line up with your forearm, just as though you were walking around with your arms hanging easily at your sides.

Your elbow should be bent at about 90 to 120 degrees by the time your hand passes directly under your chin. The exact flexion of your elbow will be determined by the amount you roll your body during your stroke. If you are quite flexible in your shoulders and torso, your hand will move more easily into the still water. If your roll is less pronounced, you'll have to bend your elbow more radically to compensate.

If you are new to swimming, you will probably need to work on exaggerating the reverse S-shaped scull. Bend your elbow radically and pull your hand way under your body so that it lines up about 12 to 18 inches under your chin.

Repeating that exaggerated scull should give you a feel for the still water—and it will certainly slow down any tendency you may have to resort to that rapid-fire, windmill arm turnover. However, you should avoid too much arm flexion, because your arm will move into the vacuum under your torso and slip toward your hip. That will result in increased arm turnover and an asymmetrical stroke. It also wastes energy.

To keep your elbow up where it belongs, pretend there is an eyeball on the tip of it. As your forearm passes beneath your shoulders and your chest, that eye should be focused outward, to the side. If it looks back or slightly downward, your elbow is probably dropping. You can monitor this particular phase of your stroke by allowing your head to drop enough to watch your arm during this inward scull. You should also have someone watch your elbow from the side, underwater.

The underwater arm motion starts with your body full rotated.

1

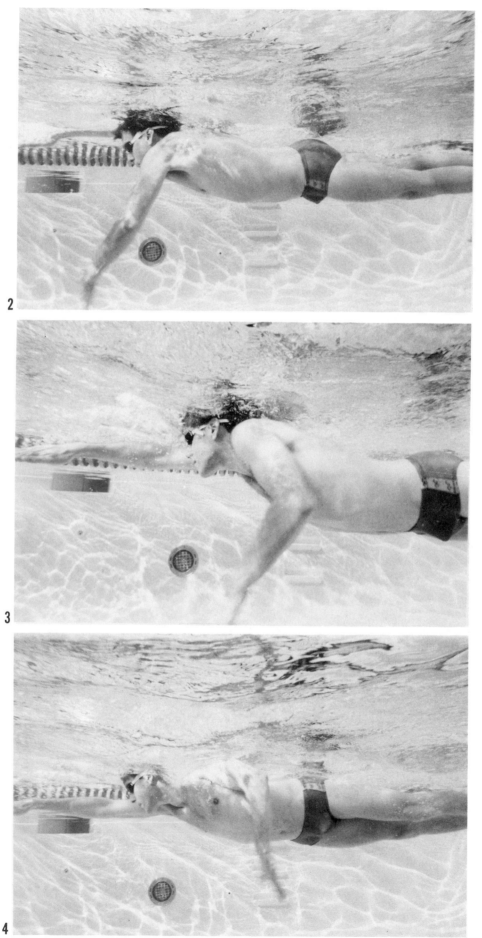

GETTING READY FOR THE FINISH

Now your hand is under your chin, about a foot beneath your chest, your wrist is extended and your elbow is bent at about 100 degrees. This is the point in your stroke at which you generate the most power. Start to extend your arm and move it outward toward your hip. That sets you up for the finish of your underwater stroke: an outward press.

THE FINISH

Before your forearm comes out of the water, your wrist should be hyperextended—bent so that your hand is all the way forward. It should be in the same position it is in when you put both hands on the edge of the pool and push yourself up to get out.

During the outward press, you gradually straighten out your arm and extend your wrist so you can lift your arm up out of the water. The movement is just like pulling your hand out of your pants pocket; your elbow comes out first, then your forearm, and finally your hand and fingers.

To simulate the proper hyperextension, imagine that you have an eyeball on your palm. It should be looking straight back toward the opposite end of the pool. Don't let your hand relax enough for the eyeball to look at your thigh, and don't flick your wrist at the last minute so that the eyeball looks up at the sky.

Your arm should be straight, with your wrist hyperextended and fingers pointing down toward the bottom of the pool. Relax your hand and rotate your finger in toward your thigh. Relax your wrist and forearm in anticipation of recovery.

As you finish your stroke, your wrist should be hyperextended.

RECOVERY

Now that you've straightened out your arm and lifted it out of the water, bend your elbow again and bring your hand up to the next point of entry. The recovery phase of the stroke gives your arm a chance to rest momentarily while you set up the next stroke.

It is important to relax as much as possible during the recovery, keeping your forearm and fingers loose. If you bend your elbow too sharply or move your hand too close to your side, your *deltoid* will tighten progressively with each successive stroke. The deltoid muscle's purpose is to help lift your arm away from the side of your body; you obviously don't want it to stiffen up while you're trying to swim. Also, if your arm is stiff or carried too close to your body, your *trapezius* will tighten. (This muscle is used to shrug your shoulders.)

If you pitch your hand in toward your hip, it will slip and cause the opposite hand to accelerate during the rest phase or the following entry. "Rushing" your stroke like that causes all sorts of problems, including erratic breathing.

To alleviate stress in your trapezius and deltoids, use a wide recovery.

Triathletes often have a poor recovery because of an asymmetrical stroke developed in open-water competition. If you overrotate your shoulders to allow a longer inhale period on your predominant breathing side, and you exaggerate your headlift in open water to overcome waves or surf and to sight buoys and markings, you will probably develop a very wide-arm or high-arm recovery. That will cause your feet to fishtail, which makes your body sway, and you'll end up spending energy compensating for that unwanted movement.

1

During the recovery phase of your stroke, relax your arms and carry your elbow fairly high.

4

2

3

5

6

STROKE CLINIC: HOW TO REMEDY COMMON PROBLEMS

1 *Problem:* Wrist does not flex properly; stays in alignment with forearm.

Remedy: Use a hand paddle and concentrate on pressing with your fingertips. That should initiate the catch and give you a feel for the proper wrist flexion. Or try an elongated "stretch stroke." When your arm is extended, allow a one-second hesitation at the catch so you can watch and feel the flexion in your wrist.

2 *Problem:* Fingers are cupped or curled under.

Remedy: Wear a paddle on the hand with the problem. That should force you to keep your fingers straight.

3 *Problem:* Catch happens too quickly after entry.

Remedy: Use a stretch stroke (make sure to count out a full second's hesitation) and visualize your hand entering the water, then sliding on a piece of ice to a full arm's extension before initiating your catch.

4 *Problem:* No feel of water on hand; can't feel pressure on your fingertips.

Remedy: Your shoulders are probably tight, which results in a flat-arm entry in which your hand is not deeper than your elbow—thus you have no leverage. Angle your hand deeper and try a closer entry spot. Try a wider entry spot (which will also alleviate shoulder tension).

BREATHING

Whenever someone asks what I think about while I am racing, my answer is always the same: relaxed breathing. During the final miles of the 1983 Ironman, I was so exhausted that I could barely hear or focus; concentrating on each breath as my feet hit the pavement helped me relax as much as possible under the circumstances, and kept me from becoming further fatigued.

I think about proper breathing during all three events, because it keeps me relaxed and helps to establish a smooth, easy rhythm. During the swim, concentrating on breathing is especially helpful in setting timing and rhythm of my stroke.

Coaching new swimmers, I have observed that many are so anxious about getting enough breath that they practically panic on every inhale. I have seen hundreds of variations of the gasping-for-breath syndrome, all of which make it more difficult to breathe and ruin your stroke at the same time.

The best way to breathe while you swim is basically the way you breathe any time you are relaxed—deep, slow, rhythmic inhales and long, smooth exhales.

WHEN TO BREATHE

The best pattern for triathlon swimming is one inhale on each stroke. That gives you a constant exchange of oxygen and carbon dioxide without building up an oxygen deficit. As you initiate your final press—or as your opposite arm completes the catch—you should turn your head to the side, with your eyes looking back slightly. (Remember that where you focus your eyes will determine the position of your head.)

THE BOW WAVE

As you swim, your body is essentially burrowing out a groove in the water. Forward motion creates a wave off your head—the *bow wave,* like the bow (front) of a ship. If you rotate your chin forward when you breathe, you'll open your mouth right into that bow wave, sucking in water instead of oxygen. When you use a head-up stroke—in training or in competition—you should inhale at the same time as you would during your normal freestyle stroke. After you inhale, you can rotate your head forward (to sight course markings) as you exhale with your mouth underwater.

Don't raise your chin above the bow wave. In addition to making you gasp for breath, it will hyperextend your lower back and cause your feet to drop, which will increase your frontal resistance.

Take a deep breath through your mouth and try to relax. You should complete your inhale as your arm passes over your head in the recovery phase. Then turn your head back into the water, focusing your eyes 10 to 15 feet ahead of you—not down—and slowly exhale through your mouth and nose.

I start my exhale slowly and easily as I initiate my catch, then breathe out more heartily at my final press. At that point, I close my mouth for a fraction of a second just before I turn my head again for the next inhale. As soon as my head is

Proper head-up stroke breathing: mouth and nose still in water, eyes rotated forward.

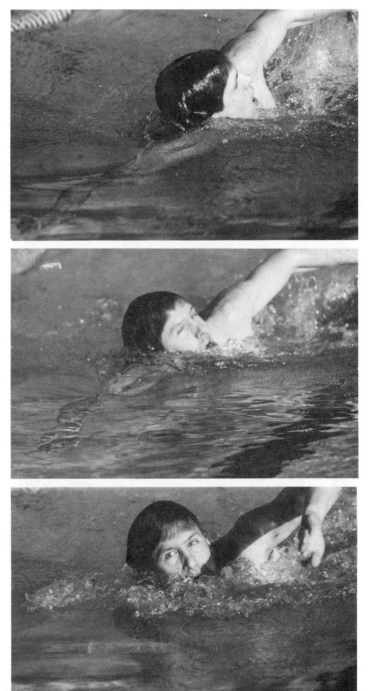

turned, I start inhaling through my mouth.

Important: Do not clinch your teeth or purse your lips when your face is underwater. Keep your lips cracked about a quarter of an inch. Don't worry about water coming into your mouth; the difference between the volume of air in your body and in the water will prevent water from rushing in.

Improper head-up stroke breathing. Head all the way out of the water, eyes looking all the way backward.

HOW TO GET THE MOST FROM EACH BREATH

1 *Keep your face and neck as relaxed as possible.* If you hold your face in a tight grimace, your neck and shoulder muscles will also tighten up. That will make it more difficult to rotate your shoulders and to roll your body in a fluid, rhythmic motion.

2 *Roll your body.* It increases the speed and efficiency of your stroke and allows a longer and less stressful inhale period. If you hold your shoulders still and turn just your head to breathe (about 90 degrees), your neck and shoulder muscles will become very tense. When you roll your shoulders, your head turns only half as far (about 45 degrees). This reduces muscular activity and tension.

3 *The more oxygen you can take in—without gasping—the better off you'll be.* The oxygen-carbon dioxide exchange on each stroke should be about 85 percent. At rest, that exchange is constant (100 percent). During freestyle swimming, most triathletes have about one second to inhale, so 85 percent of a normal breath is optimal. At that rate, no oxygen deficit will develop. As long as you don't rush your stroke, one inhale per stroke is best.

BREATHING TO YOUR OFF-SIDE

Most swimmers breathe to just one side during their freestyle stroke; I breathe to my right. In most cases, a one-sided breathing pattern is good; it allows you to set up a consistent rhythm and uses less energy than breathing to both sides. It also provides more oxygen intake because you are inhaling on each arm turnover, while an alternate breathing pattern skips a stroke between each breath.

But there are a few good of reasons you'll need

to develop the ability to breathe comfortably to your alternate (nondominant) side. First of all, in open-water swims you need to get a peek at the world around you from more than one direction so you'll know where you're going and what looms ahead of you in the sea.

Secondly, since your breathing pattern works hand in hand with your shoulder rotation (body roll), breathing to just one side will usually cause you to overroll to your dominant (breathing) side to allow a longer inhale. That will bring your arm farther out (wider) on the recovery phase of your stroke and generally cause a flatter entry and a straighter arm pull. You can end up with a sort of stroke and a half, a one-sided stroke in which one arm is way up there and the other one is relatively flat. Then you'll look like me! I guarantee you—from my own experience—that is not the most efficient way to swim!

Finally, you need to give your shoulders a break during the long, open-water swims. Breathing to your alternate side every 10 to 20 strokes will eliminate some tightness in your *trapezius* (the large muscles that extend from the back of your head and the vertebrae in your neck and chest to your collarbones and shoulder blades). It will also limit shoulder stiffness.

We will discuss alternate breathing and how to use it to your best advantage in Chapter 8.

KICKING

My advice to triathletes is threefold: (1) Don't overkick, (2) maintain a steady, easy kick and a horizontal body alignment, and (3) increase your ankle flexibility.

You really don't need a strong kick. The swim distances in triathlons are usually at least a half mile, for one thing, and you'll waste energy if you kick too hard. Overkicking for that long a time will elevate lactic acid level and draw oxygen to your *quadriceps* (the large muscle on the outside of your thigh). The net result will be a dramatic increase in overall fatigue and a reduced aerobic endurance capacity for the next two events.

Overkicking will also tire out your leg muscles—especially your quadriceps—which you want to keep as fresh as possible for the rest of the race.

The water is often quite cool, so blood is shunted from your legs to your torso and arms (which are doing most of the work) to warm them up. When you start kicking hard, it forces the blood back to your legs, to deliver more oxygen. If your blood supply is inadequate, your muscles may cramp. If you must increase your kicking, do so gradually and watch your breathing. If you start breathing hard, then you are probably kicking too hard.

However, you can't just let your legs drag behind you as dead weight. Learn to use a smooth, easy flutter kick. Every triathlete should adopt a kick that suits his or her own needs, depending upon his or her leg strength, flexibility (shoulders as well as ankles), body position, and the relative distances he or she is swimming.

ANKLE STRENGTH AND FLEXIBILITY FOR A BETTER FLUTTER KICK

Have you ever grabbed a kickboard and found that no matter how much force you used in kicking, your forward speed was ridiculously slow? Your legs may be strong from running and cycling, your body position might be ideal (hips close to the surface), yet it seems to take forever to kick just 25 yards.

Don't feel alone! Some of the strongest triathletes have a relatively ineffective kick. I certainly include myself in the non-propulsive kicker category. My problem—shared by many runners and cyclists who are trying to develop their leg speed—is limited *plantar flexion* (the ability to stretch my ankle and point my toes). Your feet are not usually stretched to that extent in running and cycling, so the muscles and tendons in your ankles and feet do not allow a loose, mobile ankle joint.

You really need that looseness for a good flutter kick. You could have leg muscles like Arnold Schwarzeneggar and it wouldn't do you a bit of good without sufficient plantar flexion. Ankle flexibility can be dramatically improved with a daily stretching program. (See Chapter 7.) You can also incorporate the use of fins in your training workouts.

Developing ankle flexibility takes a long time, so you will have to weigh how much time you are willing to spend doing it against how much your swimming speed actually improves.

BODY POSITION FOR KICKING

If you have poor ankle flexibility, try to increase the strength of your flutter kick, but kick only hard enough to maintain a good body position in the water. You should feel as though your feet are near the surface at all times, even though you will kick downward 10 to 18 inches. Try to break the surface with one heel.

During the head-up portion of a rough-water swim, you will probably find yourself kicking deeper, unless you make a conscious effort to de-emphasize your flutter kick. Before I learned to alter my arm stroke—I flattened my entry slightly so I could lift my head every three to five strokes without kicking deeper or harder—I would find myself kicking like crazy and my legs would be exhausted by the end of the swim.

In general, I try to elevate my foot just above the surface and then initiate my downward thrust by bending and pushing, from my hip. At the completion of the downstroke—when my foot is at its deepest point in the water—I sort of flick my toes as though I were trying to flick sand off the end of my feet.

Turning your toes slightly inward will increase the surface area for your downward thrust. Think of your feet as fins, with your big toes clipping each other as they pass during the upward and downward phases of your kick. It should be a fluid motion; your legs should not stop at the end of each upstroke or downstroke.

Don't worry about an asymmetrical kick, though. Most swimmers have one dominant kick per arm cycle.

TYPES OF FLUTTER KICKS

Triathletes usually use one of three basic flutter kicks: (1) six-beat, (2) two-beat, or (3) two-beat crossover. Most swimmers don't even know what type they use; it isn't a critical point of information. Just find a kick that feels best for you, make sure you keep your heels elevated, and you shouldn't have any big problems.

SIX-BEAT KICK

In a six-beat kick, there are three downward kicks with each individual arm stroke. These kicks take place during the underwater phase of the arm stroke. Usually there is one dominant kick followed by two weaker ones. Many of the top triathletes use a six-beat kick, but I would recommend using a two-beat or a two-beat crossover. I use a two-beat crossover because it stabilizes body roll and minimizes energy expenditure.

Most runners and cyclists find a six-beat kick too difficult, but if you are comfortable with it, that's fine.

As your right arm pulls through and recovers, kick downward three times with each leg. Usually you kick once with each of the three phases of the underwater pull; kick once as you start your downward press, once with your inward sweep, and once with your final (upward) press.

No matter which kick you use, you'll find that the depth of your kick will correspond to how much you bend your elbow in your arm stroke, to your natural buoyancy, and to your head height relative to the water. The straighter your arm pull, the shallower your kick; the higher your head, the deeper your kick.

Remember, as your body rolls, so will your legs. They will be kicking to the side a little bit, as well as up and down, so your hips will rotate a little bit to compensate. Try not to overroll your hips; just let it happen naturally.

TWO-BEAT KICK

The two-beat kick is fairly simple. Each time you start your inward scull with your arm, you start a downward press with your leg. You can let your legs drag—float—during the recovery and the downward press of your arm stroke.

This efficient kicks seems to be preferred by many of the top women, who tend to be more flexible than men are in their shoulders and back. Also, women tend to be more buoyant and keep their legs up a bit higher. But many of the men seem to have trouble with the two-beat kick, and so adopt the two-beat crossover.

TWO-BEAT CROSSOVER

The crossover is similar to the two-beat, but is more like a four-beat kick, because there are two dominant kicks and two minor kicks. Each of the major kicks comes at the same time as the two-beat kicks: during your inward scull. The other kicks come during the downward press of your arms, when your legs would be floating in a two-beat kick.

Most people who use the crossover kick are compensating in part for their body sway. Your legs should cross over and actually hit each other about halfway through your kick, about six inches below the surface. Be careful to avoid an incomplete kick, in which your leg doesn't extend all the way.

Cyclists and runners often kick from the knee down, using their legs underwater in the same manner as they would while running or riding. That motion traps water behind the knee on the upbeat, which means more effort has to be expended. The result is, obviously, undue fatigue.

A FINAL RECOMMENDATION

To get the most thrust for your effort, I recommend emphasizing the first kick of each arm cycle. I have noticed—even with my meager kick—that if I emphasize this initial kick I can actually feel a slight thrust forward. Even if you use a six-beat kick, you will feel the extra distance per stroke if you emphasize the initial kick during the longer (800 meters or more) triathlons.

A "FEEL" FOR THE WATER: KINESTHETIC AWARENESS

All this techanical talk about how to tilt your hands, bend your elbows, point your toes, kick your legs, and pull yourself through the water can be overwhelming, especially if you don't have a lot of experience as a swimmer. You have to actually get in the water and see how it feels to really understand how and why it all works.

For example, we've said that sculling through still water works better than pulling your arm straight through a "trough" of moving water. But can you actually feel the difference between still and moving water? Can you feel when your elbows are bent properly?

If you have to think about it, you will be at a disadvantage because you won't be able to relax, which is a key to efficiency.

In a race, it will really help you to know how well you are progressing based upon your own *kinesthetic awareness*—a sense of the movement, tension, and position of your body perceived through the nerve endings in your muscles, joints, and tendons.

Some people are naturally more sensitive to those perceptions than others; theoreticians believe that kinesthetic awareness can be a form of native intelligence. Like every other form of intelligence, however, that sense of feel has to be cultivated.

DRILLS TO IMPROVE YOUR FEEL FOR THE WATER

DRY LAND DRILLS.   One way to develop a sense of your own movement, particularly in relation to the water, is to practice dry land drills.

Standing next to the pool—or anywhere out of the water—bend over at your waist and simulate the arm pull you use in your freestyle stroke. Close your eyes so that you are just feeling that pattern and movement, rather than looking at it. Then have someone stand directly in front of you and tell you whether you are flexing your wrist too much, for instance, or dropping your elbow, or holding your head in the wrong position.

Now make the necessary adjustments—with your eyes still closed—and pay attention to how it feels. Even though you won't have the water as tension, you will be able to feel the difference as you bend your wrist or elbow a little or hold your arm a little higher. This exercise will train your motor nerves and your muscles to coordinate that specific pull pattern, and you will actually be able to recognize when it feels right.

IN-WATER DRILLS.   If you are lucky enough to swim in a pool that is equipped with underwater mirrors (at the end or on the bottom), you can watch your stroke in actual motion in the water. That is a great way to look and feel at the same time. But most pools do not have mirrors, so you will probably have to settle for watching your shadow. Swim when the sun is directly overhead or at only a slight angle. Your shadow image will be slightly distorted, but the idea is to look at gross technical points, not the fine-tuning. Check out your basic pull pattern, for example, not the degree of your wrist flexion.

FEELING YOUR HANDS IN THE WATER

Most adults have a difficult time learning to use their hands as paddles in the water. Even though I have been a swimmer for my entire life, I need to refresh my hand/water sensations from time to time. To do that, I stand in the water and practice holding my hands and fingers in different positions. I do some sculling motions and try curling my fingers underneath or opening them really wide to find out which position optimizes water tension. Often a subtle change will balance out a stroke.

For best results, go to a deep part of the pool and scull, with your arms supporting your weight. Scull vertically; get in a horizontal position with your head out of water (sort of like a breaststroke position) and scull back and forth. Don't do a breaststroke pull; scull just enough to stay afloat. The idea isn't to go anywhere. You just want to feel your hands in the water. Get used to the way it feels at different hand pitches, with your fingers spread to different degrees, with your fingers curled underneath. You'll be able to tell when the water is slipping through and when you are actually holding still water. Learn how it feels to use your hands correctly.

It also helps to use hand paddles during your swim workout at least twice a week. Start by using two paddles, then take one off and swim a few laps with just one. Then switch hands and repeat a few one-paddle laps. This drill will point out any hand slippage and will recruit additional muscle fibers. (More on the use of paddles in Chapter 6.)

HOW WELL ARE YOU DOING? (LEARNING YOUR OWN CUES)

When you're training—and racing—you need to develop your own cues about how well you are doing. Many top triathletes say that before a race they know how they want to feel at every point along the course. In addition to a projected split time, for example, they know how fresh—or tired—they should feel at each mile in order to perform on target.

Be aware of your competitors, but define your own parameters and use your own cues. If I had judged my own performance by how strong Scott Tinley looked when he passed me during the run at the 1983 Ironman, I might have given up. He didn't look half as tired as I felt! But I knew I had an internal reserve that had not yet been exhausted, and I wasn't about to be defeated while I still had anything left. (Luckily I didn't run completely out of gas until after I crossed the finish line.)

You cannot judge how well you are doing by comparing yourself to anyone else—especially when you're swimming.

Let's say the person in the next lane normally swims at a slightly faster pace than you. You decide to try to stay with him during the workout, and you succeed. You probably figure you are doing well, but it may not be true. You may have cranked up your arm speed, but if you had to spend three or four times as much energy to do it, you didn't necessarily gain anything over your past performance.

You should be able to tell how well you're doing with your eyes closed—literally. If you are in an open pool with no lane lines, try taking six or seven strokes with your eyes closed. Feel the water pressure on your hand, and the way your arms feel as they pull you through the water.

Warning: Don't try that without someone watching you, or in a crowded pool, or during a workout. You could collide with another swimmer, or worse yet, with a cement wall.

EQUIPMENT

One of the best things about swimming is that you don't have to spend a lot of money to do it. A lot of fancy equipment isn't necessary. But you will need a few items to aid in your workouts and keep you afloat.

1 *Suit:* Wearing a suit will keep you from being arrested for indecent exposure, and will keep everything in place so that you don't distract other swimmers—that's really important! All swim stores offer one-piece Lycra racing suits, which are your best bet because they allow freedom of movement yet fit close enough to keep you sleek and streamlined in the water.

2 *Goggles:* Everyone should wear goggles in training. They allow you to see your hands and arms—and everything else in the water—and keep the pool chemicals out of your eyes. It's much easier to relax when you can see and your eyes don't burn.

   Sometimes I don't wear goggles during a race, because they tend to fog up in open water, which makes it difficult to sight buoys. They also can get kicked or elbowed during a mass swim start, then they start leaking and you have to stop and adjust them or take them off. I've found that it's easier to go without goggles in cold water than in warmer, saltier water (Hawaii). Any time you go without goggles, though, it's going to be difficult to see well when you first get out of the water.

Sometimes leaky and fogged-up goggles are more of a nuisance than an asset.

3 *Kickboards:* Since heavy kicking is of limited use to most triathletes, the primary advantage of doing kicking drills with a board is to increase your ankle flexibility. Kickboards will allow you to forget about your stroke while you're concentrating on kicking.

4 *Fins:* The best way to do kicking drills is with a board and fins. It stretches your ankles and works your quadriceps at the same time. If you find that you don't have time to ride or run, you can put on your fins, go in the deep water, and do vertical flutter kicks. (Putting your hands on your head will make it more difficult and give you a better workout.)

5   *Hand paddles:* I recommend using hand paddles twice a week to check your stroke pattern. Make sure you keep your hands on the surface of the paddle; don't grip the paddle or let your thumb hang over the side. And be careful: You can put a lot of stress on your shoulder muscles and biceps tendons by leaning on your hand too long during your downward press.

6   *Pull buoys:* These are small Styrofoam cylinders you wear between your legs to keep your body afloat so you can concentrate strictly on your stroke. I don't like them because they give you a false sense of buoyancy and tend to restrict your body roll. If you need to use pull buoys to straighten out your stroke, make sure you allow your shoulders and hips to roll freely. Don't do any high-intensity speed work.

Hand paddles and pull buoys can be customized to serve as motivational aids. These belong to Scott Tinley.

4 CYCLING

When I started out as a triathlete, I had been riding my old Raleigh "in-town" bike around Davis for nearly 20 years, but I knew nothing about competitive cycling technique. I had never been on a really long ride; one 45-mile round-trip to the dam at Lake Berryessa had been my longest two-wheeled journey.

I was not schooled in the discomforts of cycling. I had never experienced riding for hours with my hands on the drops (the lower part of the handlebars), nor had I known the numerous varieties of a neck ache or the unforgettable sensation of my crotch going completely numb for an hour-and-a-half.

The swim-to-bike transition area at the Hawaii Ironman.

But I decided to invest quite a bit of money—$953 to be exact—in a racing bicycle. My friend Pat Feeney, who knew a lot about bike frames, seats, cranks, tubes, and wheels, helped me select my new bike. At the time, it seemed like a lot of money to spend, but I thought it would be a worthwhile investment because I figured I'd be riding competitively for years to come.

When I got my new bicycle, I rode every day for about three weeks—and came to the conclusion that cycling was the most uncomfortable sport ever invented. After a ride, my triceps throbbed and my legs burned inside and out. My arms had gotten kind of sore from swimming in the past, but I had never gone out and swum for three continuous hours—on a bike, there's no stopping. I just wasn't prepared for that endless effort.

Nor did I have the right equipment. I didn't have cycling shoes or gloves or padded shorts. The cold, damp Davis winter was just setting in and I rode in long underwear and sweatshirts—not exactly sleek. When I finally bought wool cycling "skins," gloves, and shoes with cleats, I was shocked at how much more comfortable I was—and more efficient. Unfortunately, it was quite a while before I learned that a few minor adjustments on my bicycle would resolve the rest of my aches and pains.

You can learn from my mistakes. Make sure your bicycle fits properly, and is adjusted for comfort as well as performance. If you wear the clothing that is designed for the sport, you will avoid the complaints that plagued me when I first started.

But no amount of equipment will save you if you don't know *how* to use it. Technique should be your main concern. Being skilled at any of the three sports is helpful to the new triathlete, but if you want to be a proficient competitor, you will have to eventually master all three.

FITTING YOUR BICYCLE

When I first bought that $953 bike, I had absolutely no indication of how it should have fit me, nor how I should have adjusted it. I didn't know where my head should be in relation to the stem, how straight my legs should be when the pedal was all the way down at the bottom of the stroke, or even how high my seat should be. The only clue I had was how comfortable I felt on the bike.

There was too much tension on my arms, my neck was in a knot, my crotch alternated between sore and totally numb, and my feet were always asleep. When I figured out how to adjust my bike, my technique and efficiency improved, along with my comfort.

When fitting your bicycle, your basic considerations are the frame (including the top tube length), seat height, handlebars, and handlebar stem.

FRAME

Your first consideration in fitting a bicycle is finding the right-sized frame. Have a knowledgeable person look at your position on a bike, measure your legs, arm, and torso length, and recommend an appropriate frame for you. Any reputable cycling shop should be able to help you. Unless you are very small or very large, you should be able to find a stock frame that fits.

Most people seem inclined to get bigger frames than they need, particularly if they are

An ideal triathlon bike performs well under racing conditions and holds up under the rigorous demands of training. Centurion designed my signature bike to my specifications. (Photo by Mark Clifford)

accustomed to touring. But a racing frame should be slightly smaller than a touring frame. When you stand over the bike, there should be a couple of inches between the top tube and your crotch. When seated, you should be able to extend your leg fully on the downstroke, so that you can lock your knee—you can adjust your seat height for a perfect fit.

A good way to fit a frame is to sit on a stationary apparatus, such as a wind-load simulator (see "Equipment," page 72). Have the shop mount the bike you are considering on the simulator, and take it for an in-store test ride. That will give you an idea of how it will feel on the road. Don't be afraid to stand up, adjust the seat, simulate varied terrain.

Once you have determined the size that fits just about right, you might want to try a half-size smaller for an optimal racing frame.

Look for a lightweight, relatively stiff frame. You'll have to learn to handle the rigid, pounding ride of a stiffer frame, but you will appreciate how much faster it is when you race. (It is faster than a softer frame because it doesn't flex when you apply pressure, so the frame isn't absorbing your torque/energy.)

Don't go crazy trying to find the lightest bike ever made. America's top cyclist, Greg LeMond, suggests using a frame that is sturdy enough to hold up under the rigorous demands of road racing. Overall weight is important, but a few bored-out holes in your brake handles never won a race for anyone.

Custom frames can be designed to your exact specifications, but they are costly and not necessary for the beginner. As a wise frame builder once said: "One hour of good technique is worth a thousand dollars of custom frames."

TOP TUBE LENGTH

An important consideration in choosing a frame that fits properly is the length of the top tube. Though road or time trial frames are built fairly uniformly in terms of the angles, some bicycles do feature a slighter longer top tube than others of the same basic dimensions. I recommend a long top tube (relative to your torso length) for triathletes, because it allows you to stretch out a bit more so that your upper body is more relaxed when you start to run.

However, don't select an extremely long top tube, because it will shift too much weight over the handlebars, putting excess stress on your triceps (which are already somewhat fatigued from the swim). If you have a slightly top-heavy build, you should use a standard-length top tube.

The optimal measurements of your frame will depend upon the length of your own torso. If you can't find a frame with a long enough top tube to suit you, you can achieve a similar effect by using a longer handlebar stem.

SEAT HEIGHT

After you have found a frame that fits, there are several other adjustments you may need to make for a perfect fit. First, you need to adjust your seat height so that you are properly positioned over the frame when you ride.

I have often heard cyclists complain that triathletes use poor technique and are improperly positioned on the bike. What many of these cyclists don't realize is that triathlon cycling is based on different considerations than pure road racing. When Greg LeMond finished the cycling portion of the World's Toughest Triathlon, for example, he was finished for the day—his one third of the relay was over with. But before Scott Molina even started that same ride, he had already swum nearly two-and-a-half miles, and after the bike ride was over, he still had to run a marathon. Obviously, Molina had to modify his technique to allow the best possible ride without totally exhausting his legs for the run.

One of those modifications is seat height. Conventional road racing position is relatively low, to facilitate fast spinning. However, many top cyclists are following the example of Tour de France champion Bernard Hinault—adjusting their seats higher for a more powerful down-stroke.

A higher seat is best for triathletes for three reasons: (1) You can get more power on your downstroke with your leg fully extended, (2) it takes some of the stress off your *gluteals* (but-tocks muscles) and alleviates tension when you start to run, and (3) it relieves pressure from your *vastus lateralis* (upper quadriceps) so your leg can extend more fully and comfortably dur-ing the run.

To position yourself correctly, sit on your bicy-cle and put your heel on the pedal spindle; when your foot is at the bottom of the stroke, your leg should be almost straight. You should be able to lock your knee with your heel just below the pedal, or parallel to it.

One final note about checking the height of your seat: Make sure that you wear your cycling shoes when you make the determination. Some shoes have thicker soles than others; cleats also add some height.

HANDLEBAR STEM

To check for the best length of your handlebar stem, get on your bicycle with your hands on the drops and look down. You should be looking directly over the stem shank. In that position, you should be able to stretch out without putting too much weight on your shoulders.

If you are heavily muscled in your shoulders, or if you are a woman with large breasts, you may want to use a slightly shorter stem, so that your weight is partially shifted away from your shoulders. Otherwise, your arms, back, and shoulders will be unnecessarily fatigued after a long ride.

When I first started riding, my legs didn't get tired, but my triceps felt worn out. It didn't make any sense to me at the time, because I knew I had strong arms from swimming and weight lifting. But when I rode downhill, I leaned too far forward; when I got to the bottom, my arms were so tired that they were shaking.

To find the best handlebar stem length, put your hands on the drops and look down.

Finally I realized that my seat was pointed down too much and my stem was a little bit too long. I made those two adjustments and raised the stem height slightly, and the problem was resolved.

Your stem height should be about even with your seat height. In fact, you might find it advantageous to adjust it a little higher during a race, because if you ride too low while wearing a hard-shell helmet (required at most triathlons)—with your hands on the drops, your chin tucked fairly tight, and your eyes focusing downward over your front wheel—it will put a lot of stress on your trapezius and neck muscles.

Road racers didn't have to wear helmets until 1986, when the United States Cycling Federation (USCF) ruled that hard-shell headgear would be required at sanctioned races. Now cyclists will also have to consider this sort of neck and shoulder fatigue when they are racing.

HANDLEBARS

If you have a background in swimming or another strength-oriented sport, you probably have fairly broad shoulders and a large girth, and you'll need a wider handlebar than other people. Using a 40-centimeter handlebar drew my elbows and shoulders in so that I was really streamlined, but it also restricted my breathing. When I am riding with my hands down on the drops, I want my arms out just a bit farther so that I can breathe properly; I switched to a 42-centimeter handlebar, and it made a noticeable difference. Even though my frontal resistance (to the air) was greater because my arms were out wider, I think it was certainly compensated for by the fact that I was able to breathe much more easily. Also, my upper-body weight seemed to be distributed more evenly, so cornering was much easier.

Riding with your elbows slightly outward is not the most aerodynamic position, but it will allow you to breathe more easily.

RIDING POSITION

A reporter once described former Olympic cyclist John Howard as looking like a praying mantis because he rode so hunched over his bike. Obviously you don't want to curve your spine that much, but you don't want your back to be stiff and straight, either. One of the keys to good racing is being able to relax. The best cycling position is one that allows you to ride efficiently while keeping your body as relaxed as possible.

You should try to ride with your back slightly flexed. That should be relatively easy on your shoulders; periodically moving your hands from the drops to the brake hoods will also alleviate some stress.

John Howard (right) passes Chris Hinshaw in the 1984 Ironman. His "praying mantis" position didn't keep him from registering the fastest bike split and finishing fifth overall.

HAND POSITION

Triathletes should try to ride with their hands on the drops most of the time, because it is aerodynamically advantageous. But when you do move your hands to the brake hoods, it will allow you to sit up a little more and redistribute your weight on the seat. Although many people choose to race in that position—probably because it seems more comfortable and their hands are closer to the brakes—it is not a good idea for people who are top-heavy. It puts more weight on your triceps and brings your body forward, which can unduly fatigue your arms, neck, and shoulders by the time you start to run.

However, riders who are more bottom-heavy may find that racing with their hands on the brake hoods—with elbows flexed more—is more comfortable and less tiring in the long run. You have to experiment based on your own body type and how your position seems to affect your performance.

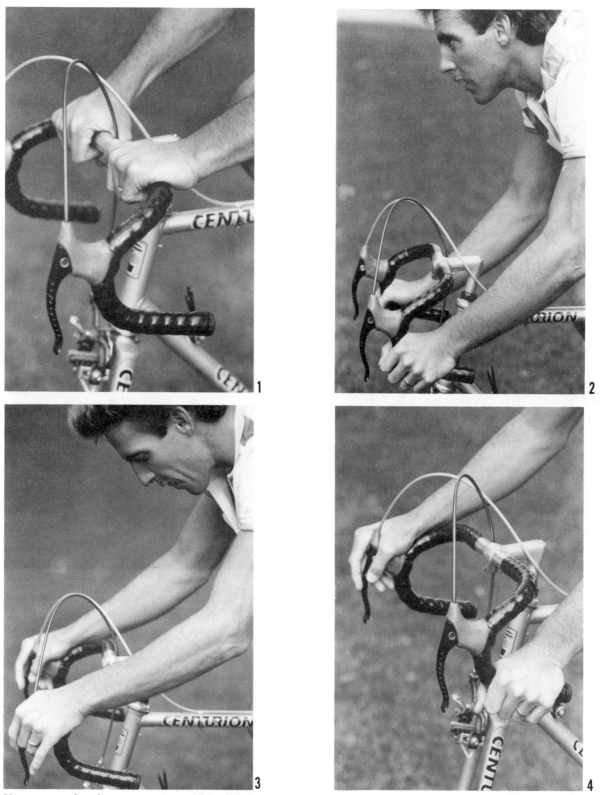

Varying your hand position occasionally will help you relax during a long race. A close grip (with elbows flexed and shoulders fairly low) is good for time trialing and climbing. You can also place your hands on the drops, the brake hoods, or one on the drop and the other on the brake hood.

ELBOWS AND ARMS

Your elbows should be slightly flexed and your hands should be fairly relaxed, with your fingers loosely wrapped around the drops. Don't grip so hard that your knuckles turn white; that will not give you any more control and it will tighten up your hand and forearm muscles.

As a general rule, you shouldn't move your hands close together, toward the stem. It will detract from your steering control, and your hands will not be close to the brakes. However, some triathletes prefer that position for gradual climbs; it allows them to pull on each down-stroke, which rests the back and triceps.

During the 1984 Ironman, I stayed relaxed by keeping my elbows slightly flexed, varying my hand position and wiggling my fingers around from time to time. I don't usually wear gloves in a race, so it is especially important to keep my fingers and hands supple.

RELAXING YOUR UPPER BODY

To relieve the pressure on my back and hands—and to break the monotony—I move around quite a bit. Every four or five miles I take my hands completely off the handlebars and shake my arms out a bit, which relaxes my shoulders as well. I wiggle my fingers around, too, to avoid any numbness.

All of this adds to the relaxation of my whole upper body. One thing you absolutely want to avoid is being cramped up on top before you even start the run.

Another way you can relax is to roll your head around. Just make a circular motion two or three times in one direction, then two or three times the other way. Occasionally look down and slightly back toward the seat; this will alleviate stress in your upper spine.

FOOT POSITION

This is one area in which I learned a lesson. I had been advised by road racers to ride with my feet pointed straight ahead, so that's what I tried to do. But I walk (and run) like a duck—it's simply my anatomy—and this straight-ahead foot position was extremely hard on my hips and knees. Eventually I began to have trouble with my *vastus medialis* (the muscle extending down your thigh to your kneecap) on the inside of my knee.

(I have noticed that this is a common problem for swimmers and runners who become triathletes. They tend to have poorly developed vastus medialis muscles, and if they are pushing too big a gear—below 75 rpm's—or their seat is extremely high with feet pointed inward, their knees will rotate inward at the bottom of their stroke. This stresses the tendon and the kneecap.)

The best way to find out your own optimal foot position is to loosen up your cleat and allow your foot to move around while you ride 10 or 20 miles. You will eventually find the proper foot position for your individual anatomy, just as you do when you walk.

If you notice that your pressure on the pedal changes during your stroke, you may need to adjust your cleat. You should also pay careful attention to where the ball of your foot is in relation to the axis of the pedal.

If your cleat is too far back on your shoe—the ball of your foot is too far over the pedal spindle—you'll end up pointing your toe too much at the bottom of your stroke. It will feel almost as though your toes are rolling over the pedal. Your toes will actually flex inside your shoe, which may cause cramping in your arch. It can also cause your *gastroenemus* and *soleus* (calf muscles) to shorten and knot up, which can bring about extreme pain and calf cramps during the run.

If your cleat is too far forward on your shoe—the ball of your foot is not over the spindle at all—you'll end up pushing too hard to initiate your downstroke. That will put undue pressure on your patellar (knee) tendon and your quadriceps and cause a lot of unneccessary fatigue.

Sometimes adding a prescribed orthotic (or a slight lift or pad) on one side will correct uneven foot pressure.

DIFFERENT STROKES: CYCLISTS VERSUS TRIATHLETES

In a road race, cyclists ride in pace lines or packs. They have to use explosive bursts of energy to break away or attack. In a triathlon, however, packs and pace lines are categorically eliminated with the no-drafting rule.

The bike leg of a triathlon is a time trial—you are riding alone. You don't have the advantage of drafting, nor do you have to break away in a sudden burst.

CADENCE

You will probably find it better to train at a slower cadence than a cyclist would. (See Chapter 6.) When I first started riding, cyclists told me I should pedal at 90 to 110 pedal revolutions per minute. But I have found that such a fast cadence may not be best for triathletes. If you

have to travel a certain number of miles, and it takes a certain number of wheel revolutions to get there, is it really better to spin the pedals an extra 5,000 revolutions just to get to the finish in the same amount of time?

The answer is not cut-and-dried. Obviously

you can't use such a high gear that your legs tire out in the first few minutes, but there is a diminishing return if your cadence is so fast that you exhaust your fast-twitch fibers. Since triathlon training is more aerobic in nature, you are better off using a slower cadence.

The optimum range for a triathlete is between 80 and 90 revolutions per minute. (This will vary depending upon your leg weight and the hills you encounter.)

CIRCULAR VERSUS ELLIPTICAL STROKES

Though most cyclists use a smooth, circular stroke when they race, triathletes should concentrate on long, elliptical strokes. Don't press straight down from 12 o'clock (the top of the pedal revolution) to 6 o'clock (bottom). Press out, instead, to 3 o'clock, then pull back slightly with your heel to 9 o'clock, then pull up again and back out to 3 o'clock, etc.

ANKLE FLEXION

At the top of your stroke, your ankle should be flexed so that your foot is fairly flat. As you press slightly forward in your elliptical stroke, push forward with your toes. Don't roll your foot too far forward over the spindle; keep your weight on the ball of your foot.

When your foot is between 3 and 6 o'clock, tug slightly with your heel to initiate your upswing. Thinking about the upstroke at that point—rather than pushing down hard then stopping—can really help you maintain a smooth rhythm. I find this particularly helpful

When your foot is at 9 o'clock (applying the greatest amount of pressure) extend your ankle no more than 120 degrees. Do not extend farther than that, or you might develop calf cramps.

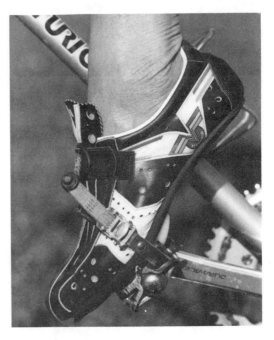

after a hill or a sudden increase in acceleration for some reason. When I face those *mumuku* crosswinds at the Ironman, I concentrate on my elliptical stroke to regain my momentum.

At the bottom of your downstroke, extend your ankle 150 degrees. Do not point your toe, as in the photo above.

RELAXING YOUR FEET AND LEGS

I think my ability to relax on the bike has helped my running performance more than anything else. I find that no matter how long the races—or how severe—I am able to relax my leg muscles enough on the bike to avoid that dead, heavy feeling when I start the run. Even though my legs do get fatigued, they are relaxed enough for me to get into my running rhythm within the first half-mile—at most races. There have been exceptions, such as the 1983 Ironman where it seemed to take forever to pick up my pace, but being relaxed after the bike ride has been an appreciable advantage for me at almost all of my successful races.

The following drills will help you relax your legs while cycling. You can practice them when you're training as well as racing.

1 *Alternate leg rests:* When you start to get tired during a race, concentrate on pedaling five elliptical strokes with your right leg, letting your left leg rest. Repeat with your left leg while your right leg rests. Continue that pattern: four right/four left, three right/three left, two right/two left, then back to every other stroke.

Pedal very lightly with the resting leg and wiggle your toes around. Hyperextend your toes, try to lift your heel up inside your shoe, and let your foot slide back and forth. That helps the blood flow more freely to your feet, preventing numbness and cramping. Loosen your toe strap from time to time to avoid numbness on the outside of your foot just prior to running.

This drill allows your legs to rest up. It has helped me increase my tempo noticeably (a mile and a half faster per hour). It is especially helpful when you're coming off of a section of rolling hills, and you are back on the flats again, but you've lost a little momentum—or your rhythm—from the climb.

2 *Mid-stroke leg rest:* Relax your legs on part of the stroke rather than working consistently all the way through it. Work the down part, then relax on the upstroke, or work from 3 o'clock to 9 o'clock, but allow yourself several cadences where you relax your legs. Emphasize complete elliptical revolutions.

3 *Calf stretches:* Stand up from time to time. On the flats, stand up and push your hips forward and drop your heel down to stretch out your calf. This is good when you first get on the bike, because your calves are usually tight from pointing your toes while kicking during the swim. If your ankle extends too much at the bottom of your stroke, your calf will tighten even more. So I try not to ride for more than 20 to 30 minutes without stretching.

Sometimes when I'm standing up on my bike, I shift into a larger gear and slow my cadence just a little bit, but actually increase my speed. Then when I sit back down and return to the gear I have been using, it actually seems easier.

HILL CLIMBING

The secret to successful hill climbing, I've learned, is not just how fast you get up the hill—it is also how fast you can top it off, come back onto the flats, and get back into your regular cadence. You can lose a tremendous amount of time if you have trouble on a hill, and you can make up even more if you are prepared for it. Learning how to use hills to your advantage is one of the best skills you can have as a competitive triathlete. (See Chapters 6 and 8.)

That's something I work on a lot. I try to maintain a steady speed going up the hill and once I get within 50 yards of the top, I actually accelerate slightly. That increases my lactate level quite a bit and I start breathing harder, but as soon as I get to the top, the lactate starts diffusing back into my bloodstream, my heart rate goes down, that burning sensation in my legs subsides, and I resume my speed.

Regaining your momentum is a key factor in successful hill climbing. It will be much easier for you when you have trained your oxidative fast-twitch fibers to respond aerobically. (The training program in Chapter 6 includes workouts to achieve that goal.) However, don't rely on a one-minute effort at the top of the hill to save your race—virtually all of the top triathletes ride the entire hill fast.

IT'S EASIER IF YOU STAND UP

For most triathletes, it's easier to get up the hills if you "get out of the saddle"—stand up. You'll use your energy more efficiently that way, and avoid overloading your quadriceps. I have seen a lot of triathletes grinding it out over the hills like many road racers do—sitting down. However, some of the world's finest cyclists, including Greg LeMond, tend to stand more than they sit.

When you're standing, you should hook your ring finger and middle finger underneath the brake hoods, with your index finger wrapped around the brake and your thumb over the top. Your little finger is slightly relaxed. You can use a subtle pulling motion to give you a little more torque; as you step down on the right side, for example, pull a little bit with your right arm and allow the bike to rock slightly to the side so that your body will be directly over the pedals.

For gradual climbs, slide back in your saddle and grip the handlebars close to the stem if you are going to remain seated. However, it is usually better for triathletes to stand up.

CHOOSING GEARS

Make sure you're not in too large a gear or the muscles in your back will shorten quite a bit, your gluteals will tighen up, your stomach will protrude forward, your pelvis will shift forward, and you'll end up using your arms too much.

Once again, it is very important to know yourself, understand your abilities and your body type. Tailor your gearing to your own needs. If you are a powerful, aerobically strong triathlete, and you are able to assess the severity and length of the hill as within two or three minutes' total effort, you will probably be able to go up it fairly quickly, top it off fast, and get back into your regular rhythm without much trouble. But if you are predominantly a fast-twitch, white-fiber body type, you'll probably want to start off in a much easier gear—start slowly and build up your effort over the hill.

In your training, it is critical that you understand your body type so that you can understand your strengths and weaknesses—and capitalize on your strengths when you are doing the cycling leg. (As you train, you will discover exactly what your strengths are.)

When you're going up a hill, you can sometimes stay in the same gear, depending on the steepness. Your cadence will usually slow down to 50 or 60 rpm's. In short climbs with a 2 to 5 percent grade, you may find it easier to gear up a little bit and maintain your speed. If the hill will take longer than a minute and a half, though, gearing up will cause your lactate level to rise sharply. You have to experiment and learn what works best for you.

Once you get to the top of the hill, as you get ready to start your descent, shift into a larger gear to increase your speed right away. Once you sit down on the downhill, get your speed up to maximum, then try to relax your legs by spinning easily.

Don't lock your legs up and hold them in a fixed position on a long descent after a climb; that will prevent lactate from diffusing back into your bloodstream for use as a fuel. Keep up your

spinning—60 to 80 rpm's—on the descents, even if you're not engaging any gears.

Try to come off the hill as quickly as you can. And remember to start the climb slowly, because you're going to reach your maximum breathing rate after about a minute and a half, which will cause your lactate level to rise. But if you maintain a steady tempo, you will stabilize the oxygen/carbon dioxide exchange. You may actually be able to increase your cadence a bit.

During hill climbing, I concentrate on being very relaxed and breathing with my diaphragm—letting my stomach go out on the inhale and in on the exhale. If you are using the wrong gear, it will impair your breathing rate.

Dan Harper's (opposite page) downhill position is extremely aerodynamic, but it can be unstable; Scott Tinley (above) is also aerodynamic with his head tucked, but he has more control because his hands are wider and down on the drops; the third triathlete (right) is sitting up far too high.

RIDING IN THE WIND

Like everybody else, I hate riding in the wind. You can never win; if you fight the wind, you're going to lose. I just try to relax and to stay as low as I can in front. If I am following a line or a relatively straight course, I'll lift my head once every 10 or 15 revolutions to look ahead 100 to 200 yards—then I tuck it again.

When I do raise my head to see what's in front of me, I look at the road surface to see if there are any major obstructions (a piece of wood, shattered glass, dead animals, etc.) and if there is nothing visible, I put my head back down as close to the stem as I comfortably can. At that point, my frontal vision is limited to about five feet, which can be frightening in an unfamiliar area.

At the Hawaii Ironman, I try to stay very low, because there is generally a front or cross-wind—or both—the entire time.

Occasionally, though, I treat the wind as a force just like a hill; I stand up. Even though it increases my frontal resistance, it allows me to stretch my body out and get some relief from the tension of riding huddled over the bike. When you are standing up on the flats against a wind, you may want to move into a larger gear.

The dangers of the wind are fairly obvious. In addition to slowing you down, a strong crosswind can virtually blow you over or off the road. When you are riding downhill against the wind, be sure to hang on a little tighter to the drops.

Jo Anne Ernst rides out of the saddle with her hands on the drops to regain her speed against the wind. This position is also good for short hills.

USING YOUR BRAKES

Get used to using your front brake when you are going fast and you want to slow down. Don't apply it too sharply or you'll go right over the handlebars—not a fun thing to do. But if you hit your back brake on a turn, your back wheel will slide out quite a bit. Apply the front brake first, then as your bike begins to slow, lightly apply the back brake.

I sometimes pump my brakes a little bit and it doesn't seem to alter the line of my bike as much as a steady application.

When you are leaning into a sharp turn, allow your downhill leg and knee to move out slightly. That will help you corner a little more smoothly. You can also let your downhill elbow go out just a little bit and lean over the bar to the opposite side. But don't resist the motion of the bike; as soon as you elevate your body, the bike will straighten out and you could easily get in an accident.

REPAIRS

Let's face it, if you are out on a triathlon course and anything major goes wrong with your bicycle, you will not be in much of a position to fix it—unless your bike has a side-car that carries a complete tool and spare parts kit! Unlike cycling road races, the no-assistance rule in almost all triathlons forbids any outside help at all, even borrowing a tool to make your own repair.

There are no spare wheels, no pit crews, and no mechanics in a triathlon. That was certainly a poignant lesson for Mark Allen when his broken derailleur forced him out in the October 1982 Ironman—he was a close second (behind me) at the time. Ironically, I suffered the same fate in a race Allen eventually won: the 1985 Nice Triathlon. On race morning I discovered that the spokes had been broken on one of my wheels, and I had to make a last-minute switch to an inferior training wheel. The tire was poor, and it flatted on the hilly course, where it was unsafe to put on a new sew-up (tubular) tire that might come unglued on a 50-mph downhill.

FLAT TIRES

It is not impossible to change (or fix) a flat tire during a race, even though it can be extremely frustrating. At the 1982 Malibu Triathlon, Scott Molina was virtually on the homestretch—on his way to a prize-money victory—when one of his tires flatted. He stood at the side of the road, trying to pump up his tire for several minutes while other riders passed him by. I know exactly how discouraged he felt. After several minutes—and even more riders—he gave up.

The best way to learn how to fix a flat is to practice when there is nothing at stake. When Bill Bryant went to Hawaii as the bike mechanic for now-defunct Team J. David, he made them practice fixing flats over and over while he timed them. His theory was that it was useless to spend months training to ride the bike course three or four minutes faster, just to lose it all by spending 10 minutes fixing a flat tire.

Reading instructions is not the ideal way to learn this skill. Go to a bike shop, or have a friend show you exactly how to do it. Then practice changing your tires—before they go flat—so you will be an expert at it when the need arises.

Flat tires come with the territory.

Clincher tires (see page 73) are less prone to flats than sew-ups, but they take much longer to repair (and they are not as fast). You have to wedge the bad tire off the rim with tire irons, then install the new tire (or fix the old one), then pump it up. Sew-ups are glued to the rim; you just pull them off and stick another one on.

The correct pressure for your tires will be indicated on the tire sidewall. But if you don't carry a gauge—most people don't—you can test it by trying to squeeze the tire between your thumb and forefinger. If you can depress it, you need more air. You should always carry a pump; it will fit right on your frame.

If you have an aversion to bicycle pumps—and you want to save a lot of time—you can buy CO_2 cartridges, much like the ones used to put the fizz in carbonated water, that will fill your tires with air in a matter of seconds. John Howard used those in the 1983 Ironman, when vandals covered the bike course with carpet tacks, but it didn't do him much good—after two flats, he ran out of spare tires. *C'est la vie.*

MINOR REPAIRS

Even if you can't realistically make many repairs during a race, it is a good idea to know how to take care of basic repairs when you train. On long rides, it is especially important to be able to fix your bike well enough to get to the nearest telephone, if not back home.

Most reputable bicycle shops offer information about basic repairs, and many offer classes and clinics. Ask your local triathlon organization (see Appendix C) where to find such classes.

EQUIPMENT

All the bicycle manufacturers claim they have the lightest, most aerodynamic components on the market. Some may be better than others, but in the end it's the rider—not the bike—that wins a race. Losing a couple of pounds and tucking your head in tighter will help you far more than a flashy brake that's smoothed over to avoid catching wind or black "Hollywood-go-faster" rims.

But there are certain basics, in addition to the bicycle itself, that will make cycling easier and more productive.

CLOTHING

I'm not an expert on cycling clothes, nor would I qualify as a fashion consultant, so I hesitate to make concrete recommendations as to the type of clothing you should select. You will have to see what feels best and works best for you. But there are some basic components necessary to any triathlete's cycling wardrobe. You should have stiff-soled cleated cycling shoes, close-fitting cycling shorts, padded cycling gloves, a helmet, and sunglasses.

1 *Cleated cycling shoes* lock your foot into place on the pedal, and are said to increase riding efficiency by as much as 25 to 30 percent. Most cycling shoes are leather (usually black, for some reason) and they come with fixed or adjustable cleats. If you choose adjustable cleats—as most triathletes do—you will be able to try different foot positions on the pedal, and find the best one for you. Fixed cleats are nailed or screwed into place on the shoe, and must be totally removed to be adjusted.

2 *Shorts* are available in many stretch fabrics and colors, and should be tight-fitting. They usually have a chamois or padded crotch, to add a little comfort on those long rides. You can also get wool, cotton, or Lycra tights (sometimes called "skins") to keep your legs warm in the winter. Many sports apparel companies now feature all-purpose sports tights (with foot stirrups) that can be used for running and cycling. However, they do not usually come with a chamois or padded crotch.

Some triathletes like to wear one-piece skin suits for one, two, or all three events, but I really don't recommend it. If a skin suit is tight enough on top to offer any aerodynamic benefit, it inhibits your breathing. Also, if it has a chamois crotch, it can chafe and be stiff and uncomfortable while you're running; if it doesn't have a chamois, it will be uncomfortable for cycling. There is a lot of experimentation in the triathlon clothing field, but so far, no one-piece suit has worked for me in the three different sports.

3 *Padded gloves* are like shock absorbers for your hands. I don't always wear them, but most people find that they are essential to a comfortable ride.

4 *A hard-shell helmet* has become a fact of life for cyclists, whether they like it or not. Until 1986, road racers wore leather "hairnets," (soft, open-construction helmets that look almost like a catcher's mask) as protective headgear. But compelling head injury and death statistics prompted USCF officials to change their rules; hard-shell helmets are now required at all USCF-sanctioned events, as they have been for several years at triathlons. There are many varieties available; check your local bike shop.

5 *Sunglasses* are a boon for all three sports. They cut the glare, even on overcast days, and allow you to relax your eyes and facial muscles, which in turn relaxes your neck and shoulders. I always wear them.

TIRES

There are two basic kinds of tires—tubular (sew-ups) and clinchers. A clincher tire must be used with a clincher rim, on which the tire is fastened in basically the same way that an automobile tire is mounted on its wheel. A tubular tire is completely enclosed and is glued to the wheel. Most cyclists and triathletes use tubular tires because they are thought to be lighter and faster. However, they do puncture much more easily than clinchers, and can also be very slippery on wet roads.

The walls of tubular tires are usually made from silk or cotton. The silk ones are very slippery in wet weather, and are more subject to expansion and/or contraction with changes in air temperature. I was riding on silk tires at the rainy 1985 Japan Ironman, and I crashed because the silk didn't have enough surface tension on the wet pavement. I managed to get up and finish the race, but my hip was injured and I couldn't run for some time afterward. That interruption in my training program affected my performance for the rest of the season. I'm switching to cotton!

PARAPHERNALIA

If I tried to list all the gadgets that you can get for cycling, it would require an entire catalog. So do your own shopping, but be sure to include the following items: (1) a water bottle and a water bottle holder for your frame, (2) a pump, and (3) an odometer with a stopwatch so that you can monitor your intervals (interval training is discussed in Chapter 6).

You can get anything you want, from a stereo system to a programmable air horn. I personally suggest you stick to basics on your racing bike—I have yet to see a bike with streamers and a portable TV crossing a triathlon finish line!

5 RUNNING

s a triathlete, you are likely to experience a rude awakening the first time you hop off your bike with visions of running your best-ever 10 kilometers. Your legs have undergone an incredible transition—they feel as though they have turned into cement. If you have a running background, you may be particularly shocked by the tightness you feel in your quadriceps after what seemed to be a smooth bike ride.

I have seen aspiring ex-runners zip through the swim and power through the bike, only to come prancing out of the bike-to-run transition on their toes, looking more like they were doine a painful rendition of *Swan Lake* than the final leg of an endurance event. Unfortu-

A triathlon can be made or broken during the run.

nately, it doesn't feel as amusing as it looks, especially when someone passes by you in an apparently effortless trot.

Running fast and efficiently in a triathlon is one of the keys to successful racing. Since running is usually the last event in a triathlon, it can make or break you. Yet you start out with a handicap: the fatigue you have accumulated from the two previous events. Even if you have a solid running background, chances are you have not developed your quadriceps or upper body muscles used during the first two events of a triathlon.

Running, by itself, utilizes primarily your *hamstrings* (the muscles on the back of your thigh) for lift and drive and your quadriceps to stabilize and support your knee joint during a run. But during the first stages of a triathlon, your upper body—which is virtually undeveloped if all you usually do is run—has had a major workout. Your back, shoulders, and arms have been vigorously stressed during the swim, and again during the bike ride. It's easy to understand why even the most talented runners can have a tough time finding a comfortable stride when they get to the critical final phase of a triathlon.

Never take running for granted. Many triathletes are far faster runners than I am—on paper—but have not been able to perform as well during a race. I have worked at developing my upper body and my quadriceps, so that I recover quickly when I get off the bike. I start the run with an advantage—I am simply not as tired.

During the run, you can clearly see the advantages of cross-training. Building your upper body and quadriceps makes you more powerful in the water and on the bike, cuts down on cumulative fatigue, and even gives you an extra edge in the run, where you can use your arms for added power.

Top sprinters use their arms as well as their legs; the faster they move, the faster their arms pump. At the end of some of the longer triathlons, such as the Ironman, a lot of runners drag along with their upper bodies completely stiff. Their shoulders are drawn, their arms fall limply at their sides, and their legs move at a very slow pace.

In future years, as triathletes develop a better understanding of training—and of the three sports as modified components of one overall sport—running times in triathlons are going to drop dramatically. The gap between personal best times for a given distance and times during a triathlon run (of the same distance) is going to narrow. The top triathletes are presently running within a minute to a minute and a half of their best 10-kilometer times. That's quite a remarkable accomplishment.

There's no mystery to becoming a skilled triathlon runner. Learn proper technique and train yourself to run longer and faster under triathlon circumstances. (Training techniques and special considerations are discussed fully in Chapter 6.)

BODY POSITION

The first thing I think about when I start my run is body alignment, not because I want to look good, but because it can determine how well I run, especially when I'm tired. A reporter once described me as "burning holes in the pavement" with my eyes during the Ironman run. That may present an image of someone who is so exhausted that he can't hold his head up, but I actually lower my head deliberately. It allows me to lean slightly forward and land softly on my heels—though I wouldn't say I look particularly soft. I look more like a stampeding buffalo.

Where you focus your eyes determines the position of your head, which in turn determines the position of your body. You should focus on a spot 40 or 50 feet ahead of you, occasionally glancing upward to view any turns or changes in the course. Try not to look upward too often; it can shift your pelvis and hips forward, causing you to land harder on your heels.

During the 1983 Ironman run, I was so tired that I had a hard time concentrating on keeping my head down. I could hear my feet slapping the pavement as my pace slipped into a slow plod. When I lowered my gaze, it made me lean forward just enough to realign my body properly and pick up my pace. (Unfortunately, during the final five miles, all semblance of efficiency stopped. I was mentally and physically drained.)

You can check your posture by looking at your shadow from the side if the sun is near setting. Or if you are running past a store or shopping center, peek in the plate glass windows—but be discreet!

Don't lean too far; 5 percent is plenty. Don't bend forward or backward, and don't arch your back or bend over at your stomach. When I start my runs, I try to concentrate on drawing my pelvis back, as though I were starting a sit-

Mike Norton demonstrates correct body position, looking down slightly so that his body leans forward about 5 percent.

up motion. Just drop your chin slightly to initiate this response.

When you get off the bike, your back and spine are flexed from your bent-over cycling position. Your shoulders and trapezius are tight from being hunched over, as are your hip *flexors* (the muscles that allow your legs to bend at the hips). You should push your pelvis slightly forward when you get off the bike, letting your head come up to stretch out your back a bit. During the transition, while you are seated, look downward, then upward to stretch your back.

RELAXING YOUR FACE, NECK, AND SHOULDERS

You'll have a more efficient run if you are relaxed. Conversely, scowling or grimacing will tighten your neck and shoulder muscles. Common occurrences such as blisters on your feet or squinting into the sun can cause you to clench your jaw and stiffen your *sternocleido-mastoids* (the large muscles on either side of your neck that extend from behind the ears down to the junction of the breastbone and collarbones).

Since your trapezius muscles eventually meet up with your sternocleidomastoids, your neck, shoulders, and chest tighten up when you grimace. Your arms will pump higher, your shoulders will rise even more, and soon your whole body will be in a knot—all because of a scowl on your face.

I always try to keep my face as relaxed as possible—regardless of the conditions—whenever I train or race. Every quarter-mile I consciously drop my shoulders, relax my face, and let my cheeks just feel loose. Occasionally I roll my head around just a little bit, and that also seems to alleviate some of the tightness. It is vital that your upper body be relaxed, not just so that you'll feel more comfortable (which you will), but so that you can use your arms to your best advantage while you're running.

USING YOUR ARMS AND HANDS

It is important to get your arms moving as soon as you start the run. Unfortunately, it is not easy to do that when your shoulders are tight from the swim and the bike ride. Following are some hints that will help you.

DOS

1 Swing your arms forward, but keep the movement in your lower arms to avoid working your heavier upper arms and shoulder joints.
2 Keep your elbows bent at about 90 to 110 degrees and your hands loosely cupped. Put your thumb on top of your index finger rather than clinching your hand into a fist.
3 Keep your arm movement rhythmic and easy.

Keep your elbows bent at 90 to 110 degrees.

Proper hand position. Note the thumb on top of the index finger.

DON'TS

1 Don't bring your hands out too far in front of you.
2 Don't cross your arms in front of you.
3 Don't bring your arms up high, in front of your face; your hands should stop at the midline of your torso.
4 Don't swing one arm wider or higher than the other; it can cause you to sway from side to side with each stride. You will probably have to concentrate on uniform arm carriage at first, but it will eventually become an unconscious effort. This side-to-side sway can also be caused by one of your legs being shorter than the other, or a particular tightness in one side of your body.

HOW TO RELAX

Your arms can help you relax when you run. Every four or five minutes, drop your shoulders and shake out your arms and fingers. It will relieve some of the tightness accumulated in your upper body.

I drop my shoulders and shake out my hands and fingers to relax (1984 Ironman).

KEEPING IN STRIDE: WHAT TO DO WITH YOUR FEET AND LEGS

The point of the following information is not to make you feel like a robot when you run, but to remind you that the key factor in triathlon running is efficiency—keeping fatigue in every muscle down to a minimum so that you can perform to the maximum. Every bit of energy you save by not lifting too high, extending too far, slapping your heel too hard, or reaching for too long a stride is energy you have available to run faster, all the way to the end.

STRIDE LENGTH

Your back will feel tight when you get off your bike, along with your pelvis and hip flexors. They're not stretched out enough for you to start off with a long, comfortable stride. If you try to regain your stride length too soon, you'll be fighting a losing battle against your own body. (More on this in Chapter 8.)

If you are training in all three sports, I recommend starting out with a shorter stride length than you would usually use, and concentrating on developing a smooth rhythm and breathing pattern. You can gradually lengthen your stride.

The mechanics of stride are fairly simple: in order to achieve a longer step, you have to lift your leg higher in front and extend it farther in back. That's what sprinters do—but not for hours and certainly not after swimming and cycling.

Even some of the top triathletes utilize a long stride and a high kick during races, but that puts too much stress on their hamstrings, so that they eventually lose their effectiveness, or get cramps in their hip flexors, or both. They could be faster in the long run if they would increase their stride frequency (how often their legs turn over) and decrease stride length.

I "shuffle" when I run, keeping my stride short and my knees low, so that the bend in my hip is at about 120 degrees at the most. That way I don't tire out my hamstrings from all that high lifting or wear out my hip flexors from reaching out for a longer stride.

A long stride and high kick (above) puts too much stress on your hamstrings; a shorter stride (left) with faster leg turnovers is more efficient for triathlon running.

PLANTING YOUR FEET ON THE GROUND

I try to land on the heel of my foot for just a second, then roll to the ball of my foot, then push off hard from my big toe. I concentrate on moving quickly from my heel so that I can spring off my toes. One of the worst feelings you can have during a run is that your feet are almost sticking to the ground, slapping your heel on the pavement.

It's natural for your calves to feel tired during a triathlon run—they've already been stressed during the bike ride. But try to keep your heels on the ground for as short a time as possible.

When you make contact with the pavement, draw an imaginary line down the center of your body onto the road, almost like the dotted white line that divides the lanes. Plant each foot just slightly off the center of the line. Don't let your feet stray too far out from the imaginary line, nor cross over the center of it.

2. Roll to the ball (outside) of your foot.

1. Land on the heel of your foot.

3. Push off with your big toe.

BREAKING THE MONOTONY

There is no set formula that has to be followed every second you are training and racing. It's good to vary your stride from time to time and drop your hands down, look up, look around, land on your heels, land on your toes. Momentary breaks from the rhythm you have established give you a mental boost as well as a physical break. This subtle change recruits a different set of muscle fibers, which gives the more commonly used fibers a respite.

People always ask me what I think about, how I keep from being bored or tired during a long race. I have no magic formula or secret mental tricks. I just think about my breathing and my technique. I don't meditate or chant or visualize myself winning the race or use any other method of distracting myself from what I am doing at that exact moment. I don't fret about the past or worry about the future—I concentrate 100 percent on the present.

That means I allow myself to enjoy the environment around me, the people I see along the way, and the feeling of exhilaration I get when I know I am putting out my utmost physical and mental effort. I do chat with people along the way and look around at the scenery, but I don't let it distract me from my task at hand. I always bring my thoughts and concentration back to the race, and to my technique.

There are many ways to break the monotony of a long run; Patricia and Sylviane Puntous maintain proper form while keeping each other company.

BREATHING

As we've already seen in the chapters on swimming and cycling, breathing is really important, and the rhythm is different for each of the three sports. When you make the swim-to-bike transition, your breathing automatically changes because you are no longer in the water with breathing dictated by your stroke.

But when you switch from cycling to running, the breathing change is more subtle. There is a tendency to get off the bike without concentrating on breathing any differently. Within a very few minutes, the physical demands of running can give way to hyperventilation, which makes you feel as though you are anaerobic, even if you are keeping to a relatively slow pace. That can really be disarming—you can't figure out why you feel so tired when you're going so slow.

You should be aware of your breathing during every phase of a triathlon. Every transition involves a change in your breathing. When you make the bike-to-run transition, make sure you are breathing with your *diaphragm* (the muscular partition between your chest and your abdomen). Try to take slow, deep inhales through your mouth and long, slow exhales through your nose. Ideally, your breathing will be relatively slow and very rhythmic; you should be able to say three or four words out loud without hyperventilating.

HILL RUNNING

I am not sure that running "killer hills" is particularly beneficial for triathletes. It's not running uphill that is so treacherous on the body—although it is extremely demanding—it is the downhills that can really hurt you. When you run downhill, the impact on each foot strike is dramatically greater than it is on level ground.

Of all the triathlon sports, running is the most physically demanding, because you have to move your entire body. When you ride a bike, you sit on a seat and move only your legs, and when you swim, you are floating. Pumping the blood from your heart to all your extremities (when you are running) is a lot of work for your heart. It is especially tough on hills, because you have to pump your arms harder and lift your knees higher.

But if you live in a hilly environment, you will obviously have to learn to live with hills. Following are some tips that should help you:

1 When you're going uphill, increase your forward lean quite a bit, and try to stay on the balls of your feet rather than landing on your heels. Using your arms more and lifting your knees higher will also help. Your energy output is increased on the uphills and your recovery is slightly slower on the downhills, so you will need to carefully assess your pace and adjust it if necessary. Since you use your quadriceps on

When running uphill, bring your arms up higher.

the uphills, it is a good idea to strengthen them as much as possible. You can supplement your strength training by standing up often on your bike during training rides.

2 When you're heading downhill, your instinct is probably to lean back and put on your brakes, but it's better to lean very slightly forward, lengthen your stride, kick your heels higher behind you, and let the hill carry you down. If you're not a daredevil, you may not feel particularly comfortable about the prospect of falling flat on your face, so be very careful to be in control each time your foot lands on the ground. Running downhill forces your leg muscles into eccentric contractions; the trauma and force of impact are tremendous. You should exercise extreme caution. The heavier you are and/or the longer your stride, the greater the impact.

3 Once you get down the hill, the important thing is to get back into your normal rhythm. Try not to slap your foot on the ground, stay as light on your feet as possible, use your calves for foot extension, and shorten your stride again. Don't worry about your speed dropping; think about your head position, focus your eyes, get your arms moving, and ease back into your flatland mode.

STRETCHING

We'll discuss weight training and stretching in depth in Chapter 7, but it is worth stating at this point that stretching before you run is not a good idea, unless it is an extremely subtle stretch. You can start off a run with some long-stride walking, backward walking (pointing your toe in slightly to allow your muscles to begin warming up), and then slowly getting into your stride. After you have run at a slow, relaxed pace for three or four minutes, *then* stop and stretch. Your muscles will be warmed up a bit.

After you run, you should stretch slowly and easily, and perhaps walk for several minutes to cool down. A hot shower immediately afterward will also relax your muscles.

1. Hamstring stretch: Bend over and reach behind your leg, exhale slowly, slide hands down toward calves. Bend knees as you straighten up.

2. Also a hamstring stretch: With knees bent, bend over at waist while exhaling, reach toward toes slowly—do not bounce. 3. Quadriceps stretch: Reach behind and grab the top of your foot, pull foot up toward buttocks, bend over slightly to increase stretch. 4. Hip and gluteal stretch: Grab ankle and foot, draw up toward hip, lean forward slightly.

EQUIPMENT

The most obvious—and indispensible—item of running equipment is a pair of suitable shoes. Every person has different feet and different problems, so you'll have to experiment until you find the shoe that is right for you.

When you buy shoes, you'll need to consider: (1) your overall size and weight, (2) your weekly running mileage, (3) whether the shoes are for racing or training, (4) how much ankle support you need, (5) how much cushion you prefer, and (6) your individual quirks.

If you pronate too much or are a heavy foot striker or run very long distances, you may need a shoe to compensate. Any reputable running shoe store can help you find a suitable shoe, but if you have special problems, you may need to see a podiatrist for advice.

6 A PLAN FOR ALL SEASONS: YEAR-ROUND TRIATHLON TRAINING PROGRAM

**M**ost people think of the four seasons as winter, spring, summer, and fall, but I divide my year into four training "seasons"—pre-season, pre-competitive, competitive, and post-competitive. The pre-season phase (about two months) is a time for getting into shape after my annual month of rest; during the pre-competitive period (three months) I gear up for racing; competitive season training works hand in hand with racing (five months); and the post-competitive phase (one month) is a cool-down period leading to my one month "off."

This year-round involvement is one reason journalists have called triathlon a "lifestyle

sport." You can't show up for spring training in March and expect to play the game in April. But riding your bicycle nonstop from January to December is not the answer either—you have to have a plan.

Each year, I have a set of long-term goals and a plan for achieving them. The plan is broken down into short-term objectives—goals for each "season" and for each week of that season. Let's say my long-term goals are to do well in several short races and to try to win an Ironman-distance race at the end of the season. The short races will fall before the long one, and will serve as meters for my progress toward my end-of-season goal—I learn something at every race.

Meanwhile, my workout schedule is designed to help me meet my goals in the amount of time I have available. I start with a time trial (1,500-meter or 1,650-yard swim, 10-mile bike, 3-mile run) to determine where I stand and how far I have to go in my training program. Then I figure out what I need to do to make the necessary progress in the least amount of time.

Your workout schedule will be determined the same way, keeping in mind your overall objective for that phase, your level of skill and fitness, your time trial results, and the amount of time you can spend training.

If you are starting at a minimum fitness level, you will have to increase your overall strength and endurance before you plunge into a comprehensive triathlon training program. Do not, however, increase the duration of your overall workout by more than 5 percent every two weeks. For example, if in your first week of training you are able to ride comfortably for two hours, do not exceed that time the following week, but add 5 percent—six minutes—to your ride for the third and fourth week. This incremental increase is especially crucial in running, which taxes all of your physiological systems far more than cycling or swimming. If you want to increase your running workout by more than 5 percent, intersperse vigorous walking breaks during which you monitor your heart rate so that it doesn't drop below 60 percent of your maximum (see page 23).

MAXIMUM RESULTS IN MINIMUM TIME

My training philosophy used to be "more is better." I thought my performance improved in proportion to the amount of time I spent training, regardless of the quality of that effort. My method seemed to work fine—I capped off my 1982 season with a decisive Ironman victory that included the fastest split times in all three events. I felt as though I was sitting on top of the triathlon world. There were a few other guys who wanted that seat, though, and their mega-mileage programs soon equalled—or exceeded—mine. I needed a new edge.

During the 1983 season, I still wanted to be the best, but I just didn't feel like spending seven or eight hours a day—every day—training. I had to figure out a way to spend a lot less time and still get the same results. It turned out that a lot of other triathletes felt the same way. As more short-distance triathlons are taking place, the novelty and appeal of Ironman-distance races are starting to wear thin; many people simply don't have the time—or want to spend it—for long, long training workouts. Training techniques must be refined to be more conducive to the actual races. That means more quality and less quantity.

I started (in 1983) by defining my parameters—the constant factors around which I would design my program.

HOW TO DEFINE YOUR PARAMETERS

The key to success in triathlons is efficiency, but it is important to remember that there is a big difference between efficiency and shortcuts. Before you can develop your ideal program, you must establish what you want and what you have to work with. Take the time to answer the following questions: write them down for future reference.

DEFINING YOUR PARAMETERS

1 *What are your exact goals?* Start with an overall goal and break it down into smaller objectives.

   A *Long-term:* What do you want to accomplish this year? Which races do you want to complete? What is your end-of-year target for your personal time trial?

   B *Seasonal:* Within each of the training seasons listed above, what do you hope to do?

   C *Short-term:* What do you want to accomplish this month? This week?

2 *What is your physiological makeup?* As an athlete, your raw material is your body. You have to consider your body type when you design your training program. What type are you?

   A Are your muscle fibers predominantly fast-twitch or slow-twitch? There are two ways to find out: a muscle biopsy (which is highly accurate) and your physical responses (which will give you a rough idea). If you recover rapidly on short-rest interval sessions—with 5 to 60 seconds' rest between repeats—you are probably endowed with an abundance of slow-twitch fibers. If you are better at short, fast events—repeats of 30 seconds to 2 minutes with equal rest—your fast-twitch fibers are probably predominant. Another test is how you feel after strenuous exercise. People with more slow-twitch fibers tend to feel a general dull ache, while people with more fast-twitch fibers usually experience localized/specific muscular soreness.

B   Other factors are your present VO_2 max, anaerobic threshold, resting heart rate, stroke volume, cardiac output, blood volume, and capillary density. (See page 24.) Most of these must be measured in a lab. These measurements are all indicators of your aerobic capacity, and will improve with training.

3   *How much time do you have to train?* To compete in triathlons—even short ones—requires a minimum of one hour per day, four days per week. If you can put in more time than that, you can expand your program. But remember, it's quality, not quantity, that counts. Most people think of "quality" training as speed work, but that is not necessarily true. I define "quality" training as a consistent program that integrates the five types of training—explosive speed, sprint race, VO_2 max, anaerobic threshold, and distance.

4   *What are your strengths and weaknesses?*

A   Do you already have a strong event? If so, you should emphasize the other two in training. Don't fall into the trap of building on your strong sport and neglecting the other two; the days when one strong sport would carry you through a triathlon are long gone.

B   Are you better at climbing hills than holding a steady speed on the flats? Do you get started a little slowly, but then steadily whittle down the gap until you catch the leaders? Do you get your second wind just as other are starting to fade?

One of Scott Molina's greatest strengths is climbing hills.

TRAINING BASICS

In outlining my 1983 program, I tried to consider everything I had heard from coaches and physiologists or read in books; I wanted to create the most comprehensive, efficient program possible. I asked the following questions, and the answers eventually helped formulate my own training program.

1   *What is the "hard/easy" theory?* Books and magazines abound with advice to follow a hard day of training with an easy day. That means nothing to me, because they don't offer a useful definition of the terms "hard" and "easy." For someone who is just beginning an endurance program, doing anything for more than a half hour may be hard; for a hard-core triathlete like Scott Molina, six hours on a bike might be easy. Yet the amount of time you spend engaged in a particular activity has little or no bearing on the degree to which it stresses your physiological systems. Distance training is important in some ways, but there is a point of diminishing returns. To me, a hard workout is one involving short rest intervals, in which I really tax my anaerobic threshold, or VO_2 max training (see page 107); those workouts take half (or less) the time of a distance workout, yet they are more demanding.

2   *How hard should you push yourself?* The "no pain, no gain" mentality is far too prevalent among coaches and athletes. Pushing yourself to your limit day in and day out does not produce the best possible results. For psychological as well as physiological reasons, you have to balance your daily activities. Rest is just as important as training.

3   *Does training benefit increase in proportion to training time?* A wise old office manager once said, "Work smart, not hard." By using a mixture of training methods, I have found that I can accomplish as much in a 20-hour weekly program as I once did in 40 hours. You will reach a point of diminishing returns if you just add time/miles to improve your performance. The benefits of a "smart" training program are many: (a) You can actually perform better because you have trained all your systems, (b) you have more free time to pursue other interests, and (c) you are far less prone to injury.

4   *When it comes to training mileage, is more better?* Not necessarily. Remember: Long Slow Distance = Long Slow Progress. There is a better way to increase your speed and endurance than simply adding time and miles to your program. Naturally, you have to do a certain amount of distance training to condition yourself physically and psychologically for long-distance races. But, as swimmers have known for a long time, short-rest interval training builds aerobic conditioning much faster than merely swimming laps.

It is a refined version of the hard/easy concept; you stress and rest your heart by exercising intensely for a short period of time, then resting momentarily, then repeating the process.

5   *Can too much distance work actually hinder your speed and strength?* If you do primarily slow-twitch work, you can lose some of your fast-twitch strength. Long slow distance work develops your slow-twitch responses to the detriment of your fast-twitch fibers. You need keen fast-twitch responses at many times throughout a triathlon. The wide variety of terrain (hills, etc.) and environmental conditions (heavy winds, heat, etc.) combined with the element of competition calls for strength and the ability to surge—fast-twitch functions.

6   *Do most triathlon training injuries occur because of going too fast—or going too far?* An overwhelming majority of training injuries are due to an increase in duration—not intensity—of workouts. It is tempting, especially for a beginner, to overtrain at first.

If you are going from little or no activity to long, daily workouts, the initial results will be dramatic. You will improve by leaps and bounds at the very beginning—it is a variation on the nowhere-to-go-but-up theme. And if most of your training is aerobic, your endurance will improve in all three sports. But don't count on it for long; you will reach a plateau, or injure yourself from the sudden strain, or both. One injury can pour months of overambitious training down the drain.

7   *How often should you train?* During the pre-season, pre-competitive, and competitive seasons, you should try to train six days a week with one day completely off. (Obviously, if you don't have that much available time, you will have to use a shorter schedule.) During the post-competitive season, a five-day week is best. When you take your annual month "off," cut quality and distance back by 25 to 50 percent; don't be idle or you'll lose your aerobic conditioning. Studies show that for every three or four weeks of inactivity, it takes 40 to 60 days to regain your conditioning.

8   *How many activities should you do each day?* If you have an hour and a half to two hours (or more) each day, you should work out in all three sports every day. If you have one particularly strong event, do your strong event only four days per week and the other two all six days. However, if running is one of your weaker events, do it only four days per week; beginning runners must build their muscular and skeletal strength before they can withstand the demands of running long enough to start building aerobic capacity.

If you have less than an hour each day, set up a consistent program that emphasizes all three sports equally. You can do this by doing workouts in two events per day; do your strong event three times a week, your other two events four times a week, and take one day off. For example, let's say swimming is your strong event:

Monday—swim and bike
Tuesday—bike and run
Wednesday—run and swim
Thursday—run
Friday—bike and swim
Saturday—bike and run
Sunday—off

9   *How many types of training should you incorporate each day?* You should do no more than three different types of training (see page 103) in any one day. It will take too long to do any more than that, and it will wear you out in a hurry. However, on days when your distance sets don't take as much time, you may be able to squeeze in an additional anaerobic set, if you can physically tolerate it. The best way to judge your physical tolerance is by looking at your performance times and heart rate—primarily your recovery rate (how fast your heart rate drops after strenuous exercise). If your effort times and heart rate are somewhere close to your time trial results, you are probably within acceptable range.

CROSS-TRAINING BENEFITS

Much has been said and written about the benefits of training in three sports at once, but no one really knows for sure the extent of the cross-application. Because triathlons are essentially aerobic in nature, anything you do to increase your aerobic conditioning is going to basically apply to all three sports. This is most obviously true in the respiratory system; the ability to take in and use more oxygen will equally aid any endurance activity. But you also need to look at two other critical areas: circulatory and muscular.

Aerobic training in any sport will enhance circulatory activity—getting oxygen from the lungs into the bloodstream and to the working muscles. There will be a general increase in blood volume and capillary density. But capil-

Jo Anne Ernst started swimming and cycling, and improved her running enough to qualify for the Olympic Trials.

type of muscle fibers are being recruited for each activity. If you train aerobically, you'll improve the functioning of your slow-twitch fibers, which will help you to some extent in any sport that also uses slow-twitch fibers, such as distance running. The same is true for both types of fast-twitch fibers.

But the real question for triathletes is whether or not overall performance in one sport will actually improve by adding the other two. I don't think that question can be adequately answered yet, because so few training programs combine the three sports as one integral pursuit. However, with my current training program, I am able to swim as fast as I did in college (10 years ago) on less than half as much in-pool training.

Joanne Ernst, women's winner of the 1985 Ironman (Hawaii), is another cross-training success story. A former Stanford University track star, she reduced her weekly running from 90 to 40 miles in 1983, and added swimming and cycling. The results were positive—she cut her marathon time enough to qualify for the Olympic Trials.

lary density will increase only around muscles that are being exercised, so the transfer of that particular benefit from one sport to another is limited. Running up hills, for example, uses the vastus lateralis muscle, which is also used in cycling, so the increase in capillary density is useful in both activities. But if you don't run up many hills in training, that particular cross-benefit won't exist.

Swimming, cycling, and running are each highly specific in muscular motion. If you suddenly put a pair of running shoes on a swimmer, it is highly unlikely that he would run a 33-minute 10-kilometer; he wouldn't have the necessary endurance in the specific leg muscles used for running. But there does seem to be some carryover, as long as the same

HOW TO MEASURE "INTENSITY"

An hour of swimming is not necessarily equal in intensity to an hour of running or cycling. There is actually a fine balance between level of technical skills required and demands each sport places on the human body.

Swimming is the least physiologically demanding in that the surrounding water cools you as you work and your horizontal position makes it easier for your heart and circulatory system to deliver blood to your working muscles. But in terms of technique, swimming is by far the most complicated of the three sports. It takes three to four years for a previously inexperienced swimmer to develop optimum neuromuscular coordination in the water.

Cycling is triathlon's *juste milieu,* a "golden mean." Though the physical movements of cycling are not as complicated as swimming, the physics of a human and a machine working together are definitely trickier than running. Cycling takes more effort than swimming, but less than running. It, too, has a built-in cooling element (the wind) and a gravitational advantage (a seat).

Running technique is relatively simple to master, but don't let that fool you—running uses more calories in any given period of time than cycling or swimming. It also heats, shocks, and stresses your body much more.

So the intensity of a workout cannot be determined by the amount of time—or skill—it takes to do it. You have to consider four other factors:

1 *The distance of each workout and/or repeat.* Let's say you are going to swim for an hour—will you swim uninterrupted for an hour straight? Or will you break the hour into several segments (repeats)? How will you break it up—will it be three 20-minute swims, six 10-minute swims, three 10-minute and six 5-minute swims?
2 *The rest interval between repeats.* How much time will you rest between the actual exercise? What is the ratio of work to rest?
3 *The number of repetitions.*
4 *The speed of each effort.*

YOUR PERSONAL TIME TRIAL

When you first start training, and before each new training season, do a time trial to determine your maximum output at that time. You will use the results from the time trial to assess your performance as you progress.

Run and cycle on flat roads or trails, so that you don't unnecessarily tax your anaerobic systems. If you are a beginner at any of three sports, start at a moderate pace for the first five

to seven minutes, then slowly pick up your pace. More experienced triathletes should start moderately fast for the first two minutes, then go all out.

The standard distances I use are:

1 Swim: 1,500 meters or 1,650 yards
2 Cycle: 10 miles
3 Run: 3 miles

Beginners may need to scale down those distances at first. If you are new to any of the sports, you may want to try one third of the prescribed distance, for example. However, you should keep building your strength and endurance so that you can do the standard distances comfortably by the end of the preseason.

For each type of training in the year-round triathlon program, you will work at a prescribed percentage of your maximal output. (Maximal output is determined by your most recent time trial.) When you do explosive speed training, for example, you will work out at a pace that is equal to 95 to 120 percent of your time trial pace; for distance training, on the other hand, your workouts will be done at 65 to 80 percent.

As your fitness and skills improve throughout the year, your time trial results will also improve, and you will have to go faster to work at those percentages. For example, let's say a particular running workout requires that you work at 75 percent. If your time trial run was 19:30 (6:30 per mile), you would have to do the workout at an 8:15-per-mile pace. But if your speed increased to 18:00 at a later time trial, that 75 percent workout would be done at a 7:30 pace.

The Personal Time Trial Record (page 96) allows you to keep a written record of your time trial effort. Do each phase of your time trial (swimming, cycling, running) on a separate day, to allow maximum performance. Record your time and pace (from the pace chart). If you are not doing the full distance, your overall times may be recorded, but they are only important in determining your pace at 100 percent effort. For each type of training, you will be asked to work at a specific percentage of that pace.

Your time trial results represent your maximum effort at the prescribed distances (1,650-yard swim, 10-mile bike ride, 3-mile run). However, you may be doing shorter or longer distances in training, so you will need to know your pace (per 100 yards in swimming, per mile in cycling and running). The Personal Time Trial Pace Chart (page 97) will help you to determine this. Please note that the swim paces listed are appropriate for novice swimmers during the pre-season. During the pre-competitive season you should figure out your own pace based on an all-out effort in a 200-yard freestyle swim; during the competitive season, base it on an all-out effort in a 500-yard freestyle swim.

R&R: REST AND RECOVERY

The best measure of your aerobic fitness is not your maximum heart rate, as many people believe; it's how fast you recover. After a maximal effort—in an explosive speed exercise, for example—your heart rate should drop by 20 percent during the first 30 seconds, and 30 percent within the first minute.

As you get into better shape, your stroke volume increases, which lowers your heart rate. I have actually noticed my pulse dropping during anaerobic threshold workouts after about 8 to 10 minutes. Knowing that my heart rate will drop dramatically after an intense effort, such as climbing a hill or riding against the wind, has been a keen psychological—as well as physical—advantage for me during races. According to lab tests at the University of California, my maximum heart rate is 172 and within a minute of strenuous exercise, it was down to 99—a 42 percent drop.

You should check—and record—your pulse before each exercise session, as well as during and after. Keep tabs on your most important muscle. Remember that the amount of R&R you need is a function of your body type, as well as your level of fitness.

People who have a predominance of fast-twitch fibers will need 20 to 30 percent more rest on aerobic sets, and may also have to reduce the distance somewhat. In coaching Masters swimming, I found that many of the anaerobically inclined swimmers would not fully recover during the workout, or sometimes by the next day. You will never improve your performance by grinding yourself into the ground.

PERSONAL TIME TRIAL RECORD

SPORT	PRE-SEASON	PRE-COMPETITIVE	COMPETITIVE	
		SEASON*		
SWIM 1,650 YD				TIME
				PACE
CYCLE 10 MI 16 KM				TIME
				PACE
RUN 3 MI 5 KM				TIME
				PACE

*No time trials are necessary during the post-competitive season.

PERSONAL TIME TRIAL PACE CHART

SWIM—1,650 YARDS		CYCLE—10 MILES		RUN—3 MILES	
TOTAL TIME	PACE/100 YD	TOTAL TIME	MPH	TOTAL TIME	PACE/MILE
35:45	2:10	40:00	15	30:00	10:00
34:22	2:05	37:30	16	29:00	9:40
33:00	2:00	35:20	17	28:00	9:20
31:37	1:55	33:20	18	27:00	9:00
30:15	1:50	31:34	19	28:00	8:40
29:25	1:47	30:00	20	25:00	8:20
28:52	1:45	28:34	21	24:00	8:00
28:03	1:42	27:20	22	23:00	7:40
27:30	1:40	26:05	23	22:00	7:20
26:40	1:37	25:00	24	21:00	7:00
26:07	1:35	24:00	25	20:30	6:50
25:18	1:32	23:04	26	20:00	6:40
24:45	1:30	22:13	27	19:30	6:30
23:55	1:27	21:25	28	19:00	6:20
23:22	1:25	20:41	29	18:30	6:10
22:33	1:22	20:00	30	18:00	6:00
21:59	1:20	19:21	31	17:30	5:50
21:10	1:17			17:00	5:40
20:37	1:15			16:30	5:30
19:48	1:12			16:00	5:20
19:15	1:10			15:30	5:10
18:25	1:07			15:00	5:00
17:52	1:05			14:30	4:50
17:03	1:02			14:00	4:40
16:30	1:00			13:30	4:30
15:40	:57			13:00	4:20
15:07	:55				

One way to check your day-to-day recovery is to monitor your resting pulse. Before you get out of bed each morning, record your heart rate. If it is elevated the day after a tough workout, you may need to allow longer rest intervals.

LACTIC ACID—FACT AND FICTION

They say a little knowledge is a dangerous thing; that is especially true in an endurance test such as a triathlon, where common fallacies can divert you from proper precautions.

1   *A popular myth is that lactic acid buildup causes that crippled feeling in your muscles when you "hit the wall" toward the end of a race.* That is almost always false.

   If you took a blood sample of everyone at the finish line, you would find lactate levels only slightly above the resulting norm—2 millimoles per milliliter. During intense exercise, such as sprinting, your lactate might rise up to 12 millimoles, but during most triathlons, the increase is far less dramatic—usually from 3 to 6 millimoles at most.

   In a triathlon, lactic acid isn't much of a factor, unless there are a lot of hills and/or you are not properly trained. Glycogen depletion and dehydration are the primary causes of muscular fatigue and failure. Dehydration brings on many of the muscle cramps that are erroneously attributed to lactic acid buildup.

2   *Many triathletes don't realize that lactic acid is used as a fuel.* Contrary to popular suggestion, lactic acid is not merely an evil side effect of overexertion. You need it to sustain high-energy efforts that last from 30 seconds to two minutes. You run into problems with it when (a) your system produces it in excessive amounts, (b) you are not able to diffuse it properly to your working muscles, and (c) you cannot rap-

idly resynthesize it in your bloodstream for use as a fuel.

3   *Lactate accumulates at a much slower rate when your muscles are used to using both types of fast-twitch (white) fibers.* If you have not done any fast-twitch training and you suddenly go all out in a race, your body will not be able to efficiently use lactate for fuel. Some of that lactic acid that was produced for fuel will obviously accumulate. Meanwhile, you will use up your available glycogen rapidly, and build up an oxygen debt. The result is extreme fatigue and muscular soreness. You can avoid these problems by incorporating sprint and anaerobic threshold workouts into your training program.

4   *One way to keep lactic acid under control is to maintain proper technique.* Don't fall into the typical triathlon booby trap of sacrificing your technique when you come up against the unexpected. Many people lose their concentration when someone passes them or their own pace begins to fall off due to hills or wind: they suddenly speed up or change their style, and their muscles simply aren't used to it. The extra exertion

"Hitting the wall" is caused by glycogen depletion, not lactic-acid buildup.

summons extra lactic acid. Try to maintain proper technique no matter what.

5   *Shorter races require you to tolerate higher levels of lactate.* No matter how mentally tough you may think you are, you can't tolerate higher levels of lactate by simply believing you can overcome it. You have to become physiologically accustomed to it by incorporating sprint training into your program.

6   *Knowing that you can physically tolerate elevated lactic acid levels will give you a psychological boost.* No matter how well-conditioned you are, you are going to experience some discomfort when you put out intense effort to attack hills, ride against the wind, or surge ahead of an opponent. But if you are properly trained, that discomfort will come on slowly, and will be able to monitor exactly how much of it you want to withstand. You also will know that the lactic acid will diffuse quickly, should you choose to push even harder. That kind of control is an enormous psychological asset.

body learns to burn fatty acids rather than depending primarily upon glucose and glycogen. (Extra food also draws water into your gastrointestinal tract, which can contribute to eventual dehydration.)

In order to find out how far I can go on a small amount of food, I sometimes do my entire workout (5 to 6 hours) without eating anything except perhaps a banana or a couple of dried figs. If you try that, make sure you do it under controlled circumstances, such as a long workout that will not take you far from your home. When you run out of fuel, you can become very light-headed and disoriented; it is a good idea to learn your limits in familiar territory.

The best time to experiment is during your mini-triathlons, because you are simulating race circumstances. Find out exactly how much food you need and develop a planned pattern so that you'll never be caught off-guard during a race. There are enough variables as it

FUEL EFFICIENCY: FOOD AND FLUIDS

Most people give more thought to the kind of fuel they use in their cars than the food they put in their own bodies. As a triathlete, you can't afford to do that, or you'll virtually "run out of gas" in the middle of a race. Likewise, you can't afford to neglect your fluid intake, or you will overheat just like a car breaks down when there's no water in the radiator. (For a complete discussion of nutrition, see Chapter 9.)

FOOD

Experiment with your diet while you are training—never during a race. I try to get by on the minimum amount of food, so that my

Scott Tinley takes a drink.

is; don't make a race a nutritional guessing game.

After you have finished your workout, be sure to eat a high-carbohydrate meal as soon as possible. That will help to replenish your glycogen stores, and will keep you from feeling tired and sluggish the following day. Don't wait a few hours; eat right away.

FLUIDS

A few years ago, there was a lot of excitement over electrolyte replacement fluids, and several commercial brands became available at aid stations and in stores. They soon replaced Gatorade and de-fizzed Coke as the choice of most amateur marathoners.

Though you do lose trace amounts of minerals during exercise, the degree to which electrolyte drinks are helpful in races under 12 to 15 hours is debatable. Most experts agree that you should take in about 2 grams of glucose per 100 milliliters of water, and perhaps up to $1/10$ gram of sodium. I prefer plain water.

THERMOREGULATION: HOW TO COPE WITH HEAT

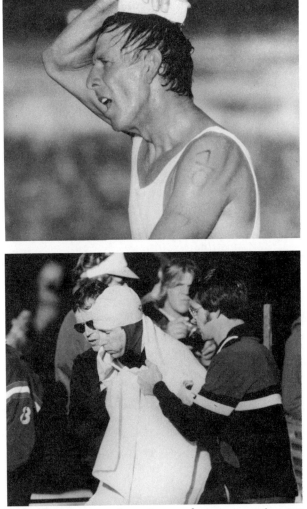

In a triathlon, you have to guard against getting too hot—or too cold.

Heat and humidity have been the demise of many otherwise well-prepared triathletes, especially in ultra-distance races. Some of the best competitors—including Mark Allen and Scott Molina—have been been reduced to walking or dropping out entirely in the muggy tropical heat of the Hawaii Ironman.

Allen said he had gotten dehydrated during the 112-mile bike ride; Molina explained his own problem as "faulty air conditioning." Any way you look at it, one conclusion is unavoidably true: *If you are going to race in the heat, you have to train in the heat.*

If you are going to be cycling or running in the afternoon sun during the race, you should train during that same time of day. Try to simulate every aspect of race conditions when you train. It takes six days to two weeks to become fully acclimated to the heat, so allow yourself plenty of time before a race to get used to working out in that particular environment.

The "air conditioning" to which Molina referred is the ability to transfer heat from your body to the air, via your cardiovascular system. Some people's genetic makeup allows them to cope with heat more readily than others, but no one is immune to hyperthermia. I can handle heat fairly well, which has helped me greatly in the Hawaii Ironman, but I have also reached the finish line light-headed and dizzy—it is a frightening feeling.

When you become hyperthermic—overheated—your stroke volume decreases, so your heart rate and respirations increase. Many people respond to that apparent shortness of breath by tensing up and panting even more, which worsens the problem considerably. *Pay special attention to relaxed, deliberate breathing when you are training or racing in the heat.*

HOT TIPS: BEATING THE HEAT

1 *Eat more food.* You may have less of an appetite in warm weather, but your body

Mark Allen wears a visor to protect himself from the intense heat in Hawaii.

actually burns more glycogen than it does in the cold. By increasing your intake of complex carbohydrates, you will prevent some of the additional fatigue and soreness of hot-weather racing.

2 *Drink plenty of ice-cold water.* When I train in the heat, I drink about 20 ounces of ice-cold water (40 to 50 degrees) before a run or bike ride. The cooler the water, the more it will lower your internal body temperature. You may feel a little bloated at first from the volume, but in temperatures of 90 degrees or more, you'll use the excess fluid within a few minutes.

When I was in junior high school, our football coach thought that depriving us of water during practice would make us "tough." Actually, it made us thirsty and sick. Mostly, though, it made us realize that our True Grit coach must have been out of his mind. I don't know what happened to the rest of the cotton-mouthed warriors, but I filled my greasy helmet with water and sipped surreptitiously. The only thing more disgusting than drinking out of my helmet was not drinking at all!

3 *Wear a light visor.* It will keep the sun off your face, as well as out of your eyes.

4 *Go soak your head! (. . . and arms and neck).* When you are running, try to stop from time to time and hose yourself down. This wet outer "shield" will cool your skin as you run, especially if there is a breeze.

DO WOMEN REALLY "ONLY GLOW?"

Remember the old saying, "Horses sweat, men perspire, but women only glow?" The man who made that observation obviously didn't know any female athletes! Of course everybody sweats—the question is, do you sweat enough? Medical studies indicate that many women don't sweat as readily or profusely as most men. Since perspiration is a vital cooling mechanism, some women may need to be especially careful to take preventive measures when racing and training in the heat. Drink plenty of cold water, wear a sun visor, avoid excess food intake, and pace yourself according to your level of fitness.

WEIGHT LOSS IN THE HEAT

At the fat farm, they stick people in sweatboxes to shed a few pounds of water so they'll become believers in the lose-weight-fast system. At a triathlon, no sweatbox is necessary. But be careful about weight loss in the heat; a drop of as little as 3 percent of your overall body weight can significantly elevate your rectal temperature.

Hyperthermia can creep up on you, especially if you are on your bike, and the sun is beating down on you with the wind at your back. Keep taking in small amounts of food and fluids, and concentrate on staying as cool as possible. It isn't merely a matter of comfort; it could save your health.

ALTITUDE TRAINING

There are some benefits to training at high altitudes, but beware: Working out at 8,000 feet isn't going to make you any stronger when you come back down to sea level. If you go to Colorado and train in the Rockies for six months, for instance, you might perform better at a low-altitude race—but that would be true after training *anywhere* for six months, regardless of whether it was in the Mohave Desert or on Mount Everest.

The true advantage of altitude training is, of course, in altitude racing. Every type of training prepares you for the race conditions it simulates. So six months in the Rockies will definitely give you an edge over people who have been training for six months at sea level *if the race is at 8,000 feet*. But when you come down to their turf, the odds will be even.

ADVANTAGES

1 *The main benefit of high-altitude training is that it increases the concentration of hemoglobin in your blood* to compensate for the reduced oxygen available in the atmosphere. That aids in the transport of oxygen to your working muscles.
2 *Climbing the hills increases strength in some of your major muscles.*

DISADVANTAGES

1 *You are more prone to dehydration* because the air is generally dryer than at lower altitudes. Be sure to take in plenty of water.
2 *You must work at a lower intensity* than at lower altitudes; the reduced oxygen ("thinner air") means that you must increase your respirations, which makes your heart work harder at the same rate of exertion.

WHAT IS THE OPTIMUM ALTITUDE?

The best of both worlds is about 4,000 feet, where the stresses are a little greater than at sea level, but not so taxing that you have to cut back on your intensity.

THE FIVE TYPES OF TRAINING

There are many different ways to train, depending on who you listen to, but these are my tried-and-true methods. Though each approach is designed to improve a distinct func-tion, there is always some overlap. Think of it as a spectrum from aerobic to anaerobic. Combining all five methods will allow you to compete closer to your anaerobic threshold for a

SWIMMING PACE FOR THE FIVE TYPES OF TRAINING

PACE/ 100 YD	EXPLOSIVE SPEED (100–120%)	SPEED RACE (90–100%)	VO$_2$ (80–95%)	ANAEROBIC THRESHOLD (75–90%)	DISTANCE (60–85%)
2:10	2:10–1:48	2:24–2:10	2:42–2:16	2:53–2:24	3:36–2:33
2:00	2:00–1:40	2:13–2:00	2:30–2:06	2:40–2:13	3:20–2:21
1:50	1:50–1:31	2:02–1:50	2:17–1:55	2:26–2:02	3:03–2:09
1:40	1:40–1:23	1:51–1:40	2:05–1:45	2:13–1:51	2:46–1:57
1:30	1:30–1:15	1:40–1:30	1:52–1:34	2:00–1:40	2:30–1:46
1:25	1:25–1:10	1:34–1:25	1:46–1:29	1:53–1:34	2:21–1:40
1:20	1:20–1:06	1:29–1:20	1:40–1:24	1:46–1:29	2:13–1:34
1:15	1:15–1:02	1:23–1:15	1:33–1:18	1:40–1:23	2:05–1:28
1:10	1:10–0:58	1:17–1:10	1:27–1:13	1:33–1:17	1:56–1:22
1:05	1:05–0:54	1:12–1:05	1:21–1:08	1:26–1:12	1:48–1:16
1:00	1:00–0:50	1:06–1:00	1:15–1:03	1:20–1:06	1:40–1:10
0:55	0:55–0:46	1:01–0:55	1:08–0:58	1:13–1:01	1:31–1:04

CYCLING PACE FOR THE FIVE TYPES OF TRAINING

PACE/ MPH	EXPLOSIVE SPEED (100–120%)	SPRINT RACE (90–100%)	VO$_2$ (80–95%)	ANAEROBIC THRESHOLD (75–90%)	DISTANCE (60–85%)
15	15–18.0	13.5–15	12.0–14.3	11.2–13.5	9.0–12.8
16	16–19.2	14.4–16	12.8–15.2	12.0–14.4	9.6–13.6
17	17–20.4	15.3–17	13.6–16.2	12.8–15.3	10.2–14.4
18	18–21.6	16.2–18	14.4–17.1	13.5–16.2	10.8–15.3
19	19–22.8	17.1–19	15.2–18.0	14.2–17.1	11.4–16.2
20	20–24.0	18.0–20	16.0–19.0	15.0–18.0	12.0–17.0
21	21–25.2	18.9–21	16.8–20.0	15.8–18.9	12.6–17.8
22	22–26.4	19.8–22	17.6–20.9	16.5–19.8	13.2–18.7
23	23–27.6	20.7–23	18.4–21.8	17.2–20.7	13.8–19.6
24	24–28.8	21.6–24	19.2–22.8	18.0–21.6	14.4–20.4
25	25–30.0	22.5–25	20.0–23.8	18.8–22.5	15.0–21.3
26	26–31.0	23.4–26	20.8–24.7	19.5–23.4	15.6–22.1
27	27–32.4	24.3–27	21.6–25.6	20.2–24.3	16.2–23.0
28	28–33.6	25.2–28	22.4–26.6	21.0–25.2	16.8–23.8
29	29–34.8	26.1–29	23.2–27.6	21.8–26.1	17.4–24.6
30	30–36.0	27.0–30	24.0–28.5	22.5–27.0	18.0–25.5
31	31–37.2	27.9–31	24.8–29.4	23.2–27.9	18.6–26.4

RUNNING *PACE FOR THE FIVE TYPES OF TRAINING*

PACE/ MILE	EXPLOSIVE SPEED (100–120%)	SPRINT RACE (90–100%)	VO₂ (80–95%)	ANAEROBIC THRESHOLD (75–90%)	DISTANCE (60–85%)
11:00	11:00–9:10	12:13–11:00	13:45–11:34	14:40–12:13	18:20–12:56
10:00	10:00–8:20	11:06–10:00	12:30–10:31	13:20–11:06	16:48–11:46
9:00	9:00–7:30	10:00–9:00	11:15–9:28	12:00–10:00	15:00–10:35
8:00	8:00–6:40	8:53–8:00	10:00–8:25	10:40–8:53	13:20–9:24
7:45	7:45–6:27	8:36–7:45	9:41–8:09	10:20–8:36	12:55–9:07
7:30	7:30–6:15	8:20–7:30	9:22–7:53	10:00–8:20	12:30–8:49
7:15	7:15–6:02	8:03–7:15	9:03–7:38	9:40–8:03	12:05–8:31
7:00	7:00–5:50	7:46–7:00	8:45–7:22	9:20–7:46	11:40–8:14
6:45	6:45–5:37	7:30–6:45	8:26–7:06	9:00–7:30	11:15–7:56
6:30	6:30–5:25	7:13–6:30	8:07–6:50	8:40–7:13	10:50–7:38
6:15	6:15–5:12	6:56–6:15	7:48–6:34	8:20–6:56	10:25–7:21
6:00	6:00–5:00	6:40–6:00	7:30–6:19	8:00–6:40	10:00–7:03
5:45	5:45–4:47	6:23–5:45	6:15–6:03	7:40–6:23	9:35–6:46
5:30	5:30–4:35	6:06–5:30	6:52–5:47	7:20–6:06	9:10–6:28
5:15	5:15–4:22	5:50–5:15	6:33–5:31	7:00–5:50	8:45–6:10
5:00	5:00–4:10	5:33–5:00	6:15–5:15	6:40–5:33	8:20–5:53
4:45	4:45–3:57	5:16–4:45	5:56–5:00	6:20–5:16	7:55–5:35
4:30	4:30–3:45	5:00–4:30	5:37–4:44	6:00–5:00	7:30–5:17

longer period of time. That is the secret to successful racing.

For each type of training, you will work at a defined percentage of your current maximum (time trial) effort. Refer to the Personal Time Trial Pace Chart on page 97 for your maximum effort pace. Find that number in the Pace column of the Pace for the Five Types of Training charts (for each sport) on the following pages. Then read across for the pace you should be working at in each type of training workout. Remember that your pre-season swimming pace may be based on a 1,650-yard time trial, but your pre-competitive season pace should be based on a 200-yard all-out effort, and your competitive season pace should be based on a 500-yard all-out effort.

EXPLOSIVE SPEED TRAINING

DURATION OF EFFORT: 5 to 30 seconds

NUMBER OF REPEATS: 5 to 10

EFFORT LEVEL: 100% to 120% of your time trial effort

ENERGY SYSTEM: ATP-CP

MUSCLE FIBERS: Fast-twitch/A (slightly oxidative)

Fast-twitch/B (anaerobic)

The idea of this type of high-energy training is to work above your maximal time trial effort in order to develop power and the ability to put forth bursts of speed. It will help you get a good, strong start on the swim, for example, and help you to be able to run up the beach after the swim for a quick transition. It will also come into play when you need a reserve of speed at the end of a race—in some triathlons, that can be critical. (I once won the Ironman by a mere 33 seconds!)

However, if you already have sufficient explosive speed, or if you are concentrating primarily on long races, you may not need to do this type of training. I do not do any explosive speed training, because I have built sufficient speed and strength throughout my years of weight training and competing in triathlons.

Also, if you are unable to do any weight training, you may substitute explosive speed training. I do not recommend that particular substitution, but it will be better than no strength training at all.

WORK/REST RATIO. After each effort, allow the prescribed recovery period before you repeat the exercise. The recovery allows you to work at a high-output level throughout the workout, which will help you to develop as much power as possible.

SWIMMING: 1 to 2 (For every 30 seconds of effort, rest up to one full minute.)

CYCLING: 1 to 3

RUNNING: 1 to 3 or 1 to 4

ACTIVE REST. Don't stop cold during your recovery period. If you are swimming, for example, don't swim 25 yards, then stop and hang on the edge of the pool for 30 seconds. Keep moving, even if it is just a slight scissors motion with your legs and subtly shaking or moving your arms. You are starting to cross into your ATP-lactic acid system at the end of an explosive speed effort, so some lactic acid does begin to accumulate.

RECOVERY RESPONSE. Start each repeat in a well-rested state. Your heart rate should be no more than 20 or 30 percent above your resting pulse when you start.

HOW TO INTENSIFY YOUR EFFORTS. As the seasons progress, you may need to intensify your workouts to exercise at the required level of effort. You should try to reach your maximum level of effort as soon as possible.

1 Tethered swimming: Work out with an elastic harness around your waist. A harness is simply a long strip of surgical tubing which is attached to the end of the pool and wrapped around your waist like a huge rubber band. You can regulate the length of the tubing so that you swim for any distance you choose.

2 Use a drag mechanism to increase the load on your arms. Usually, you would wear a drag suit. It has pockets on the inside to catch water and slow you down.

3 On your bicycle, you can roll slowly—5 to 10 mph—then using your largest gear, stand up and accelerate rapidly. Or try short bursts of speed on hills.

4 Hill running on grades of 6 percent or more will increase your intensity, as will running on a treadmill on an incline and tethered running (just like tethered swimming).

SPRINT RACE TRAINING

DURATION OF EFFORT: 30 seconds to 2 minutes

NUMBER OF REPEATS: 5 to 8

EFFORT LEVEL: 85% to 100%

ENERGY SYSTEM: ATP-lactic acid
ATP-aerobic (sometimes)

MUSCLE FIBERS: Fast-twitch/A
Fast-twitch/B
Slow-twitch

This type of training helps you adapt to high levels of lactic acid and oxygen debt. It enables you to vary your tempo during the race and to put out extra effort (on hills, for example) without depleting your glycogen stores. If you are completely rested when you begin a two-minute sprint race workout, your effort will be 50 percent anaerobic and 50 percent aerobic. Sprint race training is critical to triathletes, yet

Sprint race training helps you put out extra effort going up hills.

seems to be the most neglected type of training in most programs.

Most people think of triathlons as being entirely aerobic, but they are not. Two-hour races, which are currently the most popular in the United States, require quick transitions from event to event; you have to pick up and maintain a fast pace as soon as possible. That means recruiting anaerobic as well as aerobic energy systems.

Immediately following the swim, for example, most of the blood flow is still in your upper body and arms. Your transition movements—tying your shoes, pulling your clothes on, etc.—are also in your upper body and arms, so the blood stays there. You start the bike ride with very little blood and oxygen in the working muscles of your legs.

During the first half-mile, your respirations will increase, and lactic acid will immediately begin to accumulate. If your muscles are trained to cope with the lactic acid level and oxygen debt of that initial "sprint," it will obviously be easier for you.

Even in the longer races, you need that ability to put out extra energy so that you can climb hills, for example, without using up an inordinate amount of fuel. You have to be able to use the muscle fibers and energy systems that are appropriate for the type of effort you are expending.

WORK/REST RATIO. Same as explosive speed training, but make sure you allow enough time to recover completely. This type of training is more stressful because of the lactate buildup, so you will probably experience quite a bit of muscle stiffness and soreness from day to day.

SWIMMING: 1 to 2
CYCLING: 1 to 2 or 1 to 3
RUNNING: 1 to 3 or 1 to 4

ACTIVE REST. After a running repeat, don't stop. Run easy to dissipate and resynthesize some of the lactic acid. On the bike, never stop your cadence; gear down and keep pedaling for at least 30 seconds or a minute before you really slow down and think about checking your heart rate.

RECOVERY RESPONSE. Allow a response of 30 to 40 percent above your resting pulse.

REPETITIONS. Don't do more than five to eight repeats of this type of workout. You will be emphasizing sprint training during your competitive season, and overdoing it will cause undue fatigue for the next day's workout. If you are increasing your overall training time during the competitive season, do not necessarily increase your sprint training.

WORKOUT EXAMPLES.

1 *Running:* If you run on a track, record the distance you cover, so you can monitor your progress from week to week. Let's say you want to work at a five-minute-mile pace. That pace is equal to running a 440—once around the track—in 1:15. After you run the 440, you should allow yourself three or four times as long to recover. You can jog another 440 at an easy pace, say two minutes, then walk for another minute or two until you are fully recovered. Repeat the exercise four or five times.

2 *Cycling:* (Again, keep a record of the distances you cover and the times, so you can monitor your progress.) Let's say you want to hold a 20 mph pace; that is equivalent to a half-mile in 1:30. You might want to do five or six repeats, with six minutes of active rest in between.

HOW TO INTENSIFY YOUR EFFORTS. The idea of both explosive speed training and sprint training is to recruit as many white fibers as possible during the exercise. The number of fibers recruited is dictated by the duration and intensity of the exercise. Therefore, as you progress you will need to increase the intensity of your workouts.

1 Shift from a lower gear to a much higher gear, a larger gear that you would normally use for racing.

2 Stand up on your bike. Get your speed going—it may take 15 to 20 strokes—then sit down and try to maintain that speed in the same gear, or shift into a larger gear. If I want to get my speed up to 28 mph, for example, I stand up until I am going about 25 mph, then sit down and try to bring my speed up the remaining 3 mph.

3 In cycling and running, going up hills will help you as long as the hills are not too severe. But do not run down hills over 6 percent grade. There is too much trauma and shock to your muscular and skeletal systems. Walk down easy.

USE THE SPECIFIC GEARS AND MOVEMENTS THAT YOU'LL BE USING IN A RACE. Don't do any explosive speed or sprint race training on the breaststroke, for example. You'll be using the freestyle stroke when you race, and you want your nerves and muscles to be trained for those exact responses.

VO₂ MAX TRAINING

DURATION OF EFFORT: 3 to 8 minutes (or progressive sets up to 12 minutes)
NUMBER OF REPEATS: 2 to 4
EFFORT LEVEL: 80% to 95%
ENERGY SYSTEM: ATP-aerobic
                 ATP-lactic acid
MUSCLE FIBERS: Fast-twitch/A
                 Slow-twitch

"VO_2 max" is simply the label physiologists use to denote the maximum amount of oxygen you can take in and use during exercise (milliliters of oxygen consumed per minute divided by kilograms of body weight). Because a greater oxygen supply indicates a greater aerobic capacity, many people mistakenly assume that the person with the highest VO_2 max is automatically going to be the best triathlete. That is not necessarily true.

In 1982, Scott Tinley, Scott Molina, and I were all tested for a Pritikin Institute study; we were all within one point of each other on VO_2 max. In the races that followed, our physical capacities as triathletes came down to our respective anaerobic thresholds—along with technique, efficiency, desire, and whatever else each race threw into the equation.

Even though oxygen uptake isn't the final measure of triathletic ability, it is certainly an important asset to develop. According to Dave Costill in "The Scientific Approach to Distance Running" (*Track and Field News*, 1979), if two runners with respective VO_2 maximums of 60 and 70 were asked to run at the same pace, each would have to consume the same amount of oxygen per kilogram of body weight, but "the demands placed on their aerobic systems would be markedly different." The first runner would be using 87 percent of his VO_2 max, while the second runner would use only 74 percent. In theory, the second runner could "sustain his pace for a longer period of time and . . . tolerate prolonged runs at higher speeds" than the first runner.

This type of training takes you from anaerobic training to aerobic conditioning. It stimulates your aerobic metabolism, but at the same time it taps your anaerobic reserve. Because both energy systems are in use, your ATP can be replenished, your lactic acid can diffuse back into your bloodstream, and any food you eat can bolster your glycogen stores. Your oxygen debt can be repaid.

The major physiological advantage is that your heart pumps a lot of blood per beat and your stroke volume is elevated during the recovery, which allows more blood to be pumped during the next working phase. More blood means more oxygen. By elevating your VO_2 max, you will be able to perform closer to your aerobic capacity.

Women tend to have lesser VO_2 maximums than men because they naturally have more body fat in relation to muscle mass, and therefore less mitochondria and capillaries to transport the oxygen. However, when you consider the ratio of oxygen intake to true body weight, women's endurance potential is actually closer to men's than it appears. That is one of the reasons women are closing performance gaps in endurance sports.

Most studies on triathletes show that women tend to have about 13 to 15 percent body fat, while men have about 7 or 8 percent. There is a fine balance between being lean enough to be efficient and being so skinny that you lose muscle mass required for fast workouts.

Extra weight lowers your VO_2 max; since VO_2 max is a numerical value determined in relation to body weight, an increase in pound-

Julie Olsen shows that VO_2 training helps your time trialing ability.

age will obviously decrease the ratio of oxygen to weight—it's simple math. One of the easiest ways to increase VO_2 max—without training—is to lose some weight.

WORK/REST RATIO. These are all progressive sets, in that you build up your heart rate during the first two or three minutes, then try to maintain that work range for the last few minutes. The amount of recovery time shown below is between sets, and will vary with each sport.

SWIMMING: 1 to 1 or 2 to 1
CYCLING: 2 to 1
RUNNING: 3 to 1 or 4 to 1

RECOVERY RESPONSE. Allow your heart rate to drop 30 to 40 percent. However, in this type of training, the effort you put out in each repeat should be close or equal to the previous one—work and rest are equally important.

WORKOUT EXAMPLES. The important thing in VO_2 max training is to work for long enough to elevate your heart rate, but not so long that the effort becomes entirely aerobic.

At the 20 mph pace we used earlier, a typical VO_2 max workout would be four 1.5-mile rides at 4.5 minutes each. Between each of the 4.5-minute efforts, you should slow down for about 30 seconds. After four efforts, rest for at least 1.5 to 2.5 minutes, then do the same set again. The total duration of your workout would be about 45 minutes, including work and rest.

HOW TO INTENSIFY YOUR EFFORT. As you first start training, you may be able to do only one of the type of sets—or just one of the single efforts—described above. In order to continue to elevate your VO_2 max throughout the year, you'll need to boost your workouts. Increase the duration of the sets by breaking it into repeats as illustrated above. You may also increase your speed.

ANAEROBIC THRESHOLD TRAINING

DURATION OF EFFORT: 1.5 to 3 minutes (total workout should be 15 minutes to 1 hour)

NUMBER OF REPEATS: 8 to 50

EFFORT LEVEL: 75% to 90%

ENERGY SYSTEM: ATP-aerobic

MUSCLE FIBERS: Fast-twitch/A
Slow-twitch

Your anaerobic threshold is the point at which lactic acid begins to diffuse back into your bloodstream for use as fuel. If you slow down, you will activate your aerobic system; if you speed up, you will produce lactic acid at a faster rate than you can diffuse it. The harder you can work without exceeding your anaerobic threshold, the more efficiently you'll function.

Let's go back to our example of the two runners (VO_2 maximums of 60 and 70) in the

VO_2 max section (page 107). We saw that the runner with the higher VO_2 max was theoretically capable of running faster for a longer period of time because he was using a lower percentage (74%) of his maximum oxygen uptake than the second runner (87%). But if the second runner had trained his oxidative fast-twitch fibers, he might be fully capable of functioning for extended periods of time at up to 90 percent of his aerobic capacity, whereas the first runner might be relying on his slow-twitch fibers and be limited to 75 percent of his aerobic capacity. In that case, the runner with the lower VO_2 max would actually be able to run longer and faster.

Patricia Puntous pushed her anaerobic threshold (aerobic maximum) to the limit when she won the 1983 and 1984 Ironman triathlons.

Derek Clayton was a prime example of this. For many years, he held the world record in the marathon. He wasn't as fast as some of his competitors on paper, but he could run at 88 percent of his VO_2 max—sustaining 88 percent of his fastest per-mile time—for the entire 26 miles.

That is why it is critical to elevate your anaerobic threshold—make the most of what you've got. Use figures such as VO_2 max to guide you to a better training program, not to limit your goals.

Anaerobic threshold training is not as demanding as VO_2 max training; your day-to-day recovery will be much faster. By keeping your workout recovery times to a minimum, you are stimulating your aerobic metabolism more than your anaerobic. Your lactate levels are not nearly as high.

And because you are breaking the effort into shorter segments than in distance training, you can work at a higher intensity. This trains your aerobic energy systems to burn more fatty acids in proportion to glycogen—you become more fuel-efficient.

Working at 75 to 90 percent of your maximum effort simulates race pace, and it is equally important to simulate race conditions. Use the same gearing you would use in a race, for example. Incorporate a wide variety of terrain; vary the duration of your efforts. Train yourself to function at your anaerobic threshold in every conceivable race circumstance.

WORK/REST RATIO. The rest interval should be kept fairly short. You will be working for 1.5 to 2.5 minutes in each of the three sports, with the prescribed rest periods below.

SWIMMING: 5 to 45 seconds

CYCLING: 20 to 60 seconds

RUNNING: 20 seconds to 1.5 minutes

RECOVERY RESPONSE. This type of training provides a good indicator of your muscle fiber predominance. If you recover quickly, are able to maintain your time and distance without an elevated heart rate, and don't feel that burning sensation in your legs and arms—you are probably endowed with an abundance of slow-twitch fibers. But if you feel a muscular "heaviness" after about 8 to 10 minutes, you probably have more fast-twitch fibers—you need more anaerobic threshold training and longer recovery periods. Your heart rate should drop 10 to 15 percent.

HOW TO INTENSIFY YOUR EFFORT. You can't do the same workout day in and day out and make real progress. That will maintain your condition, but if you want to improve it, you have to tax yourself. At the beginning of the year, your anaerobic threshold may be only 60 to 65 percent of your maximum effort, but later it may be near the 85 to 90 percent range. At first, you may want to do shorter-distance efforts, or fewer, or faster with a longer rest. As the season progresses you may:

1 Increase the number of repeats.
2 Decrease the rest intervals.
3 Do the sets in a pyramid. To do this in running, for example, you can run 200 meters, then 300, 400, 500, and back down from 500 to 400, 300, 200. On the way up the pyramid, you might take 30 seconds' rest in between each effort, and on the way down try to take just 20 seconds' rest while holding the same times. You can also do that in cycling and swimming.

EXAMPLE WORKOUTS. Your anaerobic threshold times should be close to your time trial results. If you are doing five 300-meter efforts in a swim workout, for example, the total time of that set, minus the rest intervals, should equal your 1,500-meter freestyle time. For example, if you swam 1,500 meters in 20 minutes, each 300-meter effort should take 4 minutes; you would probably want to do the set on 4.5 minutes, to allow rest (4 × 300 on 4:30).

At the beginning of the year, you will need the maximum rest, but by the end of the year, you may need only one third to one half as much rest.

I consider my anaerobic threshold workouts on par if I am within 1 to 2 miles per hour of my maximum on the bike, 10 to 15 seconds per mile on the run, and 2 to 3 seconds per 100 meters on the swim.

Distance training helps you sustain effort over a long period of time.

DISTANCE TRAINING

DURATION OF EFFORT: 15 minutes to 6 hours
NUMBER OF REPEATS: Continuous effort
EFFORT LEVEL: 60% to 85%
ENERGY SYSTEM: ATP-aerobic
MUSCLE FIBERS: Slow-twitch

Distance training serves a number of purposes. It trains your body to conserve glycogen and burn fatty acids, whereas more intense work uses primarily carbohydrates. When your aerobic fitness is at a maximum level, you will start burning fatty acids (along with glycogen) as early as 10 or 15 minutes after the onset of continuous exercise. Burning fatty acids conserves glycogen and keeps you from running out of energy—"hitting the wall"—prematurely.

Distance training increases your aerobic capacity, which (a) expedites the delivery of oxygen to your working muscles, (b) increases your stroke volume, (c) brings down your resting pulse, (d) increases the capillary density around your muscles, (e) increases the mass and number of mitochondria, and (f) helps release ATP aerobically.

But one of the best things it does is prepare you psychologically for long-distance events. All your interval training will prepare your body to withstand the effort, but when you compete in a 5- to 15-hour triathlon, you have to be mentally ready as well.

A word of warning, however: Don't think you have to put in hundreds of miles each week. When I first started training, I overdid it because I didn't know any better. (Luckily, my training background was sufficient to keep me from getting severely injured.) Research and firsthand experience have proven that those

500-mile weekly bike distances not only are unnecessary and potentially injurious, they do not produce the best results. They do not train the oxidative fast-twitch muscle fibers, which you need during a race.

WHAT CONSTITUTES DISTANCE TRAINING? Any continuous effort above 60 percent of your maximum is part of your distance training program. (That includes continuous post-warm-up sets.)

PACING. When you are doing this type of training, you should be able to say a few words out loud without gasping or hyperventilating. If you are short of breath, you're pushing too hard. Go out moderately and pick up speed as you get used to the pace. If you are planning a three-hour bike ride and you have to climb a lot of hills at the beginning, or you try to keep up with a faster pack, you can deplete your glycogen stores in the first half-hour. Those last couple of hours are going to be slow and uncomfortable.

FOOD AND FLUIDS. Most of the top triathletes eat very little during a race, because they have trained their systems to conserve glycogen and burn fatty acids. When you train, you should consider nutrition as an important component.

- When you increase your distance training, you'll need to increase your carbohydrate intake. Even though your body is burning fatty acids, it also constantly uses glycogen, so you need the extra fuel source.
- After an hour or so, your body will become dehydrated unless you maintain your fluid level. Take in liquids throughout your exercise period. Cool water is best.

MAINTAIN YOUR TECHNIQUE. It is tempting to let your mind wander during a long workout; in fact, that's one reason many people enjoy distance work. But don't let that meditative feeling divert you from proper form. Train yourself to concentrate on your technique. You can meditate and visualize all you want, but without the proper technique, you'll never get anywhere.

When Scott Molina pulled away from me on mile 85 of the Japan Ironman bike course, he sped out of my sight within a couple of minutes. I presumed he was getting farther and farther ahead of me, and I started thinking about how long the race was and the fact that I had to run a marathon after I finished the 112-mile bike ride. For a brief moment, I started to feel discouraged. Then I pulled my concentration back to the present—to how I felt at that moment and to my technique—and I realized that I felt strong and competitive, no matter *where* Molina might be. So I got back down to business, and was only a couple of minutes behind Molina when I started the run. I kept concentrating on my technique, and I won the race.

It is vitally important to understand what each type of training demands of you. These reference charts summarize that information for your use in planning your own program.

PERCENTAGE OF MAXIMUM (TIME TRIAL) EFFORT FOR EACH TYPE OF TRAINING

TYPE OF TRAINING	PERCENT OF MAXIMUM EFFORT
EXPLOSIVE SPEED TRAINING	100–120%
SPRINT RACE TRAINING	90–100%
VO$_2$ MAX TRAINING	80–95%
ANAEROBIC THRESHOLD TRAINING	75–90%
DISTANCE TRAINING	60–85%

FIBER USAGE FOR EACH TYPE OF TRAINING*

*These percentages are approximations since there is an overlap in training and racing and due to the variability of body types and fiber composition.

	SLOW TWITCH	FAST TWITCH/A	FAST TWITCH/B
EXPLOSIVE SPEED TRAINING	5%	20%	75%
SPRINT RACE TRAINING	20%	40%	40%
VO₂ MAX TRAINING	60%	25%	15%
ANAEROBIC THRESHOLD TRAINING	70%	20%	10%
DISTANCE TRAINING	90%	8%	2%

ENERGY SYSTEMS USED FOR EACH TYPE OF TRAINING

	ATP-CP SYSTEM	ATP-LACTIC ACID	AEROBIC	LIPID—FATTY ACIDS
EXPLOSIVE SPEED	70%	30%	—	—
SPRINT RACE	20%	60%	20%	—
VO₂ MAX	10%	20%	50%	20%
ANAEROBIC THRESHOLD	5%	15%	60%	20%
DISTANCE	2%	5%	50%	43%

INTENSITY SPECTRUM FOR EACH TYPE OF TRAINING

ANAEROBIC				→ AEROBIC
FT_B		FT_A		ST
EXPLOSIVE SPEED TRAINING	SPRINT TRAINING	VO₂	ANAEROBIC THRESHOLD	DISTANCE
LONGER REST INTERVALS	MEDIUM REST INTERVALS		SHORT REST INTERVALS	
EFFORT:* 120%	110%	95%	85%	75% 65%

*Relative to personal time trial.

WORK/REST RATIO FOR EACH TYPE OF TRAINING

	WORK	REPEATS	REST INTERVAL (RI)
EXPLOSIVE SPEED TRAINING:	5-30 SEC	5–10	30 SEC (SWIMMING) 60 SEC (CYCLING) 90 SEC (RUNNING)
SPRINT RACE TRAINING:	30 SEC–2 MIN	5–8	1:30 (SWIMMING) 2:00 (CYCLING) 3:00 (RUNNING)
VO$_2$ MAX TRAINING:	3–8 MIN EITHER A) LONGER EFFORT (2 × 6 MIN) OR B) A (BROKEN SET) I.E. 3 × 3 MIN (2 ×). LENGTH OF THE SET AND REPEAT WILL BE DETERMINED BY THE FITNESS OF THE INDIVIDUAL. BROKEN SETS ARE EASIER TO SUSTAIN A HIGH INTENSITY. LONGER DURATION EFFORTS (4, 5, 6, 7, & 8 MIN) COULD BE INTEGRATED AS YOUR CONDITION PROGRESSES. THE RI BETWEEN THESE EFFORTS (A&B) SHOULD ALLOW A 40% DROP IN HEART RATE FROM COMPLETION TO THE START OF THE NEXT REPEAT. "ACTIVE" REST IS IMPORTANT TO DIFFUSE AND REMOVE LACTATE.		3:00 (SWIMMING) 3–8:00 (CYCLING) 30 SEC (SWIMMING) 1:00 (CYCLING) 1:00 (RUNNING) AFTER 3 × 3, THE RI WOULD BE THE SAME AS THE FIRST SET.
ANAEROBIC THRESHOLD TRAINING: SWIM DAVE SCOTT'S SET(S) WOULD BE: A) 30/50 YARD FREESTYLE ON 45 SEC, AVG. TIME :31 SEC AND/OR B) 10 × 200 YARD FREESTYLE ON 2:45, AVG. TIME 2:06	15–60 MIN. (INCLUDES RI)	8–50 THE GREATER NUMBER OF REPEATS, GENERALLY THE SHORTER THE DISTANCE, AND LESS RI. IDEAL LENGTH (1.5–3 MIN)	RI RANGE 5–40 SEC A) 5–15 SEC. RI (SHORTER NEED LESS REST WORK EFFORTS)

	WORK	REPEATS	REST INTERVAL (RI)
CYCLE A) 15 × 45 SEC WITH 20 SEC RI BETWEEN. ON ALL SETS THERE SHOULD BE "ACTIVE" RECOVERY, I.E., RUNNING 12 × 330, I DID EACH 330 IN ABOUT 50 SEC, THEN I WOULD JOG EASY UNTIL THE REMAINING 40 SEC WERE UP AND REPEAT. (MONITOR THE DISTANCE, THE REPEAT TIME, AND THE REST INTERVAL. ADDITIONALLY, THE RECOVERY HEART RATE COULD BE MONITORED.) B) 8 × 1 MILE-AVG. TIME 2:15 SEC RI 60 SEC	SAME LENGTH AS SWIMMING (ABOVE)	8–50 THE GREATER NUMBER OF REPEATS, GENERALLY THE SHORTER THE DISTANCE, AND LESS RI.	RI RANGE 15 SEC TO 1.5 MIN A) 15 SEC–45 SEC RI B) 45 SEC–1.5 MIN RI
RUN A) 12 × 330 ON 1:30 AVG. TIME 50. ON ALL SETS THERE SHOULD BE "ACTIVE" RECOVERY, I.E., RUNNING 12 × 330, I DID EACH 330 IN ABOUT 50 SEC, THEN I WOULD JOG EASY UNTIL THE REMAINING 40 SEC. WERE UP AND REPEAT. (MONITOR THE DISTANCE, THE REPEAT TIME, AND THE REST INTERVAL. ADDITIONALLY, THE RECOVERY HEART RATE COULD BE MONITORED.) B) 7 × 880 ON 4:00 AVG. TIME 2:20. ON ALL SETS THERE SHOULD BE "ACTIVE" RECOVERY, I.E., RUNNING 12 × 330, I DID EACH 330 IN ABOUT 50 SEC, THEN I WOULD JOG EASY UNTIL THE REMAINING 40 SEC WERE UP AND REPEAT. (MONITOR THE DISTANCE, THE REPEAT TIME, AND THE REST INTERVAL. ADDITIONALLY, THE RECOVERY HEART RATE COULD BE MONITORED.)	SAME LENGTH AS SWIMMING (ABOVE)	8–50 THE GREATER NUMBER OF REPEATS, GENERALLY THE SHORTER THE DISTANCE, AND LESS RI.	RI RANGE 30 SEC TO 2 MIN A) 30–60 SEC B) 60 SEC–2 MIN

WORKOUT FORMAT

Your workouts will usually follow the same pattern, regardless of the activity, type of training, or season:

Warm-up
Progressive set
Workout sets
Cool-down

WARM-UP

For any workout, you should start out slowly, working at 30 to 50 percent of your maximum effort. Warm up for three or four minutes (or until your body temperature is elevated); then stop and stretch.

SWIMMING: Mix up your strokes.
CYCLING: Stand up and stretch while riding.
RUNNING: Take short steps; don't force your stride.

PROGRESSIVE SETS

These sets increase your blood flow, allow maximum joint flexibility, and begin to elevate your heart rate, so that you are ready to exert yourself more fully. You can't just jump into a workout without the proper warm-up and progressive sets, because it will tax your systems too quickly and start draining your muscle glycogen.

WORKOUT SETS

These workout sets (see pages 123–24) are designed according to the type of training you are doing. Throughout the seasons, you will be changing the order in which you do each type of training, in order to get the maximum benefit. For example, sometimes you will do sprint race training at the beginning of your workout, when you are completely fresh, to train your muscles to get a head start in a race. Other times, you will do the sprint training in the middle of your workout, to prepare your muscles and energy systems to climb hills or surge ahead of an opponent in the middle of a race, when you are already a bit tired.

COOL-DOWN

Allow at least 4 minutes (up to 8 or 10) to cool down after a workout, before you stop completely. If you have done any anaerobic work, this cool-down period will allow the lactate to diffuse back into your bloodstream. In any case, you need to cool down gradually and stretch out in order to be fully recovered for the next day's work.

Cooling down is doubly important after a race, when you have exerted near maximum effort.

Don't cross the finish line and stop! You should jog a little, drink some fluid, and eat something very light (possibly fruit juice to elevate your blood sugar level.) Then do some easy stretches.

If you are training in the water, make sure you swim easy for a hundred yards or so to cool down and let your muscles relax. Better yet, jump into a whirlpool for a few minutes.

THE FOUR SEASONS

Rules—like records—are made to be broken. I offer my training methods because they have been proven to work for me and I definitely believe they'll work for you, but don't feel that you must follow every single detail rigidly.

You need enough diversity to keep yourself motivated, but repeat two or three workouts every two weeks so that you can check your improvement as you go along. Monitor yourself—your heart rate, your overall health, how well you recover from day to day—and do your own fine-tuning.

On an anaerobic threshold set in swimming, for instance, you may be doing eight 200-yard swims on 3 minutes (8 × 200 on 3:00). During the pre-season, your efforts may be consistently 2:30 in duration, with a 30-second rest interval. But as you progress toward the pre-competitive stage, your efforts may be down to 2:25—that's progress!

If you get bored, you may want to change the order of your weekly workout to provide variety. After all, there are no workout charts in a race—you're on your own.

My year-round training program is organized in four seasons, each of which incorporate the five types of training. Within those types of training, there are several workout options for each of the three sports, depending upon your goals, your levels of fitness, and the intensity you need to meet your goals.

Your emphasis may change throughout the year. If your goal is to do well in the Ironman in October, for example, you need to gear your training toward that all the way back in the pre-season. If your aerobic capacity isn't up to par, you should increase your VO_2 max, anaerobic threshold, and distance training. If you have a high-mileage background, but you lack speed, you may want to increase your sprint and VO_2 max training, and possibly add some extra explosive speed training.

Remember that it takes at least six to eight weeks to substantially alter muscle fiber composition, blood chemistry, capillary density, and all the other physiological components of fitness. So don't make the fatal mistake of believing you can cruise along on long, slow distance work until a few weeks before the race. And don't be afraid to redefine your goals—and readjust your training program—throughout the year.

PRE-SEASON

I don't believe in off-seasons, or lazy seasons—you just get fat and out of shape. Pre-season training may not be as intense as pre-competitive or competitive training, but it is equally as important. (Workout schedules for pre-season

training appear on pages 124–25.)

1   *Your first priority during this time of the year is to build strength.* Most training programs put off strength training until they are

already doing intense, longer-duration work-outs. I think that is foolish. Why not start out strong? Pre-season strength training serves three purposes:

  A. It increases your muscular strength in your entire anatomy.
  B. It builds particular strength in the muscles you'll use for swimming, cy-cling, and running.
  C. It prevents training injuries.

2 *This is an ideal time to work on your me-chanics and technique.* Your efficiency in any sport is not just a matter of being fit, but also a matter of employing the proper tech-nique. Both are equally important, and im-proving one generally improves the other. You should always monitor technique in every workout throughout the season, but the slightly slower pace of the pre-season allows you the time to really emphasize it.

  A. If possible, work with a coach. Triathlon clubs (see Appendix C) can usually refer you to local resources.
  B. Join a Masters swim program (see Ap-pendix B).

3 *Gradually build up your endurance.* You don't build your endurance by poking along aimlessly for hours at a time. Your workouts will combine all five types of training, and the order and intensity will change accord-ing to your purpose.

4 *Integrated training:* During the pre-season phase, structure your daily workout so that you are at your freshest for hard interval work; do explosive speed and sprint race training at the beginning of the workout. On Chart A (page 124), all three sports are done every day, six days a week.

  A. Explosive speed training is limited to two days per week for swimming and cycling, and one day for running. (If you have determined that you do not need explosive speed training, substi-tute extra technique, anaerobic thresh-old, or distance work.)
  B. Spring race training is limited to two days per week in all three sports.
  C. Since the emphasis is on strength

building, do not combine explosive speed and sprint training workouts in any one sport.

  D. The order of types of training should be: explosive speed, sprint, VO_2, anaerobic threshold, distance.

5 *Order of events:* Each day, as you do your workout, the optimum order of events is:

  A. Bike.
  B. Run.
  C. Swim.

(However, if you cannot follow that order for some reason, it is better to train out of order than not to train at all.)

When you train on the bike, you will be overloading your quadriceps muscle group (primarily the vastus lateralis and medialis) and gluteal muscles; your fast-twitch fibers are likely to become fatigued. If you do the run first, you won't be able to work as well on the bike—and vice-versa. Since cycling is less taxing than running, however, and your cycling muscles are stressed more than your running muscles in weight training (see page 136), you can ride for a much longer period of time without tiring. There is also some crossover benefit (in leg muscle strength) from cycling to running.

Swimming last will give your leg muscles a chance to relax and recuperate, particu-larly during the pre-season when the air temperature is cold.

6 *Do short mini-triathlons.* Toward the end of the pre-season, incorporate a mini-triathlon into your training schedule. The distances and number of these will depend on your goals. If you are going to be doing primarily short races (two to three hours in duration), try working up to 80 percent of the race distance by the end of the pre-season. Also, start with a few minutes between each event, then shorten those transition times as the season progresses.

If you'll be doing Ironman-distance races, you will obviously have to do more distance work, and incorporate longer mini-triathlons as soon as possible.

PRE-COMPETITIVE SEASON

During this season, you need to elevate your aerobic endurance and further elevate your strength from the pre-season levels. (Workout schedules for pre-competitive training appear on pages 125-26.)

1   *Try to increase your aerobic capacity to its maximal level.* The emphasis is on endurance, which means you will do more distance and anaerobic threshold work.

2   *Re-evaluate your strengths and weaknesses.* This is the time to refine your training program; isolate your problem areas and concentrate on improving them. If you have found during pre-season training that you have difficulty sustaining your energy on long hills, do more VO_2 max and sprint training to expand your aerobic tolerance.

3   *Integrated training:*

   A.   Do your distance work first during the pre-competitive stage. You will be doing more time trial work, where you start out at 70 percent effort and build your speed up to 90 percent—try to match (or at least come closer to) your time trial results for this season. Most of the workouts on Chart B are set up with anaerobic threshold and distance training first. Then comes VO_2, then sprint or explosive speed training.

   B.   Putting sprint race training at the end of your workout means that you will be doing it when you are already fairly fatigued. Forcing yourself to do anaerobic work when you are tired simulates conditions you'll face in a race. When you are 40 miles into a triathlon and you suddenly have to climb a steep hill or pass an opponent, you'll have to work anaerobically in a fatigued state. There's nothing more humiliating than being passed in the last half-mile of a race by an opponent who still has a burst of power left, or not being able to catch up to a competitor who has broken away during the bike race. You see the back of his shirt for the next half hour or so—it's a constant reminder that you should have been in shape for that one hill! When Scott Tinley passed me in the 1984 Kauai Triathlon, he was going about 30 mph up a hill and I felt as though I were standing still! He got to the top of the hill and looked back at me—I figured he was worried—but I knew I couldn't catch him. It was a graphic reminder that I hadn't done my homework.

   C.   Cut down your explosive speed and sprint race training in cycling and running. You will be increasing the other three types of training during this season, and that will partially fatigue your fast-twitch as well as your slow-twitch fibers.

   D.   Add more sprint training in swimming to elevate lactate tolerance for the start.

   E.   Increase weight training for maximum strength. The speed and power you cut back on the road (in the bike and the run) will be regained in the weight room.

4   *Order of events:* Bike, swim, run.

5   *Mini-triathlons:* Try to do a mini-triathlon every three weeks during the pre-competitive phase. Work on decreasing your transition/rest times.

During the competitive season, you will have to coordinate your training efforts with your racing schedules.

COMPETITIVE SEASON

Specialize. You have to coordinate your training efforts with your racing schedule, so the overall duration of your daily workouts will be decreased somewhat. Make sure that the amount of time you do spend training is a wise investment. You have already built your training base; now you will be tested in races, and each one should teach you what you need to work on. (Workout schedules for competitive season training appear on pages 126–27.)

1   *Don't overlook your need for rest.* You need to be at your best for every race. That means training properly, but not too much. Make sure you always take one full day of rest each week. You may want to reduce your program to the post-competitive level for a week out of each month. I do that often to give myself a psychological break as well as a physical rest.

2   *Integrated training:* During this time, your anaerobic threshold training should be very close to your maximal time trial effort. If you are very far out of range—over or under— maybe you should do another personal time trial to adjust your target times. In general, you should reduce your distance and VO_2 max training because the races in which you are competing will tax those systems, and you should increase the number of days that you do sprint and anaerobic threshold training. (Sprint training maintains your strength and anaerobic threshold training increases your aerobic capacity.)

On Chart C, the program emphasizes anaerobic threshold training in swimming first, since the swim is the first event in a triathlon and you need a combination of endurance and speed. But on Tuesday and Thursday, sprint race training is first, so that you work fresh and can develop your speed. (Wednesday's workout should leave your lactate levels low, so that you'll be fully recovered and able to work at the maximal anaerobic level the next day.)

3 *Order of events:* You are doing more VO_2 max and sprint training, which is very taxing. So it is important to do the longer event—cycling—first. If you are doing a lot of speed work on the bike, then you should do the swim second to allow a little more recovery time before the run. And remember, on those long days, eat enough food so that your glycogen stores don't become depleted too soon.

  A. Bike.
  B. Swim/run.
  C. Run/swim.

4 *Mini-triathlons:* Every three weeks, unless you are racing that weekend.

POST-COMPETITIVE SEASON

This is a one-month winding-down period after your racing season has ended. Some people prefer to take one month off, then the post-competitive season, leading right into the pre-season. It's up to you. (Workout schedules for post-competitive season training appear on pages 127–28.)

1 *Concentrate on distance work.* This will maintain your aerobic base, and give you a chance to repair any injuries you may have incurred along the way.

2 *Any anaerobic threshold work should be done for 20 to 30 percent less time than competitive or pre-competitive level.* Your overall intensity and duration will be less.

3 *Integrated training:* The choice is yours. Chart D is a five-day workout week with two days of rest, 90 percent distance and anaerobic threshold work, and 10 percent VO_2 max. Don't worry about interval training or the order of events. Be creative!

4 *Vary your workouts.* Just because you are cutting back and kind of taking it easy, don't get into a humdrum pace of doing everything exactly the same, day in and day out. Vary your strokes in swimming, alternate gearing in cycling, and try different paces and rhythms in running. This will work your muscles in all different ways, even though you're not working intensely.

ONE MONTH OFF

You've earned it, so enjoy it! But don't be totally inactive, or you'll gain weight and lose all that conditioning you worked so hard to achieve during the previous 11 months. You don't have to participate in triathlon sports—unless you prefer them solely as recreation—but it is vitally important to remain active and healthy.

That's one of the best reasons to become a triathlete—being healthy. Most people wonder if it takes a huge ego to compete in a rugged endurance sport such as this, but I don't think you can separate ego from health. When you are healthy, you have a good self-image.

So enjoy your well-earned vacation. Take that trip to New Zealand . . . but don't forget your tennis rackets or your running shoes!

PLANNING YOUR WORKOUT SCHEDULE

Although each individual training program will be slightly different, you can make optimum use of your time by incorporating the information in the following charts. Because triathlon training can be very demanding, it is especially important to follow these recommendations for the number of days per week to do each type of training. Remember—rest is as important as exercise.

SEASONAL WORKOUT SCHEDULES

These schedules have been designed according to the amount of time you have available to train, not your level of fitness or skill. You will determine your own program according to your personal time trial and your level of aerobic fitness. Make sure you do the types of training in the order shown for each sport.

An example workout day for a relatively proficient triathlete who has three-and-a-half hours a day, six days a week available to train might be as follows:

DAYS PER WEEK TO DO EACH TYPE OF TRAINING (ACCORDING TO SEASON AND SPORT)

	PRE-SEASON			PRE-COMPETITIVE			COMPETITIVE			POST-COMPETITIVE		
	SWIM	CYCLE	RUN	SWIM	CYCLE	RUN	SWIM	CYCLE	RUN	SWIM	CYCLE	RUN
EXPLOSIVE SPEED TRAINING	2	2	1	2	1	1	2	1	0	0	0	0
SPRINT RACE TRAINING	2	2	2	3	2	1	3	3	2	0	0	0
VO$_2$ TRAINING	4	4	2	4	3	2	3	2	2	0	1	0
ANAEROBIC THRESHOLD TRAINING	3	4	2	4	3	2	5	3	3	5	5	5
DISTANCE TRAINING	4	4	3	4	4	4	3	4	3	5	4	4

SWIMMING: ANAEROBIC THRESHOLD, SPRINT RACE, DISTANCE

WORKOUT TIME	WORKOUT DESCRIPTION
6 MIN	WARM-UP: 6 MINUTES EASY SWIM, ANY STROKE.
6 MIN	PROGRESSIVE SET: 6 × 50 ALTERNATE STROKES WITH 5-SECOND REST INTERVAL. (ELEVATES HEART RATE FOR FOLLOWING SET.)
8.5 MIN	ANAEROBIC THRESHOLD: 3 × 200 FREESTYLE, WITH 20 SECONDS REST INTERVAL. HOLD TIMES. NO REST BETWEEN THIS SET AND THE NEXT.
9 MIN	ANAEROBIC THRESHOLD: 4 × 150 FREESTYLE, WITH 15 SECONDS REST INTERVAL. DESCENDING TIMES FOR EACH SUCCESSIVE SWIM.
6.5 MIN	SPRINT RACE TRAINING: 4 × 50, WITH EASY 50 THEN 15-SECOND REST BETWEEN. (50 HARD, 50 EASY, 15 SECONDS REST, REPEAT.)
12 MIN	DISTANCE: 12 MINUTES CONTINUOUS FREESTYLE, WITH 90% EFFORT EVERY FOURTH LAP.
6 MIN	COOL-DOWN: 6 MINUTES EASY SWIM, ANY STROKE; EASIER THAN WARM-UP.
55 MIN	TOTAL TIME

CYCLING: SPRINT RACE, DISTANCE, VO₂

WORKOUT TIME	WORKOUT DESCRIPTION
15 MIN	WARM-UP: 10 MINUTES MODERATE RIDE, PICK UP PACE LAST 5 MINUTES.
20 MIN	SPRINT RACE: 5 × 3/4 MILE AT 100% EFFORT, WITH MODERATE 3/4 MILE BETWEEN. ON SECOND AND FOURTH EFFORT, STAND UP FOR THE FIRST MINUTE, THEN SIT DOWN AND MAINTAIN LARGE GEAR.
20 MIN	DISTANCE: 20 MINUTES RIDE WITH FIRST 5 MINUTES AT 70% EFFORT, MIDDLE 10 MINUTES AT 80%, FINAL 5 MINUTES AT 70%.
26 MIN	VO_2: 4 × 2 MILES AT 80%–90% EFFORT, WITH 30 SECONDS EASY RIDE BETWEEN.
8 MIN	COOL-DOWN: 8 MINUTES EASY EFFORT (70–80 RPM'S).
89 MIN	TOTAL TIME

RUNNING: VO₂, DISTANCE

WORKOUT TIME	WORKOUT DESCRIPTION
15 MIN	WARM-UP: 15 MINUTES MODERATE RUN.
14 MIN	PROGRESSIVE SET: 2 × 1 MILE. ON THE FIRST MILE, RUN AT 60%–80% EFFORT FOR 3/4, THEN 80%–90% FOR 1/4. ON THE SECOND MILE, RUN AT 60%–80% FOR 1/2, THEN 80%–90% FOR 1/2.
15 MIN	VO₂: 4 × 800 AT 80%–90% EFFORT, WITH 1.5 MINUTES EASY JOG BETWEEN.
15 MIN	DISTANCE: 15 MINUTES AT 60%–80% EFFORT.
59 MIN	TOTAL TIME

To reduce total workout time, the importance of the type of training should be evaluated. The emphasis during the competitive season is to develop race speed. However, on a four-day workout schedule, the primary importance is to develop your aerobic potential, since all triathlons are at least one hour in duration.

THE SCHEDULES

CHART A
PRE-SEASON—
SIX-DAY
WORKOUT WEEK

	MON	TUES	WED	THURS	FRI	SAT	SUN
SWIM	—	EXP VO₂ D	SRT VO₂ AT	EXP AT D	VO₂ AT	SRT D	D VO₂
CYCLE	—	EXP VO₂ D	SRT VO₂ AT	EXP AT D	VO₂ AT	SRT D	D VO₂ AT
RUN	—	EXP AT	D SRT	VO₂ AT	D SRT	VO₂	D

CHART B
PRE-SEASON—
FIVE-DAY
WORKOUT WEEK

	MON	TUES	WED	THURS	FRI	SAT	SUN
SWIM		SAME AS SIX-DAY, BUT NO SATURDAY WORKOUT					
CYCLE		SAME AS SIX-DAY, BUT NO SATURDAY WORKOUT					
RUN		SAME AS SIX-DAY, BUT NO SATURDAY WORKOUT					

CHART C
PRE-SEASON— FOUR-DAY WORKOUT WEEK

	MON	TUES	WED	THURS	FRI	SAT	SUN
SWIM	—	EXP VO₂ D	SRT VO₂ AT	—	VO₂ AT D	—	SRT VO₂ D
CYCLE	—	EXP VO₂ D	SRT VO₂ AT	—	VO₂ AT	—	D VO₂ AT
RUN	—	SRT AT	D SRT	—	D VO₂	—	D AT

CHART D
PRE-SEASON— THREE-DAY WORKOUT WEEK

	MON	TUES	WED	THURS	FRI	SAT	SUN
SWIM	—	SRT VO₂ AT	—	VO₂ AT D	—	SRT AT D	—
CYCLE	—	SRT VO₂ D	—	VO₂ AT D	—	SRT AT D	—
RUN	—	VO₂ D	—	AT D	—	D VO₂	—

CHART E
PRE- COMPETITION— SIX-DAY WORKOUT WEEK

	MON	TUES	WED	THURS	FRI	SAT	SUN
SWIM	AT SRT EXP	D VO₂ EXP	D AT VO₂	—	AT VO₂ SRT	D VO₂	D AT SRT
CYCLE	AT SRT	D VO₂	D AT EXP	—	AT VO₂	D SRT	D VO₂
RUN	D SRT	AT VO₂	D EXP	—	D SRT	AT VO₂	D

KEY

EXP = EXPLOSIVE SPEED TRAINING

SRT = SPRINT RACE TRAINING

D = DISTANCE TRAINING

VO₂ = VO₂ TRAINING

AT = ANAEROBIC THRESHOLD TRAINING

CHART F
PRE-COMPETITIVE—FIVE-DAY WORKOUT WEEK

	MON	TUES	WED	THURS	FRI	SAT	SUN
SWIM	SAME AS SIX-DAY (CHART E), BUT NO WEDNESDAY WORKOUT.						
CYCLE	SAME AS SIX-DAY (CHART E), BUT NO WEDNESDAY WORKOUT.						
RUN	SAME AS SIX-DAY (CHART E), BUT NO WEDNESDAY WORKOUT.						

CHART G
PRE-COMPETITIVE—FOUR-DAY WORKOUT WEEK

	MON	TUES	WED	THURS	FRI	SAT	SUN
SWIM	AT D VO_2	VO_2 SRT D	—	AT D VO_2	—	AT D SRT	—
CYCLE	AT SRT D	D VO_2	—	AT D	—	AT D VO_2	—
RUN	D SRT	AT VO_2	—	D AT	—	AT VO_2	—

CHART H
PRE-COMPETITIVE—THREE-DAY WORKOUT WEEK

	MON	TUES	WED	THURS	FRI	SAT	SUN
SWIM	D VO_2 AT	—	D AT VO_2	—	AT D	—	—
CYCLE	AT VO_2	—	D AT VO_2	—	AT VO_2 D	—	—
RUN	D SRT	—	D AT	—	D AT	—	—

CHART I
COMPETITIVE—SIX-DAY WORKOUT WEEK

	MON	TUES	WED	THURS	FRI	SAT	SUN
SWIM	AT SRT D	AT VO_2	VO_2 EXP D	SRT AT	AT VO_2	SRT AT D	—
CYCLE	AT D	SRT D	D VO_2	SRT AT	D VO_2 EXP	SRT AT	—
RUN	AT VO_2	D SRT	AT	D SRT	VO_2	AT D	—

CHART J
COMPETITIVE—FIVE-DAY WORKOUT WEEK

	MON	TUES	WED	THURS	FRI	SAT	SUN
SWIM	SAME AS SIX-DAY (CHART I), EXCEPT NO WEDNESDAY WORKOUT.						
CYCLE	SAME AS SIX-DAY (CHART I), EXCEPT NO WEDNESDAY WORKOUT.						
RUN	SAME AS SIX-DAY (CHART I), EXCEPT NO WEDNESDAY WORKOUT.						

CHART K
COMPETITIVE—FOUR-DAY WORKOUT WEEK

	MON	TUES	WED	THURS	FRI	SAT	SUN
SWIM	—	AT SRT D	—	AT VO$_2$ D	—	SRT D AT	VO$_2$ AT SRT
CYCLE	—	SRT D VO$_2$	—	VO$_2$ AT D	—	VO$_2$ AT D	SRT AT
RUN	—	VO$_2$	—	SRT D	—	AT D	AT D

CHART L
COMPETITIVE—THREE-DAY WORKOUT WEEK

	MON	TUES	WED	THURS	FRI	SAT	SUN
SWIM	—	AT VO$_2$ D	—	SRT AT D	—	VO$_2$ AT D	—
CYCLE	—	SRT D	—	SRT AT D	—	VO$_2$ AT	—
RUN	—	AT D	—	VO$_2$ D	—	SRT AT	—

CHART M
POST-COMPETITIVE—SIX- AND FIVE-DAY WORKOUT WEEK

	MON	TUES	WED	THURS	FRI	SAT	SUN
SWIM	D AT	D AT	—	D AT	D AT	D AT	—
CYCLE	AT D	AT D VO$_2$	—	AT D	AT D	AT D	—
RUN	AT D	AT D	—	AT D	AT	AT D	—

KEY

EXP = EXPLOSIVE SPEED TRAINING
SRT = SPRINT RACE TRAINING
D = DISTANCE TRAINING
VO$_2$ = VO$_2$ TRAINING
AT = ANAEROBIC THRESHOLD TRAINING

CHART N
POST-COMPETITIVE—FOUR-DAY WORKOUT WEEK

	MON	TUES	WED	THURS	FRI	SAT	SUN
SWIM	D AT VO_2	—	D AT	—	D AT VO_2	D AT	—
CYCLE	AT D VO_2	—	AT D	—	AT D VO_2	AT D	—
RUN	AT D	—	AT D	—	AT D	AT	—

CHART O
POST-COMPETITIVE—THREE-DAY WORKOUT WEEK

	MON	TUES	WED	THURS	FRI	SAT	SUN
SWIM	D AT VO_2	—	D AT VO_2	—	D AT VO_2	—	—
CYCLE	AT D VO_2	—	AT D	—	AT D VO_2	—	—
RUN	AT D	—	AT D	—	AT D	—	—

KEY

EXP = EXPLOSIVE SPEED TRAINING
SRT = SPRINT RACE TRAINING
D = DISTANCE TRAINING
VO_2 = VO_2 TRAINING
AT = ANAEROBIC THRESHOLD TRAINING

EXAMPLE WORKOUT SETS

	EXAMPLE	SWIM	BIKE	RUN
EXPLOSIVE SPEED TRAINING *Can do 2 or 3 sets of this interspersed throughout workout, depending on emphasis. Early in workout the fast-twitch/B and fast-twitch/A fibers will be rested; therefore the performance will be much better. If the sets are done in the latter part or middle, this will teach the athlete to use the ATP-CP reserve for the "final kick."*	*Sets of 5–10 at 100%–120% effort × 5–30 seconds w/RI of: W/R = 1/2—swim 1/3—bike, run*	*6 × 25-yard freestyle on 1 minute assuming each swim takes 20 sec ± 10 sec, then RI = 30.*	*7 × 30 "standing up w/90" easy sitting between. rpm's standing = 70–80 rpm's sitting = 70–80 Use larger gears when standing to do this type of training.*	*5 × 110 yards with easy jog of 300 yards between.*

	EXAMPLE	SWIM	BIKE	RUN
SPRINT RACE TRAINING "Active" rest interval uses lactate as fuel. During rest interval keep moving 30–40% exercise level to diffuse lactate, restore O_2 debt.	Sets of: 5–8 × 30" to 2' in duration with same rest interval or possibly longer since higher O_2 debt and lactate levels occur. Work/rest ratio should be 1 to 1 for swimming, and 1 to 2 or 1 to 3 for cycling and running.	8 × 100 free on 3, assuming swims are done in 1:30. This 1:30 pace should be 3–5 seconds faster per 100 yards than the final 1,650 broken down. Generally swimmers tolerate longer sets, need less rest, and recover quickly.	6 × ½ mile sprints. This can be done on flats, hills, rollers; however, the grade percent must be constant throughout the exercise phase so that the stress is the same, with ½ to 1 minute rest between.	6 × 300 with easy 100 meters jog then 2–3 minutes rest interval.
VO_2 TRAINING	Each set should be preceded by a progressive warmup set which will elevate the heart rate, then the set length is between 3–8 minutes. Can be repeated 2–4 × depending upon condition and emphasis of training. RI should allow HR to drop to 20–40% above resting. Check HR to determine recovery response. (The importance of the VO2 exercise is to work at a high intensity on each effort—allow enough RI.) If a broken set is used, the recovery is short between repeats to allow CP stores to replenish, but still keep the HR elevated.	3 × 150 × 2, 10 sec RI between 150s with 2–3 min RI between groups of 3.	6 × 3' efforts; may be done like this: 3 × 3' w/RI of 3' then 3 × 3' again. Intensity is important. Should be faster than time trial efforts.	3 × ¾-mile efforts. All VO_2 sets are done progressive. Too much lactate will inhibit performance if effort is 100% within first 30 seconds.

	EXAMPLE	SWIM	BIKE	RUN
ANAEROBIC THRESHOLD *Sets are aerobic, pressing anaerobic threshold.*	*Sets last minimum of 15 min. Short rest between repeats is feature of sets. Short recovery between repeats allows stroke volume to increase. Sets of 1½–3 min efforts are best but can be shorter in duration; however, rest must be very short, i.e., 5 seconds.*	*15 × 125 free with 5 sec RI. Try to hold times on each repeat. If the repeats fall off then increase the RI or pace yourself better, or select an interval based on your first and second average time.*	*2 sets of 8 × 1-mile efforts with ⅛ mile moderate between. Another way of stating the same set is: 8 × 2:45" w/20–25' sec RI. After the first set, moderate distance set could be done to allow partial recovery but teaching the body to spare glycogen and use fats, then come back to the same set again.*	*8 × 400 with 1 min RI. The pace in the "competitive" season should be close to your 3-mile time trial.*
DISTANCE *This type of training is continuous—no breaks. The pace can vary from a moderate (60%) range to a time trial effort nearing 85–90%.*	*All warm-ups are usually moderate-distance sets. Then the intensity is increased if a distance swim is done in the workout. This taxes 95% slow-twitch fibers unless the effort is in the time trial percent range. Then the fast-twitch/A are also used.*	*3 × 1200-yard swim. Try to hold a pace 1–2 seconds over 1,650 time trial per 100 meters.*	*40 miles constant.*	*8 miles constant.*

DAVE SCOTT'S SWIM WORKOUT: PRE-SEASON TO POST-COMPETITIVE SEASON* (VARIATION OF ONE SET THROUGHOUT THE YEAR.)

TYPE OF TRAINING	PRE-SEASON	PRE-COMPETITIVE SEASON	COMPETITIVE SEASON	POST-COMPETITIVE SEASON
Sprint race training	6 × 75-yard freestyle on 1:50 Each repeat was swum in 47 ± seconds. These were all-out. My stroke was falling apart at the end of each repeat. I would swim an easy 25 yards in between, then rest. My RI was about 1:30 after each hard effort.	8 × 75 on 1:45, avg. time 45. I added 2 more repeats since the emphasis during this period is to increase my endurance. Due to my better fitness I lowered my send-off time to 1:45; however, my repeats were 2 seconds faster. During this phase the sprint sets are generally put at the end of the workout. The fast-twitch/A and fast-twitch/B will both be fatigued slightly.	6 × 75 on 1:40-1:45-1:50-1:55-2:00; avg. time 43. I dropped 2 repeats and used an ascending rest interval to allow additional recovery between repeats. However, my first RI was 1:40, which was a tighter RI than the previous two phases. The purpose of this phase is to develop speed, so I reduced the number of repeats and allowed a progressive rest to allow the lactate to diffuse and my O_2 debt to recover. My times were faster.	Do not include this type of training in this phase.
ANAEROBIC THRESHOLD	8 × 250 freestyle on 3. Each repeat was swum in 2:49 ± 2 sec. Tried to hold each constant.	10 × 250; 2 on 2:45; 2 on 2:50; 2 on 2:55; 2 on 2:50; 1 on 2:45. Avg. time 2:37. The interval was done in groups of 2 with a stiff interval allowing only 8 sec recovery. Then while I was reaching my max VO_2, the interval ascended to 2 or 2:50, giving me more RI to allow my heart rate to recover slightly and the lactate to leave the bloodstream. Then 2 or 2:55. The set became moderately aerobic at the end, my heart rate was dropping, my recovery was quicker, then I descended the interval on the last 3 repeats to further tax my anaerobic threshold (only 9 RI for 10 swims).	6 × 250; numbers 1,3,5 on 2:40; 2,4,6 on 3:30. Very hard on 1,3,5. Avg. time 2:33. Numbers 2, 6 I swam moderately and recorded my heart rate during the RI. Finishing heart rate was 152 (my max is 172). Emphasized speed on the odd swims and recovered on the evens. Avg. time on evens 3:00. The pace on the odd 250s was within 1 second of my tester timed 1,650, which I use as my reference for sets.	7 × 250; 3 on 2:55; 3 on 3:15. Avg. time 2:50. Gave myself a break. Heart rate between 142–149.

*I start with a basic set in the pre-season, then modify it throughout the year according to the emphasis of each training season.

TYPE OF TRAINING	PRE-SEASON	PRE-COMPETITIVE SEASON	COMPETITIVE SEASON	POST-COMPETITIVE SEASON
DISTANCE	1,650-yard freestyle. I do not enjoy these but wanted to check my time. Last season best workout 1,650 was 17:12, which is about a 1:02 average/100 yd. So this is my goal time for the year's sets. I base my types of training percent from this time. Pre-season effort 17:51.	3 × 800 freestyle on 9:15. Avg. time, 8:38. (Pace per 100 = 1:04.8, about 2.8 sec off my tester time.) Satisfied! This set was 2,400 yards all swum at a faster pace than pre-season 1,650. The emphasis was on aerobic conditioning during this phase.	2 × 1,200 on 13:40. I tried to swim each 400 faster than the previous one by 1–2 seconds. At each split I glanced at the pace clock to check my time. They were: 1—4:20 4:16 4:16 2—4:21 4:14 4:11 This was a good "fast" distance time trial for me. Very close to my "tester" 1,650.	1 × 2,000. Swam the odd 100s hard (sort of), even 100s moderate. Didn't check total time. Occasionally on the longer distance swims I'll vary the efforts on any given segment to break the monotony.

SWIMMING TIPS

1 *Use 70 percent freestyle and 30 percent other strokes.* If you swim only freestyle, day after day, you will overuse the same muscles and tendons by repeating just one movement pattern. Mixing other strokes into your workout—or varying your entry angle from time to time—will give those muscles a respite and prevent tendinitis in the shoulder.

The best way to mix up your strokes is to alternate the sets and/or the repeats. On the anaerobic threshold sets, for example, if you are doing 5 × 100, you might swim the 5th, 10th, and 15th repeat backstroke or breaststroke. You will still get the physiological benefit of the short-rest interval training, but your muscles will get a rest. You can also alternate sets, by doing an entire set with a back or breast stroke.

Warning: Rotating your feet outward on the breaststroke kick puts stress on the ligaments inside your knee. Use a very narrow whip kick or a dolphin kick instead.

2 *Occasionally do some hypoxic training.* Hypoxia is an inadequate supply of oxygen in your lungs and blood—oxygen debt. This oxygen deficit occurs when you breathe bilaterally for an extended period of time, or on every third stroke (or fourth arm pull). Your heart rate increases 5 to 10 percent. Normally, you try to avoid operating in this oxygen-starved state, but there are times during a race (when you first rush out in the swim, or when you have to breathe bilaterally to navigate, etc.) when a slight oxygen deficit is unavoidable. Therefore, you should train your system to cope with it.

Do hypoxic training only on distance or moderate anaerobic threshold swims; don't do it at all if you have any heart problem or if it gives you even a slight headache.

Swim one lap breathing every arm cycle,

and the next breathing bilaterally. Your heart rate will remain elevated throughout the regular lap, which will boost your aerobic capacity.

3 *Drink fluids during your swim workout.* Most people don't think about dehydration when they swim because they are surrounded by water. When you are wet on the outside, it's easy to forget that you may be dry on the inside. I keep a bottle of water by the pool; I go through about a pint and a half during a one-hour swim workout. Drinking during your swim workout will also help prevent cumulative dehydration during the rest of your day's training.

4 *Don't rush your warm-up.* I like to warm up at no more than 30 to 40 percent of my maximum effort. After 200 to 300 yards at a very easy pace, I gradually lengthen each stroke so that my heart rate goes up. Then I change my stroke pattern slightly to in-

crease flexibility in my shoulders. The final phase is a progressive set that leads into my actual workout. Don't skip any part of your slow, easy warm-up; if you push yourself, you will build up lactate and your overall performance will suffer. If you swim after cycling and/or running, allow even more time for the warm-up.

5 *Don't skip the cool-down at the end of your workout.* If you jump out of the pool, take a quick shower and rush back to the office without an adequate cool-down period, you will be stiff and sore the next day (or for the next activity).

6 *Learn to breathe on both sides.* Even though bilateral breathing isn't the most efficient way to swim, you will need to be comfortable breathing to either side during an open-water race to navigate properly, and to avoid getting mouthfuls of water in choppy conditions.

Though riding in packs is prohibited at triathlons, there are some advantages to training with a group.

CYCLING TIPS

1 *Select gears that allow you to maintain about 85 revolutions per minute.* During the pre-season, you may want to gear down to about 80 rpms (to save your white-twitch fibers) when you are doing anaerobic threshold, distance, and VO_2 max training. Vary your gearing to simulate the widest variety of racing conditions.

2 *Using wind-load simulators:* Using a wind-load simulator (a stationary apparatus to which you attach your own bicycle) helps you increase your speed and allows you to work on technique during those cold and rainy winter months. You don't get the actual wind resistance that you would outdoors, nor do you develop bike-handling skills, but if you vary your gearing and stand up just as you would on a variety of outdoor terrain, you can achieve effective results. You cannot dissipate your body heat as well as you would outdoors, though, so make sure you turn on the fan to partially simulate the cooling effect of the wind.

3 *Don't worry about a drop in performance during the winter.* In cold weather, your blood is drawn to your torso to keep your vital organs warm—it is an unavoidable survival mechanism. Your legs and arms, therefore, suffer from a slight decrease in circulation and available oxygen, which will ultimately result in a decrease in your overall speed. Don't worry about your times; as long as you work at the appropriate percentage of effort for that season, you are making progress. You will find that your speed picks up noticeably when the warm weather comes back around.

4 *Lycra skin suits inhibit breathing.* They may look great, but there is a major problem: they are skintight and they trap the heat. I can barely breathe in them. When you swim, ride, and run, you need all the oxygen you can get. I prefer to wear cycling shorts with a jersey or singlet that is loose enough to allow me freedom of movement and breathing, but fitted enough that it doesn't billow in the wind. In the 1984 Ironman, I wore a netlike singlet with a small, elasticized pouch sewn to the back. The wind could blow right through it, and I kept cool and comfortable throughout the race.

5 *Though riding in packs is strictly prohibited in triathlons, it can be useful in training, as long as there is a planned drafting pattern.* If the pack riders are slightly faster than you, and everyone follows a consistent drafting pattern, you will have to work harder than usual to keep up (which will boost your anaerobic threshold training), but you'll get a little extra rest while you draft. The obvious disadvantage is that it doesn't stimulate triathlon race conditions.

6 *For short races, it is critical to (a) know the course, and (b) know how to corner.* Ride the bike course before the race so that you know every turn and every hill. Pick the best line to follow on race day, and ride it several times so that you can practically ride it with your eyes closed. If you can corner effortlessly and skillfully, you can save a lot of time on a bike course.

On your training rides, get used to riding with your hands on the drops and your head low, so that you will be comfortable in that position during a race. Lift your head every 50 yards or so to look forward, and try to keep a straight line. Keep your hands and fingers as relaxed as possible.

RUNNING TIPS

1 *If you are sore, don't stop.* The hardest thing for triathletes to overcome in running is the stiffness they feel from cycling. The temptation may be to stop, but that will just make the soreness worse. Running at a moderate pace, with a short stride (30 percent less than normal) will

actually diffuse some of the lactate and help relieve the stiffness.

2 *Always start off with a very short stride.* For the first mile, run with steps that are at least 30 percent shorter than your normal stride. After a mile, stop and stretch your hamstrings and quadriceps for three or four minutes. Then continue your workout.

3 *Don't run in a rigid, upright position.* Look down slightly to shift your posture slightly forward. Swing your arms loosely to allow your deltoids and trapezius muscles to relax.

4 *Vary your workout with fartlek training. Fartlek* is Swedish for "speed play." Since a triathlon is run on the road—not on a track—there are many kinds of terrain. If you do all your training runs in controlled circumstances, at the same speed, with the same rest intervals, you will not be prepared for the diverse demands of triathlon running. Fartlek training affords that variety. Do your VO₂ max and anaerobic threshold training on hills, flats, tracks, roads, etc., so that your speed varies.

5 *Pyramid (or ladder) training makes a workout more interesting.* Every couple of weeks, interject a pyramid workout into your routine. Start with a 220, for example, then run a 330, 440, 880, 1320, then a mile, then back down again. Keep track of your heart rate, your workout times, and your rest intervals. When you repeat the routine two weeks later, you will be able to chart your progress.

6 *You don't have to run the full race distance in training.* Distance runners tend to be preprogrammed to believe they have to do a 20-mile training run to be prepared for a marathon. I don't believe that. If I can run half the distance hard and feel relatively fresh at the end, I know I'll

have no trouble doubling the distance in a race.

7 *Define your workouts in terms of duration; base the speed on your personal time trial.* Set your workouts like swimming workouts, so that the duration of a set includes work and rest. Track running workouts are typically defined by the speed of the effort alone, i.e., 8 × 1-mile on 7:30 (eight 1-mile efforts at 7.5 minutes, with an undefined rest period). That predetermines your pace, and may limit or overstress you.

8 *Incorporate "accelerations" into your workout.* Pick up your pace for a prescribed distance, then back off to your warm-up pace, then pick up your pace again. Repeat that pattern a few times. This is primarily an aerobic workout because there are no rest intervals, but your system is taxed at a variety of intensity levels.

9 *If you aren't able to ride your bicycle because of cold weather or lack of time, you can increase your quadriceps strength by "bounding."* Lift your knees really high, pump your arms high, and spring off of each foot as though you were running up a hill. Do several bounding sets in your sprint race training to work your gluteals as well as your entire quadriceps muscle group.

10 *If you use weights of any kind in your workout, do so only for a limited time.* Most people are better off losing weight than adding it, but if you want to accelerate your heart rate briefly by using weighted gloves or shoes just remember that your technique is very important. The beneficial effects are minimal for most people, but if you have a limited amount of time, it might help somewhat. Make sure you concentrate on your form.

7 WEIGHT TRAINING AND STRETCHING

In the not-too-distant past, weight lifting brought to mind comic-book advertisements about 98-pound weaklings who were tired of getting sand kicked in their faces, and wide-screen views of Annette Funicello giving Frankie Avalon a big, wet kiss at the oceanside gym in *Beach Blanket Bingo*. To a slightly older generation, it conjured images of Jack La Lanne ripping the Los Angeles phone book in half with his bare hands, after which he proved his Herculean strength by swimming from Alcatraz to San Francisco—handcuffed.

Contrary to the muscle-bound stereotype, however, the benefits of weight training extend far beyond publicity stunts and Mr. Universe pageants. You can increase your

Weight training has given me the extra strength to swim, bike and still do well in a long run.

strength and power greatly, without building bulging muscles that ripple under your body shirt. For triathletes—particularly those without a swimming background—increasing upper-body strength is essential for top performance in all three events, as is increasing leg strength for cycling and running.

Most of the top triathletes are faster runners than I am, yet I have been able to pass them at the end of triathlons, much to the surprise of many speculators. It is a matter of strength and efficiency; if I haven't accumulated as much fatigue during a long swim and bike ride, I have more strength for the run.

One of the key factors in triathlon efficiency is upper-body strength. I have worked at it since my swimming and water polo days in college. I had to—most of the other players were bigger than I was, so I compensated for my size by lifting weights and becoming at least as strong as they were.

Though my emphasis has shifted from power to strength—I have shed some of my bulk—I still supplement my triathlon program with consistent weight training. Even after a long triathlon swim, my muscles recover very quickly due to my strength training program. I have never started the bike race with a fatigued upper body.

Most people do not realize that cycling requires strength—and endurance—in your arm, abdominal, shoulder and back muscles, so they are not prepared for the shock to their upper bodies when they get on their bikes. Obviously, fortifying those muscles will help prevent that cumulative fatigue, and will enable you to start the run fresher.

Many accomplished runners have been similarly shocked at how poorly they perform in a triathlon run. Their shoulder and arms are so stiff from the first two events that they can't assume the form needed to pick up their normal rhythm and pace. Conditioned distance runners are trained to deal with extreme fatigue in their legs at the end of long runs, but they aren't trained to start out at the very beginning of a run with cumulative full-body fatigue from a long swim and bike ride.

Proficiency in a single sport does not guarantee efficiency in a triathlon. You have to develop full-body strength to complement other attributes of triathlon conditioning—endurance, flexibility, technique, and mental preparedness. In this chapter, we will outline strength exercises that specifically complement each of the sports, and establish a well-rounded weight training program which you can adapt to suit your own needs.

HOW CAN YOU DETERMINE YOUR OWN PROGRAM?

All triathletes should take several factors into account when developing an optimal weight training program:

1   *Consider your individual background.* If you have done mostly anaerobic sports—such as football, baseball, sprint activities, or weight lifting—additional strength work can actually be detrimental to your triathlon training program. However, the program outlined in this chapter emphasizes injury prevention and a balance of strength training that will complement any triathlon training program.

2   *As you do more aerobic work, your strength level will decline.* When I switched from 60 percent anaerobic exercise (in swimming and water polo) to about 80 percent aerobic exercise (triathlon), my strength fell 20 to 30 percent, using a one-repetition or one-push maximum lift as a measurement. Even though my explosive strength decreased, however, my middle distance swim times (500 to 1,650 yards)

improved. My additional aerobic training in cycling and running enhanced my endurance in swimming; I no longer needed that concentrated power.

3   *A triathlon strength training program will not build big, bulky muscles.* A lot of women (and some men) are apprehensive about weight training because they fear it will develop massive bodybuilder muscles. That will not happen if you follow the triathlon training program in this book, unless you have an extremely high testosterone level or have already built up muscle mass with years of strength training. The strength workout I recommend takes up such a small percentage of your overall triathlon training time—three or four times a week for 30 to 45 minutes at most—that it will not overwork your muscles enough to build bulging muscles. Although most competitive triathletes have more muscular mass and definition than cross-country runners, they are nevertheless very lean.

4   *Weight training conditions your nervous system as well as your muscles.* Since motor neurons carry impulses that "shock" your muscle fibers into twitching, neuromuscular coordination is an essential component of overall strength. After the first three or four weeks of weight training, you will probably experience a vast improvement in the ability of your nerves and muscles to relax and work together. It is like swimming—when you first get in the water, you are usually somewhat tense, but eventually you develop a subconscious, fluid stroke pattern.

5   *You should frequently vary your routine.* By changing your workout regularly, you use your nervous system in conjunction with many different muscles, which expands your overall neuromuscular coordination. Vary the types of exercises, the rest durations, the number of repetitions, and the number of sets.

HOW DOES WEIGHT TRAINING BUILD STRENGTH?

The goals of a weight-training program are:

1 *to increase the force your muscles exert,*
2 *to allow your muscles to reach maximum effort more rapidly,* and
3 *to increase the amount of time your muscles can sustain their maximum level of exertion.*

The idea is to increase the number and frequency of *motor units*—motor nerves and muscle fibers—which are stimulated during a given period of time. A single nerve impulse can charge hundreds of fibers at once; a rapid series of multiple-fiber twitches can generate maximum force quickly and for a long period of time.

A supplemental weight-training program will increase and balance strength in all your working muscles, so that your nervous system can recruit a wide variety of fibers. When one group of fibers begins to fatigue, another group will be prepared to relieve them.

BENEFITS OF STRENGTH TRAINING

1 *It increases your bone density.* Studies have shown that there has to be tensile force on the bones or joints to increase bone density. Swimming doesn't apply that sort of impact, so many older swimmers are prone to osteoporosis (brittle bones). Running will help alleviate the problem to some extent, but weight training is a measured, safe way to do the same thing.
2 *It strengthens the ligaments and tendons that surround the joints.* Ligaments connect bones to other bones, and tendons attach bones to muscles. Weight training will increase their strength and size.
3 *It increases joint mobility.* Tendons are relatively elastic, so the increased strength

and size (see 2, above) allows joints to move better. Including stretching exercises will enhance muscular flexibility as well as joint mobility.

WHAT DO NERVES HAVE TO DO WITH STRENGTH?

Nerves are messengers from the brain, which ultimately controls every physical response. If motor nerves don't "tell" your fibers to twitch, your muscles won't contract. That's what any kind of training is all about—teaching your nervous system, by repeating certain movements, to get the right messages to your muscles.

Those messages include:

1 *the number of fibers to be recruited,*
2 *the type of fibers* (slow-twitch, fast-twitch/A, fast-twitch/B),
3 *the order of recruitment* (see 2, above), and
4 *the frequency of contractions.*

All of those nervous system functions are dependent upon training. Your nerves will do only what they have been conditioned to do. Let's say, for example, you are climbing a steep hill on your bike. Your legs are conditioned for slow-twitch activity—you are capable of riding for extremely long periods of time on the flats—but you rarely ride hills. Before you even reach the top of the hill, you feel exhausted, your legs feel stiff, and you can't figure it out—if your legs are so strong, why do they feel so weak?

Your nervous system has been trained to deliver electrical impulses to your slow-twitch fibers during your long, flat training rides, but the steep hills require your Type A (oxidative) fast-twitch fibers. Since your nervous system has had little experience delivering impulses to your fast-twitch fibers, it carries out that task slowly and inadequately.

Varying your program will train your nervous system to recruit all three types of muscle fibers as needed, so that you can master a variety of terrain, distances, and intensity of effort in a triathlon.

BENEFITS OF A VARIED WEIGHT-TRAINING PROGRAM

In addition to the neuromuscular advantages cited above, a varied weight-training routine will also:

1 *Balance your strength.* You won't overdevelop one area and neglect another.
2 *Reduce injury potential.* You'll work many muscle groups and employ many more fibers, which will reduce the stress on any single muscle group.
3 *Prevent overtraining or "staleness."* No matter what exercise you are doing, your muscles reach a point of diminishing returns in any given period.
4 *Help you maintain your motivation.* When it comes to lack of motivation, I am an expert! When you train alone, as I do 70 percent of the time, it is easy to pull the covers over your head and go back to sleep when that alarm clock rings—especially if you are doing the same old routine, day after day. Changing your workouts makes it more fun.

KINDS OF STRENGTH

There are three basic types of strength:

1 *Isometric*—a static muscular contraction.
2 *Isotonic*—dynamic contraction (concentric and eccentric).
3 *Isokinetic*—accommodating (variable) resistance, in which the force varies with the change in muscular length.

All three words are formed from the Greek prefix *isos,* which means equal or constant. Combined with the root word *metron,* isometric means equal (fixed) measure; add *teinein,* and isotonic means equivalent tone; with *kinein,* isokinetic means equivalent motion.

All three principles should be combined in a well-balanced weight-training program. You will probably concentrate on isotonic training, because it is generally more advantageous and the equipment is readily available. However, isokinetic training is an ideal supplement for all three triathlon sports, because you can identically simulate the movements of a freestyle stroke.

The best balance for triathletes is 70 percent isotonic, 20 percent isokinetic and 10 percent isometric.

ISOMETRIC

An isometric—static—contraction is one in which there is a constant measure of tension against the muscle. The muscle is lengthened; you are working against a fixed object, such as putting your hands on either side of a door frame, and pushing.

ADVANTAGES:
· It doesn't require any special equipment.
· If you are weak in one area, such as the catch on the freestyle stroke, you can simulate the exact position in an isometric exercise. Exerting a great deal of tension will probably increase your strength in that position.
· For cycling, you can simulate the fixed position of your triceps, elbow position when your hands are on the drops or brake hoods, and the position of your neck, shoulders, and upper back.
· For running, you must hold your arms semiflexed, which can be very tiring. You can simulate that exact arm position in an isometric exercise.

DISADVANTAGES:

· Pushing as hard as possible in a fixed position elevates your blood pressure tremendously.

· It only increases the strength for the particular angle at which you are pushing.

· It takes a long time. If you have to simulate the angles for every motion in all three sports, you've got a long job ahead of you.

· To get an increase in strength, you have to work at 60 to 70 percent of your maximum for six seconds, which is extremely difficult to measure. Pushing too little will not achieve the desired results, but pushing too hard will sap your strength. (I recommend 6 to 10 repetitions, 6 to 10 seconds per phase.)

ISOTONIC

This is the most common type of strength training. It involves a dynamic contraction, in which the muscle is toned—enhanced—by equally lengthening and shortening it during exercise.

A biceps curl is a dynamic contraction; it involves a full range of motion, from a full concentric contraction (pulling the weight up) to a full eccentric contraction (lowering it back down).

ADVANTAGES:

· Equipment is readily available. Barbells, Universal, and Nautilus are all based on the isotonic principle.

· It enhances the strength of the entire muscle, not just at one particular angle (as opposed to isometric).

DISADVANTAGES:

· Since muscles contract at varying percentages throughout the entire range of motion, the maximum tension occurs for only a brief period of time—at the weakest point of your lift. On a biceps curl, your weakest point is when your arm is

completely straight—your elbow flexion is 180 degrees. The maximum strength on an isotonic lift is reached at about 115 to 120 degrees. Once you move the weight past that, the effort becomes progressively easier, especially considering the momentum. You have to deliberately lift the weight at a slow, controlled pace to get the proper benefit.

· Eccentric contractions increase the stress on joints, tendons, and muscles. This type of training can dramatically elevate your blood pressure and fatigue your muscles near failure, if you do not monitor your workouts very carefully. *If you have any sort of heart condition, you should do this type of training only under the supervision of your doctor.*

ISOKINETIC

Isokinetic training is relatively new. It provides maximum (equal) resistance throughout the entire range of motion. This is accomplished by using equipment that exerts variable resistance according to the percentage that the muscles are contracting throughout that particular motion.

ADVANTAGES:

· You can simulate the exact motion and speed of the activity for which you are building your strength. On a swim bench, for example, you can simulate the freestyle pull pattern. You can increase the tension so that it is greater than the effort you expend in the pool, thereby increasing your strength faster and more efficiently.

· You don't get the muscular stiffness and soreness that sometimes comes from isotonic lifting.

DISADVANTAGES:

· The equipment is not always accessible.

· It is difficult to monitor your workout unless the machines you are using come equipped with an electronic calibration instrument to measure your output.

WEIGHT-TRAINING "SEASONS"

Strength training is a supplement to your overall triathlon training program; it follows the same seasonal progression—pre-season, pre-competitive, competitive, and post-competitive.

PRE-SEASON

During the pre-season, you will gradually increase your strength to prepare you for the more rigorous demands of pre-competitive training. You will incorporate isotonic, isokinetic, and possibly isometric training, doing one more set of each exercise than in the preceding (post-competitive) season.

Because you are also working to increase your endurance during the pre-season, you may find that the prescribed weight-training regimen is too stressful. If so, reduce the amount of weight and the number of sets, and increase the number of repetitions.

PRE-COMPETITIVE

Strength work emphasis is greater during the pre-competitive season than at any other time during the year. You will do the maximum number of sets and repetitions during this season, and incorporate isotonic, isokinetic, and isometric (optional) training.

COMPETITIVE

Because you are racing as well as training during this season, you should reduce your strength work to allow ample rest for competition. You will be emphasizing higher-quality speed work in the pool and on the road. Consequently, you must deemphasize the quantity and intensity of your work in the weight room.

At this juncture, swift daily recovery is critical to continued progress.

During the competitive season, you will do isokinetic workouts four days per week, with isotonic no more than three. (Isokinetic work doesn't make you as sore.) You may choose to eliminate isotonic workouts altogether, and increase the intensity of your isokinetic work. In any case, you should reduce your total number of sets to your pre-season level.

If you already have a strong/muscular build, you may want to vary your strength program one day each week, by using 20 to 30 percent less weight and doing a maximum number of repetitions on each set. If you are a beginner or need extra strength, do the opposite process: add 20 to 30 percent more weight and reduce the repetitions to six or eight.

Whatever you do, make sure that you always allow two full days of rest prior to a race.

POST-COMPETITIVE

Maintain your strength and endurance, but give yourself a rest. For each exercise, do one less set than you did during the competitive season. Do isotonic exercises only two or three days per week. If you are quite fatigued following the racing season, you may reduce the weight, but follow the competitive program (in terms of sets and repetitions). This is a good time to work on your form and technique. Isokinetic work is good because it will maintain your strength while allowing you to practice the proper motions for each sport.

This is the basic strength-training program I recommend. The charts that follow are in seasonal order, from pre-season to post-competitive. The pre-competitive season chart outlines the basic program; all the other seasons' programs are modified from that chart as indicated.

STRENGTH PROGRAMS BY SEASON

PRE-SEASON
1. DO EXERCISES 1–7.
2. DO ONE LESS SET THAN THE PRE-COMPETITIVE SEASON.
3. START ISOKINETIC TRAINING ONE DAY PER WEEK.

PRE-COMPETITIVE
NOTE: THE PROGRAM FOR ALL FOUR SEASONS IS BASED ON THIS CHART, SINCE STRENGTH EMPHASIS IS GREATEST DURING THE PRE-COMPETITIVE SEASON.
1. DO EXERCISES 1–8.
2. DO NUMBER OF SETS SHOWN BELOW.
3. DO ENTIRE STRENGTH WORKOUT (INCLUDING ISOKINETIC) FOUR TIMES A WEEK.
4. IF THE STRESS IS TOO GREAT, DECREASE TO PRE-SEASON LEVEL TO ALLOW RECOVERY.

COMPETITIVE
NOTE: NO STRENGTH TRAINING FOR TWO FULL DAYS BEFORE A RACE.
1. DO EXERCISES 1–8.
2. DO ONE LESS SET THAN PRE-COMPETITIVE.
3. DO ISOKINETIC TRAINING FOUR TIMES A WEEK.
4. a. IF YOUR ANAEROBIC STRENGTH IS SLIGHTLY DOWN, DO ENDURANCE STRENGTH TRAINING ONE DAY A WEEK. (20%–30% LESS WEIGHT, MAXIMUM REPETITIONS.)
   b. IF NOT, THEN INCREASE THE WEIGHT 20%–30%, WITH 6–10 REPETITIONS.
5. EVERY FOURTH WEEK, DECREASE WEIGHT AND INTENSITY TO THE PRE-SEASON LEVEL.

POST-COMPETITIVE
1. DO EXERCISES 1–4.
2. DO TWO LESS SETS THAN PRE-COMPETITIVE.
3. DO ENDURANCE STRENGTH TRAINING ONE DAY A WEEK.

EXERCISE		REPS	SETS	RIBS* (AFTER a & b)
1.	a. BENCH PRESS	12–20	5—1 WARM-UP 3 SAME WEIGHT 1 CHANGE GRIP	50 SEC TO 1½ MIN SWING ARMS GENTLY
	b. UPRIGHT ROWING AND BENT-OVER ROWING	12–20	4—1 WARM-UP 3 SAME WEIGHT	
2.	a. MILITARY PRESS (SITTING)	10–16	4—1 WARM-UP 3 SAME WEIGHT	50 SEC TO 1½ MIN
	b. LATISSIMUS PULL-DOWN	10–16		
3.	a. QUADRICEPS EXTENSION (PULL BAR TO 110° BEFORE STARTING)	15–25	4—1 WARM-UP 3 SAME WEIGHT (ALTERNATE LEGS)	1½ MIN—WALK AROUND SLOWLY STRETCHING
	b. HAMSTRING CURL	15–25		
4.	a. TRICEPS EXTENSION	8–12	DESCENDING SET OF 4	50 SEC TO 1½ MIN
	b. BICEPS CURL		DESCENDING SET OF 3 (ALT. CURL HAND UP & BRACHIORADIALIS)	OPEN AND CLOSE FINGERS, WIGGLE FINGERS
5.	a. LEG EXTENSIONS (UNIVERSAL, NAUTILUS)	30–50	3	50 SEC TO 1½ MIN
	b. HAMSTRING CURLS	15–25	3	
6.	a. TRICEPS (DUMBBELLS)	8–12	3	NO REST
	b. ABDOMINALS	†		
7.	a. BACK	15–20	3	50 SEC TO 1½ MIN
	b. ABDOMINALS (MINI-UPS)	15–20	3	
8.	a. TRICEPS (TWO-ARM DUMBBELL PRESS)	8–12		NO REST
	b. CALF RAISES			

*RIBS—REST INTERVAL BETWEEN SETS. (AFTER a & b)
†UNTIL EXHAUSTION—HOLD STATIC ON LAST TWO FOR 5–10 SECONDS

HOW TO GET THE BEST RESULTS

To get the maximum benefit from a strength-training program, you must tailor it to your needs. You must decide which of your muscles need to be strengthened for triathlon competition. Determine how much power you need in an endurance sport. Test your present level of strength and fitness. Determine how often you should lift weights or use variable resistance machines, and when you should do your weight room workouts.

1   *How many days per week should I do strength-training exercises?*
   A   If you are a beginner, you will get the maximum benefit from a three- or four-day program; if your schedule won't allow that many days, twice a week will suffice. More experienced triathletes can work three to five days per week, depending upon their individual needs.
   B   Once a week will hurt more than it will help; the meager benefit you get is not enough to offset the soreness.

2   *How many sets (and repetitions within each set) should I do?* Refer to the charts; the number of repetitions and sets varies with each exercise. The charts are established for your pre-competitive season, but you will do basically the same workouts with fewer sets during the remaining seasons.

3   *How much weight should I use?* This will vary for each individual, depending upon your body weight, level of fitness, and experience. If you are a beginner to weight training, you should probably start each exercise with a test set: Do the complete motion without any additional weight. If it is a barbell exercise, for example, go through the motions with just the bar. Then add one weight incrementally until you feel a slight resistance. Within a week, you will find the amount of weight that produces results but doesn't make you unduly sore.

4   *How much "power" do I need in a triathlon?* You are not going to be running a 100-yard sprint in a triathlon; the exercise is done at a moderate speed for a long period of time. So your weight-training program should match that demand. You have to balance your aerobic endurance and anaerobic power.

When you do isokinetic training—simulation of a freestyle stroke on a swim bench, for example—work at a faster pace than you would during a triathlon. Isotonic work, on the other hand, should be done at a moderate pace, being careful not to jerk the weight. (Hesitate slightly at the beginning and end of each contraction.)

Don't be surprised if your strength decreases slightly as your aerobic fitness increases. I used to play a lot of basketball—I could leap like Michael Jordan and stuff a golf ball through the hoop. Then came triathlons. I maintained my strength-training program, but I switched my emphasis to my oxidative fibers rather than my explosive anaerobic ones. It helped me win the Ironman a few times, but it sure wreaked havoc with my ball game—now I can barely slap the net!

You have to give up some anaerobic power to be a better aerobic athlete.

5   *Where should weight training fit into my overall workout?*
   A   *Pre-season:* Since most of your strength work is geared toward your upper body, it is a good idea to do your weight training before you swim. That way, you can diffuse some of your blood lactate during your swim workout, and your muscles won't be as sore the next day. This obviously will hurt your swimming performance slightly, but it is a compromise that will pay off in the long run.

B   *Pre-competitive season:* Your overall training emphasis is on endurance work during this season, so it won't matter if your fast-twitch fibers are fresh for running and swimming. Do your weight training before you swim.

C   *Competitive season:* Run and swim first, then do your weight training. That way, your fast-twitch fibers will be fresh for the intense run and swim workouts emphasized during this season.

D   *Post-competitive season:* This is a more relaxed training season, with very little intense work, so it is best to do your weight training before you swim.

HOW TO AVOID THE UNAVOIDABLE: SORE MUSCLES

Because weight training is chiefly strength- and power-oriented, rather than aerobic, your muscles are going to get sore. And the newer you are to weight training, the quicker you will feel it. That's a fact of life. Even when you become accustomed to the routines, you will develop some muscle and joint stiffness any time you increase your load (increasing weights or number of repetitions).

It is possible, however, to prevent excessive soreness by using active rest between sets (swing your arms easily, or if you have been exercising your legs, walk around the room and do some easy stretches). You should also vary your workout for one day every two weeks by making any of the following adjustments:

1   *Use lighter weights and more repetitions.* When you experience fatigue from strength work, use lighter weights, and increase the number of repetitions beyond the maximum for heavier weights. If the maximum is 25, for example, reduce the weight low enough to do 30 to 60 repetitions (depending upon the exercise).

2   *Change your grip.* When you change your grip on the bar, you recruit different muscle fibers, so you won't be constantly overworking the same group on each successive set.

3   *Reduce the total number of sets.* Or take a day off entirely.

4   *Do the sets with dumbbells instead of barbells.* The strength balance will be slightly different, but you still emphasize the same muscles by using a single arm motion or using dumbbells simultaneously.

5   *Alternate the order of your exercises.* Though the order indicated on the charts is most advantageous, it is good to shuffle it from time to time.

EXERCISES

One important thing to remember about all of the exercises below, is that *you must breathe properly.* Inhale during the recovery, and exhale during the exertion. Do not hold your breath under any circumstances—it will build up tremendous pressure.

If you are doing biceps curls, for instance, exhale as you are lifting the weight up to your shoulder. Start to inhale as you begin to lower the weight, and finish the inhale as your arms are fully extended. Most people do exactly the opposite, which will not properly oxygenate your working muscles.

(If your exercise involves an eccentric contraction, e.g., lowering the weight in a bicep curl, you should inhale and exhale continuously throughout the movement.)

Each of the following exercises is listed with an alternate. You will always do both together—a few sets of the first exercise followed by a few sets of the alternate. The number of repetitions and sets corresponds to Chart E, for the pre-competitive season. You should adjust those figures according to the training season.

1 BENCH PRESS AND ROWING

BENCH PRESS

SETS: 5 (1 warm-up, 3 same weight,
    1 grip change)
REPETITIONS: 12 to 20
REST: 50–90 seconds between sets
MAJOR MUSCLES: triceps, deltoids

HOW TO DO IT. Grip the bar so that when it rests on your chest, your elbow is flexed at 90 to 120 degrees. Press the weight from that point (on your chest) to a full arm's extension. If you are just beginning the exercise, take the weight with a straight arm, then lower it slowly.

SETS.

A. The warm-up set will generally be 20 to 40 percent less weight, with the same (12 to 20) number of repetitions. If you prefer to do more reps, be sure the weight is light and your speed is moderate. Do not do so many that you start building up lactate, which will produce a heavy, stiff feeling in your muscles.

B. Do three sets using the same weight. For example, do three sets of 12 to 20 reps, using 100 pounds of weight each time. You may find that the exact number of reps will decrease on each successive set.

C. For the fifth set, change your grip. Moving it wider will put more stress on your deltoids and pectoralis; moving it closer (hands 4 to 6 inches apart) will isolate your triceps. I recommend the closer grip,

because there is more triceps work in swimming, and because your triceps tend to fatigue from being in a locked position when you ride with your hands on the drops for a long period of time.

REST. After each set, rest for 50 seconds to a minute and a half. This is an active rest; swing your arms easily to relax the muscles.

ALTERNATING EXERCISE. After the rest period, and before the next bench press set, do the alternate rowing exercises below. Repeat that pattern until you have completed all of the sets—bench press, upright rowing, bench press, bent-over rowing, bench press, upright rowing, etc.

1

1. Bench press position: start in a straight-arm position, with hands 8–12 inches outside shoulder width. 2. When the bar is lowered to your chest your elbow flexion should be about 120°. 3. *A wide-arm bench press,* which works your pectoralis muscles more, puts stress on your wrist. Press the weight all the way up until your arms are fully extended. 4. For a close-grip bench press, which works the triceps more, place your hands 4–6 inches apart on the bar.

UPRIGHT AND BENT-OVER ROWING

SETS: 4
REPETITIONS: 12 to 20
REST: 50 to 90 seconds
MAJOR MUSCLES: brachioradialis, biceps
HOW TO DO IT.

A. *Upright rowing:* Stand up straight, with your arms extended and your hands gripping the bar four to six inches apart. Draw the bar up to your chest (close to your chin), then lower it again. If you have discomfort or tension in your back, do the exercise with your shoulders against the wall; move your hips out slightly so that most of the weight is against your scapulas. This will prevent further hyperextension of your back.

1

2

3

Upright rowing: Start with a straight back, arms, legs, looking forward. Draw the weight up underneath your chin. Elbows are pointed outward, not in toward your side or back. Be careful not to use a close grip, which will put a lot of stress on your wrists. Draw the weight all the way up to your chin (or the top of your shoulders), then lower it again.

B.   *Bent-over rowing:* Bend at your waist (90 degrees). Grip the bar widely, with your hands 6 to 12 inches outside your shoulder width. Then draw the weight up to your chest. If you have any back problems, support your head while doing this exercise. Do not jerk the weight or you may hyperextend your lower back.

REST. The rest is the same as the bench press—50 seconds to a minute and a half.

1. Bent-over rowing. Start with the weight on the ground. Grip the bar 6–12 inches outside the width of your shoulders. 2. Draw the weight up to your shoulders. As you draw the weight up, stop when the bar hits your chest, then lower it back down. 3. This can also be done on a bench with your head resting on the end of the bench. Place your head on the bench or bend your knees slightly to reduce stress on your lower back. Make sure you use a light enough weight.

2 MILITARY PRESS AND LATISSIMUS PULL-DOWN

MILITARY PRESS

SETS: 5 (1 warm-up, 3 same weight, 1 grip change)

REPETITIONS: 10 to 16

REST: 50 to 90 seconds

MAJOR MUSCLES: triceps, deltoids, back muscles

HOW TO DO IT. The grip is similar to the bench press, with your elbow flexed at 90 to 120 degrees when the bar is on the back of your neck. Press the weight to a full arm's extension, then lower it carefully, so that you don't jar your spine. As in the bench press, the closer your grip, the more it isolates your triceps; the wider your grip, the more it works your deltoids. It also works your back, so be sure to keep your stomach fairly tight to avoid hyperextending your lower back. (But relax enough to breathe.)

SETS. For the warm-up, use 20 to 30 percent less weight; same number of repetitions.

REST. 50 seconds to a minute and a half. Active rest. Swing your arms loosely.

ALTERNATE EXERCISE. See next exercise, latissimus pull-down. Same number of sets, repetitions, and rest.

Sitting military press. Start with the weight behind your head. Grip the bar 6–12 inches outside the width of your shoulders. Press the weight to a full arm's extension over your head.

LATISSIMUS PULL-DOWN

SETS: 4 (1 warm-up, 3 same weight)
REPETITIONS: 10 to 16
REST: 50 to 90 seconds
MAJOR MUSCLES: latissimus dorsi, biceps, deltoids, brachioradialis, scapular

HOW TO DO IT. When your arms are pulled down behind your head, your elbow should be flexed at about 130 degrees. Make sure your grip is not too wide—it should be 6 to 12 inches beyond shoulder width—or you will overstress your biceps and deltoids. While most swimmers have amply developed biceps and can tolerate a wide grip, most runners and cyclists are not used to that kind of stress.

SETS. Same as military press.
REST. Same as military press.

Latissimus dorsi pull-down. Grip the bar 6–12 inches outside your shoulder width. Don't go too far outside your shoulders or it will put undue stress on your biceps tendon and your shoulder girdle. From a straight position, pull the bar down behind your head until it rests on the back of your neck. Then let it up again slowly.

3 QUADRICEPS EXTENSION AND HAMSTRING CURL

QUADRICEPS EXTENSION

SETS: 4 (1 warm-up, 3 same weight)
REPETITIONS: 15 to 25
REST: 1.5 minutes
MAJOR MUSCLES: vastus medialis, quadriceps

This exercise is done on a Universal or Nautilus (or similar) leg extension apparatus. I used it to rehabilitate my knee after I got chondromalacia (softening of the cartilage below the kneecap) at the 1980 Ironman. I recommend it to runners and swimmers to build up quadriceps and because it locks the kneecap and vastus medialus in place.

HOW TO DO IT. Sit with your hips flexed at 90 degrees. Put your hands on your stomach and grab the bench underneath. Place your legs under the ankle pad. (Most machines are preset so that your knee is at a 70- to 90-degree angle, which puts undue stress on your patellar tendon.) Pull the leg piece up with your arms—getting slight assistance from your legs—until your knee is at a 110-degree angle. Release your hands and continue to extend your legs. Alternate leg presses to simulate a cycling and running motion.

SETS. On the final set, during the last few repetitions (18 to 25), bring the weight up so that your leg is fully extended. Lock it for 5 to 10 seconds, then bring it back down again.

REST. For a minute and a half between sets, move your legs, walk around, stretch your legs. Then do the hamstring curl.

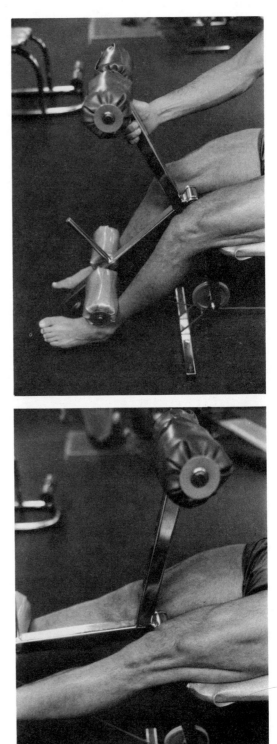

Quadriceps extension. This is done on any type of leg press machine. Draw the weight up with the aid of your arms so that your legs are starting at about a 120-degree bend. Then extend your legs out to a full locked extension. This locks the patella in the groove and locks the vastus medialis and lateralis into their fully contracted state.

HAMSTRING CURL

SETS: 3

REPETITIONS: 15 to 25

REST: 1.5 minutes

MAJOR MUSCLES: hamstrings, gluteals

HOW TO DO IT. This is the opposite of the quadriceps extension. Keep your stomach on the mat. Be sure not to flex your back.

REST. Active rest. Walk around, easy leg stretches.

Hamstring curl. Use a lighter weight on this exercise; your hamstrings are generally 40–60 percent weaker than your quadriceps. Start in a straight-leg position and curl the weight up so that your legs finish at about an 80-degree bend.

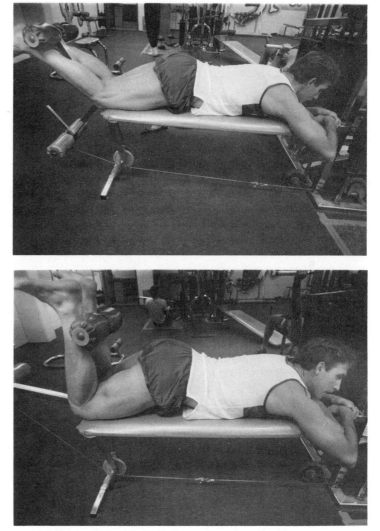

4 TRICEPS EXTENSION AND BICEPS CURL

TRICEPS EXTENSION

SETS: 4 sets, 2 times (decrease weight on each set)
REPETITIONS: 8 to 12
REST: 50 to 90 seconds
MAJOR MUSCLES: triceps

I do these exercises in descending-weight sets (reducing the weight on each successive set). Since one muscle group is isolated, fatigue sets in quickly; decreasing the load on each successive set allows you to keep up the frequency without exhausting yourself for the next exercise. (It tires the fast-twitch fibers first, then the slow-twitch.)

HOW TO DO IT. Grip the lat bar (on a Universal or similar system) closely (hands 6 to 10 inches apart). Keep your wrists straight—don't bend your hands up or down. Keeping your arms in close to your body, pull the bar down until your elbows are flexed at about 120 degrees. Then straighten your arms to a full extension; the bar should be down to your thighs.

SETS. Start with a warm-up set (using very light weights) or go right into your main set if your arms are already warmed up from the previous exercise. On each set, reduce the weight by 5 pounds, with 8 to 12 repetitions.

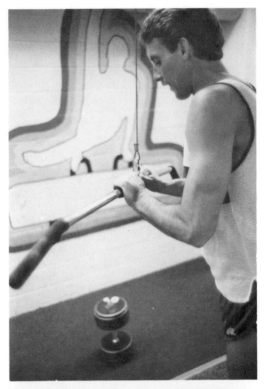

Standing triceps extension. Use the latissimus dorsi bar. Start with your elbows flexed about 80 degrees, then press the weight all the way down to a full arm extension. At the end of the extension, be careful that your wrists are not flexed. My wrists are shown hyperextended. Flexing your wrists at the end will cause you to lean over the top of the bar which will use your forearm rather than your triceps.

REST. Rest for a minute and a half between sets. Open and close your hands, and wiggle your fingers. Then shake your forearms lightly. Then do the alternate exercise below—biceps curl—between each set of triceps extension.

Reverse bend-over triceps extension. Reduce the weight from the standing triceps extension. Do not lean into the bar. Grasp the bar with your hand 4–6 inches apart, starting with your hands at the back of your head, then press to a full arm extension in front.

BICEPS CURL

SETS: 3 descending, 2 times (triceps, then biceps)

REPETITIONS: 8 to 12

REST: 1.5 minutes

MUSCLES: biceps, triceps, brachioradialis

HOW TO DO IT. Alternate the curls: first rotate your hands upward (thumbs up), then move your hands so that your palms are facing upward (thumbs out). On the hands-upward position, your arms are at your side, and you draw the weight up thumb first. (See photo.)

SETS. Same as triceps extension.

REST. Same as triceps extension.

Biceps dumbbell curl. Hold the weight with a straight arm, then draw it up (in a curling motion) to shoulder height. The biceps curl can also be done with a barbell. Grip the bar 2–4 inches outside shoulder width at a full arm extension and draw it up to shoulder height. To eliminate any back hyperextension, place your shoulder blades up against the wall and move out with your feet.

5 LEG EXTENSIONS AND HAMSTRING CURL

LEG EXTENSIONS

SETS: 3
REPETITONS: 30 to 50
REST: 50 to 90 seconds
MUSCLES: hip flexors, calves, vastus medialis, vastus lateralis

This exercise is done with a Universal or Nautilus leg extension apparatus, and can be interchanged in the overall workout order with quadriceps extensions. The alternate exercise is the hamstring curl.

HOW TO DO IT. Begin with your hips flexed at 120 degrees. Adjust the movable seat to that angle (no tighter), then fully extend your legs. To work your calf muscles, extend your foot as well. Bend over slightly at your waist to take the stress off your back.

HAMSTRING CURL

(See page 153.)

2

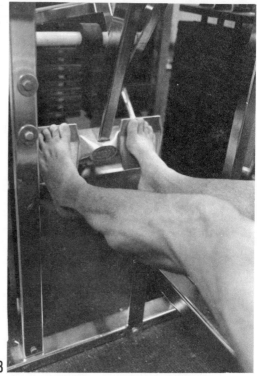

3

1

Leg extension. Start with your knees flexed at no less than 100–110 degrees. Press the weight to full leg extension with your legs locked. Using the same apparatus, extend your toes (using your calf muscles). This will help your hill climbing and reduce fatigue at the end of the bike going into the run.

6 TRICEPS (DUMBBELLS) AND ABDOMINALS

TRICEPS (DUMBBELLS)

SETS: 3

REPETITIONS: 8 to 12

REST: none; go immediately into abdominals (see page 159)

MAJOR MUSCLES: triceps

HOW TO DO IT. Hold the dumbbell vertically (see photo), and bend your elbow at about 90 degrees. Put your arm over your head, so that the dumbbell is over your opposite shoulder. Then extend your arm fully.

Single-arm dumbbell triceps extension. This can be done either sitting or standing, with your other hand leaning against the wall. Place the weight over the top of your head in a vertical alignment, then extend it to a full arm's extension. Keep your biceps close to your ear; do not allow your arm to swing out.

ABDOMINALS

SETS: 3

REPETITIONS: until exhausted; hold static on last 2 for 5 to 10 seconds

REST: none; go right back to triceps

MAJOR MUSCLES: rectus abdominis, obliques, transverse abdominis

I use these exercises as an alternative to sit-ups, which overemphasize your hip flexors. These exercises simulate the static, semicontracted state of your stomach during cycling. Strong abdominal muscles alleviate stress on your lower back and allow you to relax for easy breathing. Swimming uses these muscles in essentially the same way. If your abdominals are weak, you may hyperextend your lower back in both swimming and cycling, which will accentuate hamstring tightness during the run. Strong abdominal muscles aid all three triathlon sports.

HOW TO DO IT. I use two abdominal exercises: mini-ups and reverse sit-ups.

Mini-ups. Lying on your back, cross your arms (across your chest) and put each hand on its opposite shoulder. Flex your knees in a sit-up position, and hyperextend your back enough to slip your hand in between your spine and the floor. Then try to tighten your lower abdominals to press your spine to the floor; raise your head and shoulders about six inches off the floor. Do not jerk your head before your shoulders, as you would in a sit-up. Start with your shoulders, and let your head follow. Exhale as you are raising your shoulders; inhale at the top; then exhale again as you lower your shoulders. Each mini-up should take about three seconds.

Reverse sit-ups. With your hands on your knees (or crossed) in a sit-up position, lower your back slowly until it is on the ground.

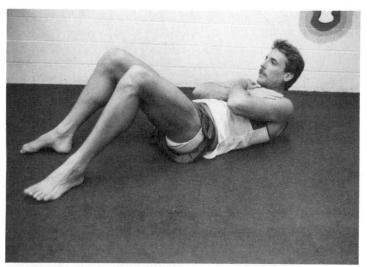

Mini-up. Bend your lower back enough to slip an arm under it. Place your hands on your shoulders, crisscrossing your arms, then tighten your lower abdominals by pressing the lower part of your spine (your lumbar spine) to the floor and tightening the rest of your abdominal cage, all the way up your abdominal cavity. Raise your shoulders, then your head. The important thing in this exercise is that you do not jerk your head first. It's a very slow, controlled motion. By the time you reach the maximum contraction your head should be only 8–10 inches off the ground. Hold that static position.

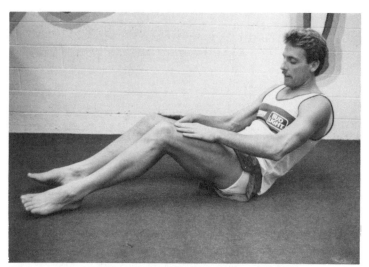

Reverse sit-up. Start in a sit-up position with your hands on your knees and slowly lower yourself down to the count of 12 (roughly 12 seconds) till your shoulders are flat on the ground. Then raise up and lower again with your hands on your knees, allowing them to slide down your thighs.

7 BACK EXERCISES WITH ANY ALTERNATE

BACK

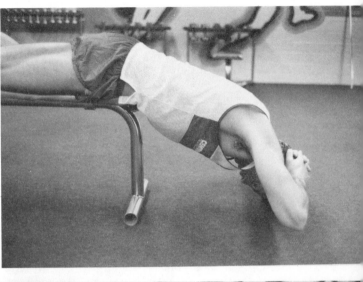

SETS: 3

REPETITIONS: 15 to 20

REST: none; go directly into any of the above exercises

MAJOR MUSCLES: postural muscles

HOW TO DO IT. Lie face-down with your legs on a bench so that your waist is at the end of the bench and your torso is completely off the bench. Have someone hold your legs down. Clasp your hands behind your neck, and lower your shoulders to the ground, then raise them up again so that your torso is aligned with the bench.

Lower-back exercises. Lie on a bench with your legs anchored, or with someone else holding your legs down. Clasp your hands behind your head. Tighten your spinal muscles and the muscles in your lower back up to a horizontal position.

Supplementary abdominal exercise to alternate with back exercises. Do this on an incline board in a sit-up position, with bent knees and hands crossed on your shoulders. Start lying down, then draw yourself up. The severity can generally be adjusted on an incline board from a couple inches to a couple feet. This exercise works your abdominals all the way up until your elbows hit your knees.

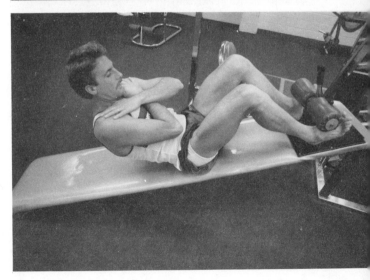

8 TWO-ARM TRICEPS PRESSES AND CALF RAISES

TRICEPS PRESSES

SETS: 2 or 3

REPETITIONS: 15 to 25

REST: use lighter weight

MAJOR MUSCLES: triceps

HOW TO DO IT. Hold one dumbbell in both hands, with the weight resting in your open palm and your thumbs overlapped. Start with the dumbbell behind your head. Your elbows should be fairly wide. Lift the weight up until your arms are fully extended. If you have back problems, do the exercise sitting down.

Sitting triceps extension (to alternate with back exercise). Hold the weight around one end of the dumbbell (at the back of your head), then press all the way up to a full extension.

Triceps press. Bend over, with one hand on a stationary apparatus. Hold your elbow in fairly close to your side; hold the weight vertically, and extend your arm fully. As you lift the weight, you are working against gravity as well. Then bring the weight back down to a 90-degree position adjacent to your knee.

CALF RAISES

SETS: 2 to 3
REPETITIONS: 20 to 30
REST: none; go directly to two-arm triceps presses
MUSCLES: soleus, gastrocnemius

If you have to do a lot of climbing during the bike race, your calves may become fatigued, which will make you more "flat-footed" on the run. Strengthening your calves will prevent some of that cumulative fatigue, and will allow you to drive off the balls of your feet when you run.

HOW TO DO IT. Put the ball of your foot on a two-by-four or an elevated step; rest your heel on the floor. Stand up on your toes, then all the way back down again.

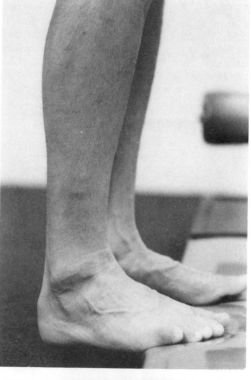

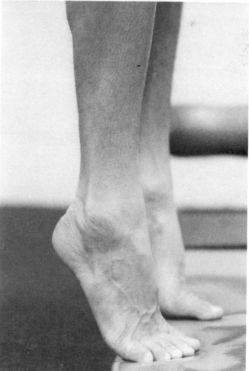

Calf raise (and ankle stretch). Elevate the ball of your foot with your heel on the floor. The Achilles is slightly stretched. Stand all the way up on your toes, then lower slowly. Do not bounce.

SUPPLEMENTARY EXERCISES

1. Rhomboid squeeze. Lie face-down on the bench with your arms flexed at about 100 degrees. Reach down and grab the dumbbells, draw the weight up until you can no longer draw it up any higher. You should feel your rhomboids, the muscles between your shoulder blades, squeeze together. You also feel this in your arms and in your deltoids. This exercise works your upper back, which can become extremely sore when you cycle.

2–6. Dumbbell flies. These exercises isolate your pectoralis and work primarily your triceps. Draw the weight down below shoulder level, then press all the way up just like you're hugging a big tree, in a circular motion, to a full arm's extension. For a slight variation, bring the dumbbells down (in a vertical alignment) until it touches your chest lightly, then press it straight up. This isolates the triceps as opposed to working the pectoralis muscle.

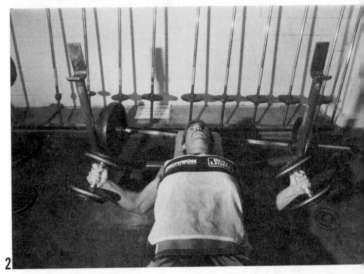

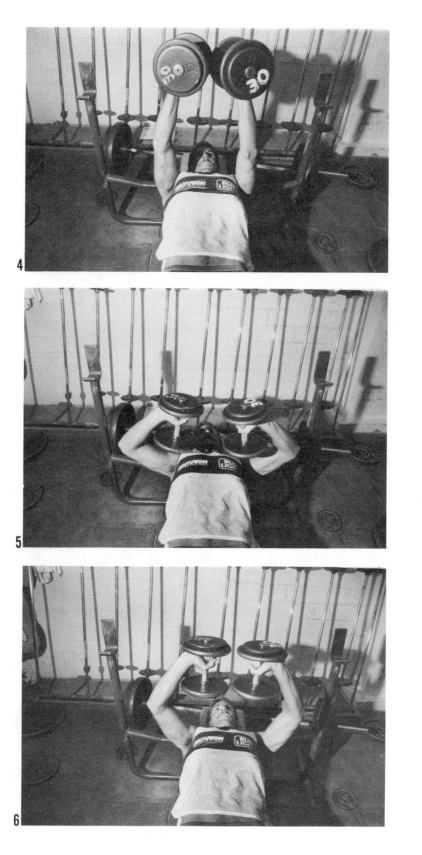

7–9. Triceps extension: Grab the weight, taking it off the floor, or have a partner hand it to you. Start with weight behind your head, then press it out at approximately 45 degrees, away from your head so that you also have to stabilize your abdominals somewhat. It primarily isolates your triceps.

10–11. Bent-arm pull-down. I do this exercise for a static contraction for my abdominals. It also works your triceps, your upper back, and your deltoids. As you raise it up, it works your lower back. It uses some of the same muscles as the downward press and finish on freestyle stroke. To start, pull the lat bar just below shoulder height, with slightly flexed elbows. Then slowly pull it down toward your thighs, bending slightly forward at the waist. Use a lighter weight than for the triceps extension.

12–13. *Bar dip.* Start with straight arms, and your feet off the ground. Lower yourself down until your elbow is flexed at about 90 degrees, then extend your arms back up. This is good for your triceps and your deltoids.

14. *Step up.* This works your quadriceps and your gluteals. It's good for hill climbing and also strengthens your quadriceps muscles for running as well. Start with the bar resting on your shoulders. Slowly raise one foot up onto the bench, then lower it back down again. Repeat the exercise with the other leg.

15. Alternating dumbbell curl. Start with a dumbbell in each hand. Draw the weight up with one arm, while the other is down; then as you lower one arm, raise the other. It is a simultaneous effort. The weight can be held vertically or horizontally.

15

Isometric "downward press." (above) Use a fixed object to simulate the catch on the freestyle. With a slightly bent wrist, keep your elbow fairly high, and pull. Hold this position 6–10 seconds. Repeat 6–10 times per set.

Isometric "finish." (right) Place your hand against the wall in the freestyle "finish" position, fingers pointing straight down towards the bottom, and press. Hold for 6–12 seconds. Make sure that you're breathing throughout the exercise. You can reverse the exercise: relax the arm, then go to the other arm. Repeat that 3–4 times.

Sculling. Your legs can be underneath in a deep pool or out in front slightly. You can cross your legs. The sculling motion is a figure-8 motion on its side. Start with your hands about two feet apart, then scull out so that your arms are nearly fully extended. This works your back muscles, your shoulder muscles, and also your forearm and upper-arm muscles.

Start with your legs straight out in front of you. As you scull with your arms turn your feet side to side (3 o'clock to 9 o'clock), keeping them above water. Works abdominals, deltoids, arms.

Feet-up drill. Start with your legs straight out in front, toes above the water. Draw your legs up to your chin, trying to keep your toes and your knees dry. This works the abdominal muscles and also simulates the freestyle sculling motion.

ISOKINETIC WORKOUT

IF COMPLETE ISOKINETIC GYM IS AVAILABLE

Follow same seasonal strength program as outlined on page 143. Do the same exercises, same repetitions, same rest intervals, etc., but use isokinetic equipment.

SWIM BENCH WORKOUT

On a swim bench, you use the exact same arm motion that you use in a freestyle stroke. Therefore, the resistance setting on the bench should simulate the amount of effort you expend in a hard (85 percent to 95 percent effort) swim workout. You will have to experiment—it may take three or four tries—to find the perfect setting, but you can establish a general estimate as follows:

A. Swim 200 yards freestyle at 85 percent to 95 percent effort.
B. Count your strokes on the last lap (e.g., 15).
C. Divide total workout time by the number of laps you swam (2:20 × 8 = about 17 seconds).
D. You should set the machine for a comparable load. In this example, you would set the load so that you could do approximately 15 strokes in 17 seconds.

You can simulate an entire swimming workout on a swim bench. For example, you could do 6 × 75 on 1:30 (sprint race training). The fatigue is going to be greater than in the pool, so you may need to reduce your overall workout time and increase your rest intervals. You can use a swim bench to supplement your regular pool training, or to substitute for it if you can't swim for some reason.

FINAL WORDS OF ADVICE

Always keep in mind that weight training is a supplement to—not a replacement for—your regular triathlon training workouts. Do not substitute a weight workout for a swim, bike ride, or run.

A few precautions will make your strength program valuable and productive:

1 *Don't overdo it.* The purpose of weight training is to build strength and prevent overuse injuries. Take your time, build up your weight load slowly, and follow the prescribed number of sets and repetitions closely. More is not necessarily better.

2 *Be consistent.* It will not do you any good to bench press a million pounds on Monday, then lie around all week until the next brutal session. Sporadic effort does not produce maximum results, and it often causes undue soreness and injuries. Complete a moderate program on a regular basis (three to five days a week, depending upon your level of fitness), and you will feel a strength increase within a few weeks.

3 *Warm up slowly.* Do easy stretches before you begin, then start with some slow, light-weight sets.

4 *Take active rest.* During your rest periods between sets, move around and keep the blood circulating to the muscles you are exercising. If you are doing leg exercises, walk around the room and shake out your legs. If you are doing arm exercises, swing them lightly and shake them out.

5 *Don't get bored.* There are hundreds of variations on the exercises I have listed in this chapter. Don't be afraid to try something new—it gives you a break from your routine and works different muscles.

6 *Keep a record of your progress with the chart on the following page.*

EXAMPLE WEIGHT TRAINING PROGRESS

DAY	EXERCISE	SETS	REPS	PATTERN	WEIGHT	COMMENTS
EXAMPLE: MONDAY	BENCH PRESS	5	10-15-14-13-10	WARM-UP 3 SAME WEIGHT 1 CLOSE-GRIP	100 LB 135 LB 95 LB	EXTREMELY TIRED ON FOURTH SET

WEIGHT TRAINING PROGRESS

DAY	EXERCISE	SETS	REPS	PATTERN	WEIGHT	COMMENTS

STRETCHING

Stretching is a preventive measure—it reduces the possibility of injury by increasing the circulation to your muscles and joints, slightly elevating your heart rate and metabolism, relaxing your muscles, and allowing a greater range of motion.

What most people don't seem to realize is that stretching can also *cause* injuries if done improperly. If you twist a muscle while attempting to stretch, for example, you can tear the muscle or pull it away from its attachment to the bone. Or if you try to stretch too strenuously without warming up, you can overstress a "cold" muscle.

If you try to overstretch, you will simply be working against yourself. Your neurological system attempts to protect you against this unwitting abuse with a physiological mechanism called a *stretch reflex*. If you stretch beyond your normal range of motion, you will start receiving sensory cues that are designed to discourage you from going any farther—it's called pain. If you start feeling more than a slight tension during your stretching exercises, take it easy—your body is trying to tell you something.

WARMING UP AND COOLING DOWN

PASSIVE STRETCHING

1 *I try not to stretch before starting an activity.* If I am running, I start with some fast walking, then I jog slowly for about three quarters of a mile before stopping to stretch. After I stretch, I resume my running workout. The same is true for swimming—I loosen up by swimming easily for 8 to 10 minutes, then I stretch in the water. Sometimes I stretch with a partner.

2 *It is also important to do some easy stretches after you exercise.* After my swimming workout, I swim a few easy laps, mixing up my strokes. Then I stand (in the water) and stretch from side to side or swing my arms lightly for 5 to 10 seconds. Do the same thing after a cycling workout, but be careful because your muscles will be very tired from contracting for a long period of time. Sudden stretches can cause muscle spasms. Never do any strenuous stretching after a workout; you will be vulnerable to a torn or pulled muscle.

STATIC STRETCHING

The best stretching exercises are static, in which you hold the stretch for about 30 seconds. Never do a bouncing stretch, like the old calisthenics teachers used to do, where you lean over and bounce your hands until you touch your toes. That can do more damage than good.

I usually stretch in a continuum of phases:

1 *Pre-stretch (warm-up)*—just enough movement to get the circulation going, such as a slight swing of the arms to start a shoulder stretch.
2 *Stretch and hold 8 to 15 seconds.*
3 *Back to warm-up.*
4 *Final stretch, holding 20 to 30 seconds.*

FLEXIBILITY

Don't expect to start right out with the flexibility of a contortionist; it takes a long time to develop maximum movement, especially if you have no background in agility-based activities or are heavily muscled. Several factors affect flexibility:

1 *Bone structure.* People who are small-boned tend to be more flexible. If you have large, heavy bones, you'll probably have to stretch five days a week to increase their muscular and joint pliancy. If you are on a three-day workout program, stretch on the off-days as well.

2 *Muscular development.* This is where the expression "muscle-bound" applies. Excessive musculature surrounds and literally locks in joints, impairing movement. Obviously, a body builder is going to have to do a lot of stretching to become an agile triathlete! An inordinate amount of strength and anaerobic work can be a detriment to a swimmer, cyclist, and runner. If you are naturally muscular, you will probably have to do more stretching exercises than a leaner person.

3 *Muscular elasticity.* This is not a trait you can develop. Certain muscle fibers are more elastic than others, and some people seem to have a greater degree of overall elasticity than others.

4 *Previous background, age, and sex.* Women tend to be more flexible than men, due to physical factors mentioned above and to their typical activities (in American culture, at least). Ballet and gymnastics produce more agility than football. And while age in itself doesn't tighten muscles, the accompanying decrease in activity does. Few of us are on the run at 30, 40, or 50 as much as we were as children or teenagers. There is some truth in the expression "Use it or lose it."

5 *Everybody has good and bad days.* When you have one of those great training days, it isn't just because you are in good physical condition, it is also because your muscles are relaxed. That is why stretching is so important; it relaxes you so that you can put your full energy into whatever you are doing.

But don't expect to respond to stretching the same way every day. If you have a particularly strenuous workout one day, you may feel slightly stiff and sluggish the next. Or if the weather is cold, you may feel relatively inflexible. Don't force yourself to reach the same point in a stretch from one day to the next. Never push to the point of pain to try to achieve flexibility—it doesn't work.

REHABILITATION

If you have been injured and are getting back into training, never try to regain your flexibility before you have regained your muscular strength and endurance. It takes a long time to mend, and to get back into the shape you were in before you were hurt. If you try to regain elasticity too quickly, you will simply re-injure yourself.

PARTNER STRETCHES

You are entrusting a part of your health to your stretching partner, so make sure you develop and maintain clear communication. The "stretchee" must let the "stretcher" know when to adjust the pressure, or if the movements aren't smooth enough. Both people must have the same goal in mind; don't let a mutual stretch become a contest over who can stretch the farthest.

Warm-up exercise. Swing your arm in a slow, circular motion over your head. This increases the blood flow to your shoulder area and stretches out your shoulders.

Lat, deltoid, triceps stretch. Reaching behind you and over the top of your head, grab your elbow, and pull it toward your spine. Reach toward the middle of the back.

Shoulder stretch. Hold your arms up over the head, criss-crossed, with your fingers clasped together. Reach up or side to side. This stretches your lats, shoulders, sides; it increases flexibility for a longer stroke.

Towel stretch. Grasp the towel with your arms out wide and straight over your head. Then slowly bring the towel behind your back so that your shoulder blades are squeezing together, or tip from side to side. This stretches your latissimus dorsi and deltoids.

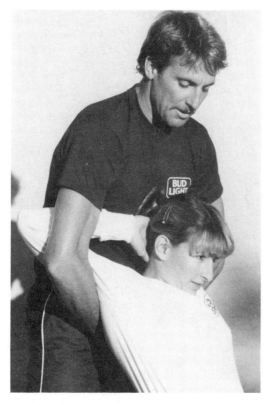

Partner stretch. My wife Anna demonstrates a lat stretch. Stand behind a partner, clasp your fingers together reaching around and over her elbows. Lift straight up and then slowly draw the elbows back to stretch your partner all the way down her side, along with her legs, stomach, and particularly latissimus dorsi (the primary mover in swimming).

Partner Stretch. Stand behind your partner and grasp underneath her biceps muscles. Lift the elbows slowly. The person who is being stretched should be very relaxed. Elbows should be drawn up to about shoulder height or slightly below, and then squeezed in slightly. This stretches the pectoralis and deltoid muscles.

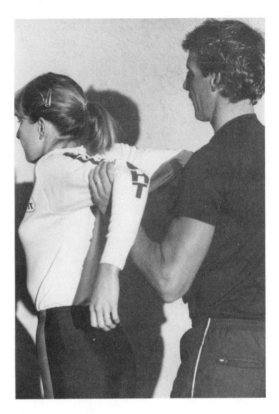

Partner stretch. Clasp your hands together around your partner's biceps muscle, lifting up and drawing the elbow slightly toward the spine. This will stretch the shoulders.

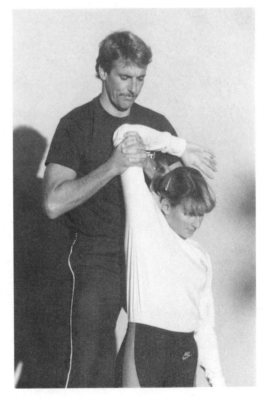

Partner stretch. With your partner's arm behind her head (supported on your shoulder), grasp her elbow and push up slowly for a shoulder stretch. Do not push too hard or too fast.

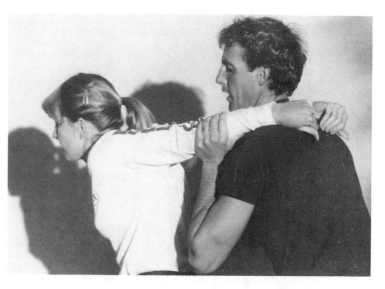

Partner stretch. Your partner should be standing against the wall. Put one hand underneath her heel, and the other hand on the ball of her foot pushing against her toes, then lift her leg up to almost a horizontal position (90 degrees). This stretches the hamstring by pushing on the toe. It also stretches the calf muscles and Achilles tendon.

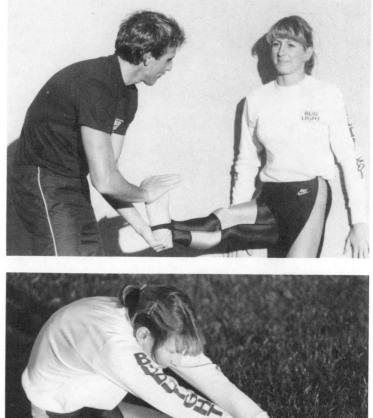

Leg and back stretch. Sitting on the ground or on a mat, grab your ankles (or the inside of your ankles or legs if you are relatively inflexible), and bend over trying to move your forehead as close to your knees as you can. This will stretch your hamstrings, your calves, and also your back muscles.

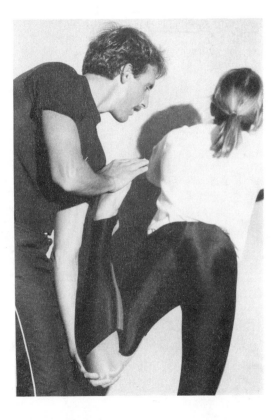

Partner stretch. Put one hand under your partner's knee, pushing on her toes with your other hand. This stretches ankles and quadriceps primarily. Lifting up on the knee allows a greater stretch in the hip flexors.

Calf and Achilles tendon stretch. Your leg should be straight, with your toe pointing straight ahead and your heel down. Push your hips forward toward the fixed object or wall. This stretches primarily your calves and Achilles tendons, but also stretches your hamstrings lightly. Allow your knee to flex a little bit to further stretch your Achilles tendon.

Ankle stretch. Place your hand on top of your toes. Pull your big toe and stretch the top of your foot. This will help the flutter kicking motion in freestyle.

WHICH MUSCLES NEED TO BE STRETCHED?

After a hard day of training, you will know which muscles should have been stretched! The soreness that builds up is an unmistakable clue.

1   *Swimming:* Shoulders are the main muscles that tighten during a swim workout. Also lats and upper back. Legs are not critical, because you shouldn't be kicking that hard, but ankle flexibility will help your kick and body stability.

2   *Cycling:* Quadriceps, calves, hamstrings, neck, and lower back.

3   *Running:* Quadriceps, hamstrings, lower back, neck, and shoulders.

8 DAVE SCOTT'S RACING SECRETS

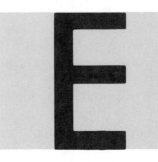

veryone dreams of having the perfect race, but it never seems to work out that way. There are so many variables in triathlons—heat, cold, water temperature, equipment, aid stations, the course itself—that actual race circumstances rarely mirror the conditions you imagine beforehand.

I have learned that lesson again and again—sometimes to my delight, other times to my dismay. At the 1983 Ironman, a totally unexpected early lead gave me the confidence to keep trying for the hardest-fought victory in my career; at the 1985 Nice Triathlon, a broken spoke forced me out of the race entirely.

The 1984 Ironman.

The breaks definitely figure into any athletic competition, but winning a race is more than a lucky roll of the dice. How you react to the breaks can make or ruin a race. You have to be prepared to change your game plan according to the opportunities—or setbacks—that appear as you go along. A triathlon is not merely a test of brute physical strength; it is a measure of your ability to adapt mentally and physically to constant change.

The most obvious of these changes are the transitions from swimming to cycling to running. In this chapter, we'll talk about some advance preparations that will save you time and trouble there. We'll also talk about the kinds of unforeseen problems that may arise during a race, and how you can minimize their effect. And, of course, you need to know how to recognize opportunities and take advantage of them. (I've become an expert at that!)

Every triathlete can be a success. If you set a goal for yourself and are able to achieve it, you have won your race. Your goal can be to come in first, to improve your performance, or just to finish the race—it's up to you. We'll go through an entire race together on the next few pages, starting at the very beginning: setting our goals.

WHY ARE YOU DOING THIS?

Before you started your training program, I suggested that you ask yourself two questions:

1   What do you hope to accomplish?
2   How do you plan to do it?

You should ask yourself the same questions for each race, and for the entire racing season. First identify your long-range goal, then the short-term objectives you'd like to reach along the way.

Don't make the mistake of centering all your hopes and efforts on one race. If anything prevents you from reaching your goal at that one event, you'll feel as though your entire effort has been wasted.

I usually set my long-range goals within a year's time—what do I want to do from June to June, or January to January? And what are the steps in between? For several years, it seemed that the Hawaii Ironman was the final race of the year, the culmination of 12 months of training and hoping. A lot of athletes put all their dreams into that one race, and a lot of them were bitterly disappointed when the heat or a flat tire or a pair of leaky goggles turned their dreams into nightmares.

In my case, an injury prevented me from racing as well as I would have liked in the February 1982 Ironman. My goal for that race was to do as well as I could under the circumstances, and hopefully place somewhere near the top. Scott Tinley was strong and fast that day—he won the race and I was satisfied with second place. But I wanted to see how well I could do without injuries. My goal for the next six months was to do as well as possible in the shorter U.S. Triathlon Series races that summer, and to come back and win the Ironman in October. Even if I hadn't won the Ironman, I would have been pleased with the fact that I met my intermediate goals at the USTS events.

HOW TO JUDGE YOUR SUCCESS

1 *Don't compare your times or your races from year to year.* Use races as stepping-stones for experience; chart your race split times, workout times, time trial results—then look at your seasonal progression. Your standing in the race isn't necessarily as important as your ongoing improvement.

If you are going through a hard time, and you compare your performance to your old races, you can become very discouraged. All during 1983, my life was riddled with personal problems and my training was inconsistent. After my poor performance at the 1983 USTS national championship, reporters—and some competitors—started hinting that my career was over. If I had judged myself based upon my successful 1982 season, I might have thrown in the towel. But I knew I could race well if I could just improve my attitude and train more consistently. So I made the most of the next few weeks, and came in third at the Nice Triathlon, then won the Ironman a few weeks after that.

You can't let the past—or other people's opinions—dictate your own assessment of your capabilities. Nor can you assume that a past victory is the best that you can do. I was in the best shape of my career when I stepped up to the Ironman starting line in October 1982. Yet I can race faster now—with much less training—than I did then. It would be foolish to look back and say, "I am only training half as much now, so I am bound to be half as efficient." Every year is a new one; there are new variables, and you have to deal with them the best way you can.

2 *Don't compare yourself to your competitors.* They provide incentive for you, so that you can meet your own goals. Know their strengths and weaknesses so you can take advantage of them in a race, but don't let the competition weigh on you.

People always ask me, "Are you afraid of Scott Tinley, or Scott Molina, or Mark Allen?" I have never been afraid of them. The only person I am afraid of when I step up to the starting line is myself, if I have not done my homework. In that case, if I worried about my competitors, I would lose my concentration and compound my problems. If you have trained properly and maintain your own standards during a race, there is no one to fear.

3 *Never look over your shoulder.* When you begin to worry about the competition, you can't concentrate on your own task at hand. In the 1983 Ironman, Scott Tinley and I had jockeyed back and forth for 23 miles of the marathon run. I was in the lead, but I was so tired that I could barely keep from falling over. When my friend Pat Feeney told me, "You better pick it up—Tinley is really moving," I wanted to sink out of sight. At that point, the last thing I needed was for someone else to look over my shoulder for me. I needed to know, instead, that there were only three miles left and that if I could just hold on to my pace, I would have the victory. To worry about Tinley would have taken more energy than I had to spare. As it was, he crossed the finish line just 33 seconds behind me.

4 *Keep your ego under control.* Maintaining your self-esteem and controlling your ego

work hand in hand. Here again, your assessment of your own accomplishments has to come from within, not from someone else's judgment. Some people will put you on a pedestal when you become a proficient triathlete, but if you allow your self-image to swell out of proportion, you are setting yourself up for a fall. While one person is basking in the limelight, another is always training diligently to defeat him. If your ego depends on believing you are better than someone else, you'll never make it.

I'll always remember a college basketball player who was a top draft pick for the pros. The promoters were building him up as a superman and flaunting his multimillion-dollar contract at a huge press conference. Reporters kept asking him how many points he expected to score per game, how many rebounds, and how many records he thought he would break. Finally he turned to a newsman and said, "Listen, I can't fly."

DEVELOPING A WINNING ATTITUDE

The way to always be a winner is never to be defeated. Go into every race with a number of objectives and evaluate your performance relative to the actual circumstances, not pre-race expectations. And remember that everyone else in the race wants to do well, too. Don't underrate your own performance because someone else does well. Ask yourself:

1 Did I do as well as I could have under the circumstances?
2 Did I perform to my potential, considering my level of ability and training?
3 Considering the above, did I compete favorably against others?

One of the things I enjoy about competing is that there is so much excitement at the start-

ing line. The competitive factor in a race heightens most people's performance; I usually expect to do 30 to 40 percent better in a race than I have done in my last two weeks of training. That becomes one of my objectives.

If I haven't been training as diligently as I should, I take that into account in evaluating a particular race. When I don't fare well against the competition, it isn't a total loss; they may have had a really good race, and I know I'll have to do more "homework" to get back into the winner's circle. When I do win, it elevates my standards for myself; to do even better, I'll have to train harder.

There's always some sort of victory, and

After the 1983 Ironman, Scott Tinley told reporters he wasn't sure if he had pushed himself as hard as he could have.

There's always some sort of victory at every race—enjoy yourself!

bly do is to judge yourself too harshly, because it takes a long time to restore broken confidence. You would be much better off congratulating someone who had an excellent race that day; it acknowledges that both of you did as well as you could.

Always analyze a race as quickly as possible, while all the details are fresh in your memory.

1 How do you feel right then, compared to how you feel when you have extended your maximum effort?
2 What were the problems you encountered, and how can you avoid them in the future?
3 Were you mentally and emotionally flexible during the race?

Don't just question your performance; take a look at your expectations. Are they realistic? And what about your training program? Is it adequate for the races you are entering? If not, you need to adjust your plan. Goals are worthless if they can't be attained.

Above everything else, learn how to be satisfied with your accomplishments along the way. There are many, many steps between swimming your first lap in a pool and finishing the Ironman. Identify the steps between where you are and where you'd like to be this time next year—write them down—and be satisfied every time you climb to the next one.

always room for improvement. If you experience a disappointment at a race, don't make too much of it. The worst thing you can possi-

RACE PSYCHOLOGY

The best way to start a race is to believe you can win. Winning doesn't necessarily mean crossing the finish line before anyone else; it means succeeding in the pursuit of one or more of your pre-race objectives. When I approach a race, I try to distinctly define three performance objectives and a plan to achieve them.

SET SPECIFIC GOALS

Going into the October 1982 Ironman, my three performance goals were: (1) to win the race under my 1980 time, (2) to start out strong and maintain the lead throughout the entire race, and (3) to achieve the fastest split times in all three events.

That was quite a big order, but I had directed all of my energy toward it for more than six months. I had trained persistently, and I knew I was physically and mentally 100 percent ready to meet my goals. That was probably the best race I've ever had, in terms of overall accomplishment. I met all my goals.

The next year, my Ironman objectives were quite different. I hadn't trained as consistently, and I had battled emotional problems throughout the season, so I adjusted my goals to be more realistic. I wanted to win, but I didn't know if that was realistic, so I aimed for (a) being completely satisfied with my race and (b) pushing myself to the absolute limits of my capabilities under the circumstances. I wanted to ignore all the negative media attention and forget about my bad races earlier in the season. With a little luck, I hoped I might exceed my own expectations.

Before each race, give yourself several ways to win. Set three goals, including at least one that challenges you to your limit. You might want to: (1) go 25 percent faster than your last personal time trial, (2) aim for your ultimate performance in all three events (meet your time trial results), and (3) be satisfied with at least two out of three events, including transitions. The goals are up to you.

At the 1983 Ironman, my goal was to push myself to the limit—as you can see, I did exactly that.

ESTABLISH A GAME PLAN

In order to compete well, you have to plan. Look at your time trial splits, your workout times, and your overall performance during the six weeks before the race. That will give you an idea of which events are currently your strongest. Then analyze the course and the race itself—the field of competitors, the climate, the difficulty of terrain, the distance. (Learn the best way to preview a course on page 190.)

When you have determined your strengths on this particular course, plan where to make your decisive moves. If you are good at riding hills, you may want to push past tiring competitors at that point, for instance.

Realize that nothing is inevitable. Don't limit yourself on the basis of any predictions—including your own. You might run much faster than your training ever indicated you could, just as an unexpected headwind might slow you down on the bike. Welcome the unexpected as an opportunity; while others may be psychologically thrown off track by a sudden storm, you can choose to ride right through it.

Try to swim, bike, and run as much of the course as possible in advance, so that you will be on familiar turf when you race. Prepare yourself mentally for the distances, terrain, and climate. Remember that you will accumulate fatigue throughout the race—do not be surprised by that or let it discourage you.

TAKE A RISK

If you never take any chances, you'll never realize your full potential. In a triathlon, that means you push harder than you ever have in a training workout. Because you don't really know what to expect when you go beyond that familiar threshold, you're taking a slight risk. It might be painful, and it might be exhilarating—but you'll never know until you try.

Every triathlete has tolerated a certain degree of discomfort during training. When you are slightly out of shape, when you go faster or farther than before, your body usually protests. But you can increase your "comfort quotient" gradually by starting out at a comfortable pace, then inching your way up to—and past—your previous limit.

If you usually run a 7:30 mile in training, don't risk premature exhaustion by starting out at a 6:30 pace. Start at 7:30, then as soon as you feel comfortable, go a little faster. Repeat that process until you're going faster than you have before. I like to train without a watch, so that I am not limited by it. I keep pushing myself to my limit based on how I feel, not how fast the watch says I am working.

Scott Tinley and I pass by each other at the 1984 Ironman. The year before, we had played cat-and-mouse throughout the marathon.

posely risk a little extra discomfort, you have won half the battle. You might not feel fresh as a daisy, but as long as you are still choosing to push yourself, you are still in control.

The oldest trick in the book is to pass a competitor looking as strong as possible, even if you can only keep it up until you're out of view. (Sometimes that tactic works great; other times your rival will do the same thing to you a mile or so up the road. Scott Tinley and I played that cat-and-mouse game for miles of the 1983 Ironman run. We both knew what we were doing, but nevertheless it pushed each of us to our top performances.)

REMEMBER: YOU'RE NOT THE ONLY ONE IN PAIN

Pain is a sensation that can be played to your advantage during a race. You can mentally wear down your opponents by never conceding that you feel as bad as they do.

Once you have made up your mind to pur-

CAPITALIZE ON YOUR STRENGTHS . . .

Know yourself. Even if you are entering your first race, you will have enough training behind you to recognize the areas in which you are most skilled. Are you a good hill climber, or are you better on the flats? Are you better at sprinting, or do you like long distances? Are you a talented runner, or do you prefer swimming?

Make a list of your strong points. Bear in mind that you will be mentally stronger—and perform better—at activities you prefer. Update the list as your skills develop. You may discover hidden talents as you go along.

. . . AND YOUR OPPONENTS' WEAKNESSES

If you are in a very competitive situation, it is important to know your opponents' strong and weak points, but don't base your race on those factors alone. Just be aware of any slight weaknesses so that you can use them to your advantage. Watch for signs of fatigue—listen to their breathing, watch their arm movement and their kick as they run—and when you know they are slowing down, surge ahead of them.

A lot of psychological warfare is waged during a triathlon, and there is nothing wrong with that. You don't know what they are thinking, and they don't know what you are thinking—it never hurts to instill a little "fear" in them!

I used to employ that tactic a lot in the swim. I would vary my speed solely to break my opponent's concentration. I would ease up a bit, and they would assume I was tired or not up to swimming any faster. Then I would suddenly surge ahead. It would confound them, at least temporarily, and make them believe I was much fresher than they were, after all.

On the cycling course, I might challenge them on a section of the course where there is really no need to challenge. On a flat section, or a rolling hill, or even an aid station, I would push ahead to gain a few extra seconds. The time might not have been much, but the psychological advantage was really worth the effort.

It is important to "read" your opponents in the heat of competition. If they are slackening their pace on a hill, for example, that is the precise time to attack. Or if you surge on the run and your opponent doesn't quite make up the gap, you can put on pressure then by maintaining or slightly increasing your speed. Even if you have to tolerate a high level of discomfort momentarily, that one particular surge might be the one that finally convinces your rival that he just can't keep up with you that day. Let them know that you will never let up.

Taking advantage of your opponents' mistakes or slight weaknesses is not cruel or ruthless; it is a healthy element of competition and part of the fun. When you use every opportunity to your best advantage, you improve your own performance and challenge yourself to higher levels.

TAPERING

There are many ways to diminish your training efforts before a race, including Kim Bushong's famous "TV Taper," in which he claimed he sat around for three weeks prior to the 1982 Ironman and did nothing but watch television and eat an occasional candy bar. I was appalled when he told that story to a roomful of reporters, and I was certain that he would fall apart during the race, but he defied the odds. He came out of the water in very good shape, led throughout the entire bike leg, and was not caught until four or five miles into the run. I didn't catch him for 10 miles!

I certainly do not recommend the TV Taper, but I do use the drastic drop-off method. You can train as you normally would up to about four days before a race.

THREE WEEKS PRIOR TO RACE

1   Do not increase your high-intensity training, speed work, or overdistance training.
2   Maintain or slightly decrease the actual time you spend training.
3   Maintain the intensity.

FOUR DAYS PRIOR TO RACE

Let's say your race is on Sunday. Your last hard workout should be on Tuesday:

1   *Wednesday:* Very easy day. No high-intensity work, no anaerobic work, no long distances. Use this as a day to recover from Tuesday's workout.

2   *Thursday:* Same as Wednesday, but add some easy hypoxic work (bilateral breathing, for example) in the pool to slightly elevate your heart rate. No intervals.
3   *Friday:* Rest day. No swimming, cycling, or running. Perhaps some easy walking; just relax.
4   *Saturday:* Easy loosen-up in all three activities. Spend 15 to 20 minutes on each, at a very low intensity (around 50 percent of your maximal effort).

It is important to exercise lightly the day before the race. It elevates your skin temperature (which increases circulation to the working muscles), loosens your muscles, and helps you shed any extra water you may have retained from the previous day's inactivity. This four-day drastic drop-off taper should suit most people, but you may need more rest if you are heavily muscled and tend to be more anaerobic. If you excel in shorter races, climb hills very well, and are more of a sprinter than an endurance specialist, allow yourself a slightly longer rest period.

BEFORE THE RACE

TAKE IT EASY

The main thing you need to do during the last couple of days before a race is relax. If you are constantly rehashing your game plan and thinking about how your muscles feel and how your competition is doing, you will go into the race so high-strung that you'll be emotionally worn out after the first half hour.

Do some other activity that has nothing to do with triathlons. Go sight-seeing or shopping, or just sit back and read a good book, but get your mind off the race from time to time. You have done all the training you can; you are as ready as you can be.

PREVIEW THE COURSE

Most race organizers provide competitors with course maps prior to the race. The more you know about a course in advance, the better off you'll be during the race. A couple of days before the race, take the time to survey all three courses, if possible.

SWIM COURSE

The course markers should be set up early enough to allow you to become familiar with all the buoys and angles.

Preview the swim course in advance to choose your own path.

1 *Survey the turns*. How many are there? Where are they? You should go out to those turning points and look around so that you will know what should be in your field of vision on race day.

2 *Find long- and short-range markers for each turn*. For example, after your first turn, focus on something on the horizon, such as a telephone tower or large tree or building. It should be something you can immediately spot by lifting your head up. When you are swimming, you will also use short-range markers, such as a buoy, boat, or a paddleboard. However, if choppy water or other swimmers block your field of vision, you will have to rely on long-range markers instead.

3 *Make sure you know what the finish line looks like*. Is it marked with banners? Is there a change tent? Where do you come in? How do you get to the transition area? It is easier than you might think to meander across a beach or lakeshore after a long swim, and miss the finish line. Don't rely on your sense of direction or pre-race instructions alone. Check it out thoroughly long before the race.

4 *Swim the course in sections*. Break the swim into several sections, swim each section, then stop and look around. There is no substitute for actually being in the water for your pre-race navigation. You can actually see what the markers will look like during the race, so you will know exactly how to orient yourself.

BIKE COURSE

If the race is long, you will need to break it into segments. Obviously, you don't want to ride all 112 miles of the Ironman bike course at once, a few days before the race. But you should try to ride the entire course, so that you know it well when you race on it.

1 *Look for all the obstacles, and pick a landmark that will remind you in advance*. If

Look for all the obstacles on the bike course.

you come across rough road, potholes, tight corners, or steep hills, find a landmark—a tree, a mile marker, or any visual reminder—*before* the obstacle, so you will be prepared for it on race day. Practice riding those individual stretches of road a few times (at least) until you have determined exactly how you want to ride through them, and are comfortable at a race pace. It is a tremendous advantage to be able to maintain—or pick up—your speed when others are slowing down.

2   *Know the turns, and practice cornering.* When you are on your preview ride, take the time to learn each turn, so that you do not have to slow down unnecessarily during the race. Not only is it a competitive edge for you, it is also safer.

3   *Choose your line.* Part of a pre-race game plan is knowing the line that is the shortest distance on the course. In running as well as cycling, the best competitors don't waste any extra energy on widely navigated corners. If you know the course, and ride it in advance, you will be able to avoid the long way around.

4   *Find the mileage markers.* The mile markers should be set up enough in advance for you to make a mental note of

them on your preview rides. It helps you to pace yourself, to prepare for upcoming obstacles, and to know when you can afford to push yourself a little harder because there is a long easy stretch ahead.

5   *Find the aid stations.* If possible, find out where the aid stations will be, so that you can consider them in your plan. It helps to know when you will be able to get more liquid (and food, if you don't carry your own) and an ice-cold sponge to squeeze over your head in the heat. You might also plan which stations you want to forgo, so that you can surge ahead at those points and gain time on your competitors who are slowing down.

6   *Try to anticipate windy areas.* This is difficult to do in Hawaii, where the winds are unpredictable. However, you can usually get some idea of where it is windiest, even if you cannot determine the exact direction of the winds.

RUN COURSE

Naturally, you don't want to run an entire marathon course at one time, so drive it in a car, then run the segments of it that are partic-

Choose the straightest line to follow on the running course.

ularly curvy, or hilly or taxing in some other way.

1   *Choose the straightest line.* Just as you did on the swim and bike courses, you need to pick your own line. The path you follow during the race should be the path of least distance.

2   *Know the turnaround points.* Make a mental note of the point at which the course doubles back. That is where you will be able to get a look at your competitors—behind and in front of you—to observe their overall condition. Are they showing signs of fatigue? Do they look strong? Since the run is the final event and your last chance to make up lost time—or hold your position—it is important to note how you are faring relative to your competitors. Do not change your plan entirely because others look tired or too good to beat, but do consider their position and overall condition as one factor in your decision. Likewise, they will be observing you, so it is a good time to practice psychological warfare (see page 189).

GET ORGANIZED

This is a good time to figure out all of the details, so that you have as little as possible to worry about on race day. For example:

1   Plan out your meals.
2   List what you need to have with you
    A   at the start,
    B   at each transition, and
    C   during each leg of the race.
3   List what you need to take care of on race morning, such as
    A   getting your bike to the start,
    B   pumping up your tires, and
    C   making sure all needed items are set up at the transition areas.

If you have a friend who can help you carry out any of the race-day details, it will make that morning much easier for you. If not, plan out the simplest program possible so that you are subjected to as little stress as possible.

GETTING READY FOR THE TRANSITIONS

Organizing your transitions well in advance will aid you tremendously on race day. If you have planned carefully and arranged your equipment according to the order in which you'll need it, you will save a lot of time and frustration.

MAKE A CHECKLIST

Write a list in a notebook, and keep it for future reference. After each race, delete items that are unnecessary and add items you may have overlooked. Note any problems you may have had in a particular transition, so that you may adjust your routine next time.

1   *Shoe selection.* Are you going to wear cycling shoes, then change to running shoes, or are you going to wear running shoes throughout the race? It is to your advantage—even in short races—to wear a stiff-soled, cleated cycling shoe for the bike race, then change to a running shoe. With practice and planning, you can get your transition down to under one minute; you can make up more than that by wearing proper shoes for cycling.

2   *Shorts selection.* Are you going to wear cycling shorts, then change to running shorts, or are you going to wear running shorts throughout? If you are prone to chafing, you may want to wear cycling shorts or a one-piece triathlon suit. In a short race—60 miles or less—I usually wear my running shorts and try to tolerate mild chafing in order to save transition time.

3   *Shirt selection.* If you wear a one-piece suit, you won't have to worry about shirts at all, but there are disadvantages to tight Lycra suits. I find that they restrict my breathing, even when I leave them un-

zipped across my chest. I prefer a cool, loose, cotton singlet while I am running. There are many types of suitable cycling tops in addition to the traditional cycling jersey. I prefer a short-sleeved or sleeveless jersey with a small pouch on the back to hold dried figs or any other food I want to carry with me. (See page 217).

4   *Food selection.* I usually eat dried figs because they are small, easy to carry, and a highly concentrated source of fuel. Many people prefer bananas. Whatever food you choose to bring along for the ride must be securely placed in the pouch on your shirt before you get on your bike. You may need to lightly tape the flap over the top of the pouch so that none of the food spills over the side.

5   *Miscellaneous items.* Anything you might want to have with you during the race must be ready for you at the transitions. Aid stations don't hand out extras like sunglasses or baby powder, so plan ahead. You might want:

A.   an extra water bottle at the swim-to-bike transition area, so you can have a drink or spray your face.

B.   a small hand towel to wipe your feet on.

C.   baby powder for the inside of your shoes (it makes it easier to slide them on).

D.   shoehorns (one for each shoe).

E.   sunglasses.

F.   a water bucket or flat pan to rinse your feet and remove any sand or small rocks.

G.   toggles or Velcro closures on your shoes.

H.   a shirt or singlet.

ARRANGING YOUR GEAR

Some races require you to make both transitions in the same area, while others have two separate areas. If you have just one area, you'll need to take that into consideration when you plan your checklist and arrange your gear. If you have two separate areas, make sure that you have two sets of any items you'll need for both transitions (towels, powder, buckets, etc.).

SWIM-TO-BIKE

1 The first thing I usually do when I come into the transition area is take a drink of water. Before the race, I have made sure the top is open on the water bottle, so I can just grab it and take a sip without fumbling.
2 I leave a small hand towel on the ground, so I can just step on it to dry my feet and get rid of any sand or rocks.
3 I have already put baby powder inside my cycling shoes and have pulled the tongues up so that I can easily slide my feet in.
4 I sometimes use shoehorns. The horns can be lightly taped to the heel of each shoe, then discarded once the shoe is on.
5 If I have to run through any mud, sand, or rocks after the swim, I set out a small bucket or flat pan of water next to my hand towel, so I can rinse my feet quickly.
6 I include a shirt. I like loose, cotton singlets.

7 Most people wear socks with th shoes, which helps prevent bl usually race without them, so the time it takes to put them on. you can lose as much or more time if a blister slows you down, so I would suggest wearing socks unless you are in a very short race.

BIKE-TO-RUN

This transition can be set up basically like the first one if the race has just one area—and if no one has trampled over your gear. If it is a separate area, as it is at the Ironman, everything you want should be in the bag you have checked in before the race. It will be waiting for you at your spot in the bike rack. My bike-to-run bag usually includes the following:

1 shoes (leave them open just enough to easily slide your foot in)
2 shorts (if the race is more than three hours)
3 singlet
4 food
5 water
6 visor

RACE MORNING

WAKE UP EARLY

Most people reach their peak metabolic rate—their heart, circulatory system, flexibility, and joint mobility are at maximum efficiency—between two and five o'clock in the afternoon. But most triathlons start much earlier than that—usually in the early morning—so you need to speed up the process.

1 *Allow yourself at least two hours to wake up and warm up before the race.* Some triathlons start so early that a two-hour wake-up call seems somewhat stoic, but your body and mind need that time to become fully alert and ready to race.
2 *Wake up slowly.* Don't bolt out of bed 45 seconds after your alarm goes off and start doing jumping jacks. Give your body time

to get used to being awake at that early hour—if the race starts at 7:00, you should be up by 4:30 or 5:00. Relax, read the newspaper, listen to some soothing music.

3   *Take a hot shower (10 to 15 minutes).* It will get your blood circulation going, warm up your skin, and accelerate your metabolism.

PRE-RACE DIET

The basic rule of thumb for eating on race day is: Less is better. Part of your pre-race preparation should have been a consistent diet that will provide most—or all—of the glycogen stores you'll need during the race. If your diet remains stable and your exercise is decreased during the pre-race taper, your glycogen level will be at a peak.

1   *Do not overeat on race morning.* Your glycogen stores will already be filled from your normal diet (see Chapter 9, "You Are What You Eat: A Champion's Diet"). A pre-race gorge will not give you extra usable fuel, but it will probably give you indigestion. Also, eating too much triggers the release of insulin, which creates a dramatic fluctuation in blood sugar.

2   *Eat food that is easily digested.* Try low-fat or no-fat foods. Before races that will last longer than three hours, I usually eat two or three pieces of lightly toasted bread without butter and two or three bananas. For shorter races, I just eat the bananas.

3   *Do not eat sugar or drink a lot of fruit juice.* Your blood sugar should be at a normal level. The idea of getting a quick lift before the race with a last-minute sugar snack is dangerously false. Eating a honey-granola bar or drinking a glass of orange juice right before the race may seem harmless, but it will cause your pancreas to secrete extra insulin, which will actually remove some of the glucose from your bloodstream. The sugar rush actually depletes energy rather than supplying it.

4   *Don't eat anything within an hour of race start.* Anything you eat will produce a slight insulin reaction, as described above. Go to the starting line feeling light and empty, with your blood sugar at a normal level.

5   *For a short race, keep food intake to a bare minimum.* All of the glycogen you need should be available, if you have trained and eaten properly before a short race.

THE PHYSICAL WARM-UP

A light warm-up before a race will allow you to start the triathlon a little faster than you normally would, without risking a painful surge of lactic acid. Your skin and working muscles will already be warm, and your respiratory and circulatory systems will be in motion. A pre-race warm-up will also increase your flexibility and overall alertness.

1   *Try to warm up 20 to 30 minutes before the race.* At most races, you have to get your race number marked on your arms and legs, inspect and check in your bicycle, and get last-minute instructions before the race. Try to complete your physical warm-up before that time. Even if you have to warm up two or three hours before the contest, a partial effect will carry over to the race.

2   *All exercise should be done at a very low intensity.* Never do any sprints or buildups prior to a triathlon. Save all of your energy for the race.

   A.   Cycle 10 to 15 minutes in a very low gear, at around 50 percent of your maximum. I like to ride 6 to 10 miles, but that may be farther than you need to go.

   B.   If you want to do some running, jog very easily for a mile or two. I usually jog two miles.

C. Swim just enough to get used to the water temperature and buoyancy. I try to swim 600 to 800 meters.

Remember that the idea is to invigorate—not exhaust—yourself. Never put out so much effort before a race that you get tired.

3 *If the water temperature is cool, skip the pre-race swim.* Most people become slightly hypothermic in water temperatures from mid- to lower 70s. If you start to shiver, get out of the water until the race begins. Bundle up; keep your head, feet, and fingers covered.

4 *Do some easy stretches.* To stretch your neck and shoulder muscles before the swim, hold your towel (one hand at each end) behind your neck and pull it from side to side. Stretch your ankles by rotating your foot with your hands; pull down on your big toe.

5 *Get a light massage, if possible.* Before the swim, massage your deltoids, lats, and upper back muscles. If you can't get someone else to give you an easy massage, do some yourself as you stretch. A light massage will warm up your skin and loosen up your muscles. It feels as good and helps as much before a race as it does afterward.

6 *A dip in a hot tub will also help.* A hot tub or hot bath will elevate your skin temperature and warm up your muscles. But don't

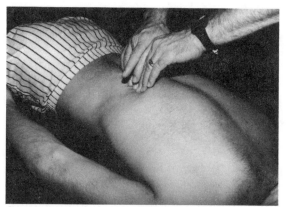
Get a massage before the race, if possible.

stay in for more than two or three minutes—more than that can dehydrate you and make you extremely lethargic.

7 *After your warm-up, stay warm.* It's better to overdress than to get a chill. Naturally, you don't want to be so hot that you start to sweat and become dehydrated, but make sure that your arms, hands, head, ears, and feet are all covered. In very warm, humid climates such as Hawaii, you'll need to wear light layers you can shed as the temperature rises, but most races start in the morning with air temperatures of 55 to 70 degrees. I always seem to be the last one with all my clothes on, but I know that it is extremely important to stay warm until the starting gun is fired.

AT THE STARTING LINE

This is it. All the preparation has been done, and now the test is about to begin. A minute or two before the gun goes off, you may immerse yourself in the water to acclimate to the temperature. But remember two things:

1 Control your breathing; don't allow your respirations to increase so that you start panting.

2 If the water is cold, stay out of it entirely until the race begins.

You will also want to mark your line—the straightest line to the buoys. Some people prefer to start out to the side of the crowd and swim a few extra yards to avoid the mad rush. The main thing is to be as relaxed as possible.

THE RACE IS ON!

PART 1: SWIMMING

For the first 30 seconds after the gun goes off, I try to block out everyone around me, and forget about anything but getting into my own rhythm. Then I start looking around, sighting buoys, markers, and other swimmers.

RACE TIPS

1 *Relax.* The most important thing to do at the beginning of any race is relax. With all of the pre-race excitement and the flurry of a mass swim start, however, you may not find it especially easy to calm down. I recommend following a step-by-step procedure as follows:

A = ALONE. Allow yourself to be alone by blocking out the competition for the first 30 seconds or so. Get into your own rhythm.

B = BREATHE EASY. Make sure you breathe with each arm cycle at first. Do not hold your head down or breathe bilaterally—you will build up an oxygen debt.

C = CONCENTRATION. Concentrate on relaxing. Talk to yourself, tell yourself silently to relax. Pay attention to every part of your body—relax your arms and shoulders, wiggle your fingers to relax your hands, inhale slowly and deeply, and do not kick too often or too strenuously.

2 *Relax your arms.* Because the water is cooler than your body temperature, your blood flow is directed primarily toward your torso, to keep your vital organs warm. Thus the circulation in your extremities tends to be relatively poor, so your feet and hands may become cold and stiff. It is very important, especially in cold water, to increase the blood flow to your arms and hands.

The best time to do this is during the recovery—when your arm comes out of the water at the end of your stroke. As your arms come over the water, shake your fingers lightly, and move them around. That will improve the circulation and relax your hands and arms somewhat.

3 *Vary your arm movement.* When you put out extra effort for a race, your lactate level rises lightly; you may feel some tightness in your trapezius, deltoids, and back muscles as your system begins to remove that lactate. You can alleviate some of this by varying your arm motion. Alternate between high and low recoveries, change your rhythm from time to time, and vary the depth of your pull. Don't be erratic, but do vary your movement once every hundred or so yards, for several strokes in succession.

4 *Don't overkick.* Keep your kick up near the surface. Most people tend to start kicking really hard when they approach the buoys; don't fall prey to that. Save your legs for cycling and running by keeping your kick light and close to the surface. You should feel your heel barely breaking the surface of the water with each easy kick.

5 *Change strokes.* At some point, you might feel excessively tight, stiff. Flip over onto your back and do a few backstrokes. This will loosen up your arm and shoulder muscles somewhat, and allow you to look around and reorient yourself. You may lose 5 to 10 seconds, but the break will benefit you by preventing cramps or neck and body stiffness that will build up during the bike leg. Flipping over to relax momentarily simulates the short rest periods you have taken between repeats in training, in that it allows you to recover slightly for the next effort.

HEAD-UP SWIMMING

The most effective type of head-up swimming is to keep your nose in the water, and roll your eyes forward. Do not elevate your entire head.

1 *Look straight ahead.* You may have to take three or four strokes with your eyes rotated forward to sight long- and short-range markers, then three or four strokes with your head down.
2 *Do not rely on anyone else.* Follow your own line. If the buoys are marked, count them as you pass, so that you will know when you are approaching the turns. Make a mental note of the significant buoys you pass, ones that are larger or specially colored to serve as markers.

DRAFTING

Drafting during the swimming portion of a triathlon is legal, and can save you 20 to 30 percent of valuable energy if you slip right behind someone else who is doing the work. But there are a few drawbacks which can outweigh the benefits.

1 *You are depending on someone else to navigate.* Your pre-race course survey is worthless if you aren't in a position to use it. You are usually better off swimming under your own power on a carefully navigated course than drafting someone else who may take you several minutes out of the way.
2 *You are stuck with someone else's pace.* When you settle in behind a faster swimmer, you have to keep up with that person in order to stay in his or her laminar flow. If that pace is too fast for you, fatigue can set in. On the other hand, the lead swimmer may slow down, and if you aren't careful, you'll end up swimming slower than you normally would.
3 *You are forfeiting your own game plan.* When you draft another swimmer, you are playing follow the leader, even if the leader's game plan may not complement your own. I have lined up with as many as 10 or 15 people behind a lead swimmer, and when someone swimming a little faster passed by, I realized that I might have been saving a little energy, but I wasn't swimming at my own optimum speed. I had joined someone else's game plan.

SYSTEM CHECKS

Throughout the swim, it is crucial to check your own vital systems. Is your breathing rate moderate and relatively easy (not gasping on each inhale)? Is your heart operating at an aerobic rate? Do your muscles feel fairly relaxed? Are your stroke length and body roll consistent with your normal training workouts?

You should occasionally interject an exaggerated crawl stroke with a slight delay after your entry, to allow your arms and shoulders to fully extend. You can also relax your muscles by doing some simple stretches while you are actually swimming:

1 *Whip kick.* This narrow frog kick will stretch your calf and Achilles tendon; the foot position simulates a cycling foot position (foot on the pedal over the spindle), thereby preventing cramping before the bike race.
2 *Dorsi flex.* On this kick, you turn your toe up (rather than slightly pointing it).
3 *Side kick.* This is similar to a scissors kick, but you don't squeeze your legs together at the finish. Kicking to the side from time to time will alleviate a lot of the stress on your hips, gluteal muscles, and quadriceps.

I alternate my kick every 30 to 40 strokes, using all of the above variations.

BEFORE THE FINISH LINE

At the end of the swim, I've often seen a tremendous flurry of people sprinting toward the finish line. What for? At that point, you should slow down and anticipate your transition instead of trying to beat someone else up the dock to gain two or three seconds over that last 100 yards. Don't waste your energy. You're much better off doing a few easy breaststrokes or backstrokes to relax and mentally change gears for the coming transition. It will also expedite the removal of lactate.

Take a deep breath, look around to orient yourself, then stand up slowly. I learned that lesson the hard way at the October 1982 Ironman. Mark Allen was right behind me on the swim, and we both sprinted in toward the finish line. I stood up abruptly, without doing any whip kicks, and as I moved up the incline ramp, I felt a twinge in my hamstring—it soon turned into a knotted cramp. I hobbled into the transition area, and by the time I got on my bike, there was a knot on my leg the size of a tennis ball.

Every time I pushed down on the pedal, the pain shot through my gluteals, radiating all the way up my back. By the time the race was over, that leg was swollen three inches larger than my other leg. I couldn't run for nearly a month after the race.

SWIM-TO-BIKE TRANSITION

Come out of the water fairly slowly. Shake your arms lightly, move your head around easily in a circular motion, and take a drink of water if you pass by an aid station on the way to your bike. Don't carry your arms tightly at your sides, or clinch your fists. And don't race to your bike; jog lightly to allow the blood to circulate freely to your leg muscles.

It is important to relax during the transitions, but don't stop your momentum entirely. Time is critical, and a minute saved in the transition area can change the final outcome of a race—especially a short one. How quickly you make a transition depends upon your goals, how closely matched you are with your competitors, and how carefully you have planned and practiced for it.

All your gear should be set out in the order you will need it. I pull on my shorts, sit down, put on my shoes, stand up, put on my shirt, sunglasses, and helmet, then I'm off.

A note for men: As soon as you get on the bike, loosen the drawstring on your swimsuit. Otherwise it will tighten up around your waist and inhibit your breathing and flexibility when you bend over in cycling position.

If you want to expedite your transition, try to streamline your needs. Time spent in the transition area must be made up on the course. Some of the "extras" that you may choose to eliminate are cycling gloves, suntan oil, and extra food. Determine your own needs; if you are very fair-skinned, for instance, sunscreen may not be a dispensable item. Tailor the transitions according to your own needs and goals.

Mark Allen starts out the 1984 Ironman bike race in a moderate gear.

Drafting during the cycling portion is illegal in triathlons.

PART 2: CYCLING

THE FIRST FEW MILES

1 *Gear selection.* Once you are out of the transition area and on your bicycle, you should start out in a moderate gear, at 75 to 85 rpm's, for the first 100 yards. You should be able to regulate your optimum spinning speed based upon your experience in training.

At the start of the bike race, your blood is just beginning to circulate back into the major muscles of your legs; it takes a while for those muscles to become fully oxygenated again. When it comes to choice of gears, you are looking for a happy medium. If you use too fast a gear, it will force your muscles to contract too fast; too large a gear will require too much strength. Choose a gear that won't require excessive effort right away, but will work your legs enough to circulate blood there.

Sit down to begin with, establish a rhythm, then stand up to start gaining speed and to stretch your calves and Achilles tendons. After that, you can shift up into the gear you know you'll be able to handle for the first part of the race. That will be determined by the severity of the course, the wind, any hills, and how you feel after the swim.

2 *Relax.* Once you have established a rhythm and pace, concentrate on relaxing your arms, neck, and fingers. Drop your shoulders to relax your trapezius, loosen your grip on the handlebars, and move your head around.

3 *Find a comfortable position.* You may want to ride a little higher in the beginning, with your hands on the brake hoods. If you hunch over right away, with your hands on the drops, you will feel extra stress on your back and neck. Start higher and ease into a lower position.

Move your hands around. Find what works best for you. I often ride with one hand on the brake and the other on the drop. It is unconventional, but it alleviates some of the stress on my trapezius.

4 *Breathe easy.* Don't pant. Take long, deep inhales; exhale slowly and rhythmically. If

I enjoy time trialing, so I try to go all-out on the flats.

any of your clothing is constrictive, loosen or adjust it so that your breathing is unimpeded.

5   *Pedal rhythmically.* The rhythm is your own; it doesn't have to be a perfectly smooth circle. I try to pedal elliptically—pushing from 10 o'clock to 2 o'clock—to loosen my ankles. Stiff ankles compound the calf tightness that can follow a long swim.

THROUGHOUT THE BIKE COURSE

1   *Know which gears you need.* If you scouted out the course in advance, you should know the turns, the hills, the long flats, and so forth. If you have done that homework, you'll recognize which gears you need for each turn and grade, and you'll know whether you need to stand up or sit down or a combination of both.

2   *Use your strengths.* If you are a better hill climber, then that's when you can really make up time. If you're better on the flats, go all out there. Remember to monitor your

effort though, since excessive acceleration will cause you to start building up lactate.

I always concentrate effort on the gradual hills—the ones that mentally grind people down. When I feel my speed dropping—on steep hills (over 11 percent grade)—I relax and slacken my pace slightly to save my energy for the gradual hills and flats, where I know I can ride fast and make up time.

3   *Use the course.* On parts of the course where other riders might be especially cautious—bumpy roads or extreme turns, for instance—I increase my speed. *But never be reckless*—you can lose more than the race if you crash. If you have a chance to preview the course, you can ride those areas in advance so that you'll be able to actually speed up when other people slow down. Even if you are not as strong a rider as some of your competitors, you can make up time that way.

4   *Top off the hills swiftly.* When I get near the top of a hill, I accelerate to the crest, then shift into a larger gear and stand up to build up speed as quickly as possible on the downhill. It is much better to do that than to get to the top of the hill and pause to wipe your brow and take a drink of water—you can lose 10 or 15 seconds that way. You should drink before you get to the hills; since you are accelerating more slowly up a hill, there is less cooling wind and more dehydration.

I always pretend that there is an extra 20 or 30 feet at the top of the hill, so that after the crest I pedal four or five hard revolutions before I back off. When I do decrease my effort, I continue spinning, so that the lactate has a chance to diffuse.

THINKING AHEAD: PREPARING FOR THE RUN

The best transition is not an instant metamorphosis, but a gradual change, like a spectrum of color. While you were swimming, you avoided overkicking, to save your legs for cycling. While you are cycling, you should modify your technique to gradually prepare you for running. During the final two miles of an Ironman-distance bike course (final half-mile on a shorter USTS-distance event), there are several ways you can condition your body for the imminent run:

1 *Gear down*. The extra race effort, especially on a hilly course, elevates your lactate level; your leg muscles are bound to feel tense, as are your back muscles. Shifting into a lower gear and reducing your speed by one or two miles per hour will remove lactate and relieve some of that stiffness.

2 *Stand up and stretch*. To stretch your back and hip flexors, stand up periodically as you ride the final miles. With your hands on the brake hoods, push your hips toward the stem and drop one heel all the way down. Hold that position for two or three seconds, then alternate heels. That stretches your calves and Achilles tendons. Then look up slightly, arch your back, drop your arms (one at a time), and shake your hands and fingers. That will give your back a much-needed stretch, and alleviate any numbness in your hands.

3 *Don't forget your feet*. Inside a stiff-soled cycling shoe, your feet are relatively constricted. Strapped tightly onto the pedals, they are locked into a fixed position for most of the bike race. If you suddenly put on running shoes and require your feet to absorb the shock of running, you may be sorely disappointed. Throughout the entire bike race, you should wiggle your toes around inside your shoes and rotate your feet forward over the pedals to change the pressure on the balls of your feet.

4 *Vary your routine*. A circular pedaling pattern utilizes the same muscle fibers on every revolution. Vary your pedaling routine every 10 to 15 minutes to give each leg

a rest. Change your foot position slightly, move your knees in and out, and alternate the power emphasis from one leg to the next. This is especially important right before the run.

ANTICIPATE THE TRANSITION

Shortly before the bike-to-run transition—100 yards or so—loosen your shoes so that the blood flows freely to your feet. Undo your toe straps and the chin strap on your helmet.

When you are 20 to 30 yards away, you can pull your feet all the way out of your shoes. That should leave your shoes dangling in your toe straps, but there is always a chance they will fall off before you get to the bike rack. If you don't want to take the risk of losing your shoes or having to run back to collect them, it is better to skip this time-saving device.

You will be seated for much of the bike-to-run transition.

As you ride up to your spot on the rack—which you should already have memorized—shake your feet and wiggle your toes, shake your legs to loosen them up a bit, pull off your helmet, and cruise into your spot.

BIKE-TO-RUN TRANSITION

When I have parked my bicycle in the rack, I immediately sit down to change my shorts and put on my running shoes. Be careful not to extend your leg too quickly or strenuously when you first sit down; after a long bike ride, your muscles may cramp with any sudden changes.

If I am changing from cycling to running shorts, I do that first. Then I put on my shoes. (Your feet may be sweaty from the long bike ride; just step on the towel you have laid out—or in your bag—to dry them.) I don't wear socks, but most people do (to prevent blisters). My running shoes are already powdered inside, the tongues are pulled up, and the lock tab on the laces is pulled out so that the shoes are open enough for me to easily slip in my foot.

The whole time I am seated, I take sips of water and pour some over my head and shoulders to cool me off.

I quickly slip my feet in my shoes, tighten the lock tab, pull off my cycling jersey, stand up, and head out on the running course with my singlet in my hand. I put on the singlet within the first 30 to 40 yards, while I am running slowly.

PART 3: RUNNING

At my first Ironman, it took seven or eight miles on my feet for me to feel that I was running. I was used to feeling light on my feet, something like the television commercials where they show a guy running down the beach with the wind in his hair. This was nothing like that—it was more like a slow-motion videotape. My legs were throbbing; I had very little sense of real motion.

Since that time, I have learned to cushion the transition from cycling to running, and it becomes easier all the time. There are a number of ways to ease into the run and improve your performance at the same time:

1 *Maintain a low, shuffling stride.* Your hamstrings haven't been used that much during the cycling portion of the race, but your quadriceps may be stiff at first. It is difficult to move right into a fluid, long stride; that requires flexibility in your quadriceps, hamstrings, and hips. After a long bike ride, those muscles will be a bit stiff, so you should keep your heels low and your stride short.

2 *Pick up speed by taking more steps.* Don't

I use my arms to set my pace at the beginning of my run.

kick your heels high to try to force a longer stride. If you want to pick up your pace, increase the number and frequency of your shorter strides. Get up on your tiptoes if need be.

3   *Use your arms.* Swinging your arms will help propel you forward. I use my arms to set my pace at the very beginning of the run, and my legs usually loosen up within the first quarter-mile or so. Bring your hands by your hip joint, rather than up by your chest. But don't let them hang at your side.

4   *Wiggle your fingers.* When your hands are clenched, your trapezius is taut, and your upper back and neck can become stiff and sore. Open your hands from time to time and wiggle your fingers to alleviate the stress.

5   *Lean slightly forward.* Because of the limited range of motion you have had on the bike, it is difficult to immediately assume a smooth runner's form. Your back, hips, and hamstrings are all tight. Try to keep from running too vertically—straight up and down—by shifting the focus of your eyes slightly downward.

6   *Enjoy your surroundings.* Naturally you have to concentrate on technique when you run, but taking in the surroundings and acknowledging the people along the course will help you to relax. Though I am often characterized as "burning holes through the pavement" with my eyes, I am actually aware of people around me while I am running. I try to alternate from sheer concentration for a while, to relaxing and talking to people as I pass, then back to concentration, and so on. It is not good to get so ingrained in your task at hand that the race becomes unnecessarily stressful.

THE FINISH LINE

Congratulations! You finished the race and hopefully met your goals. But don't just stop cold or you will be stiff and sore.

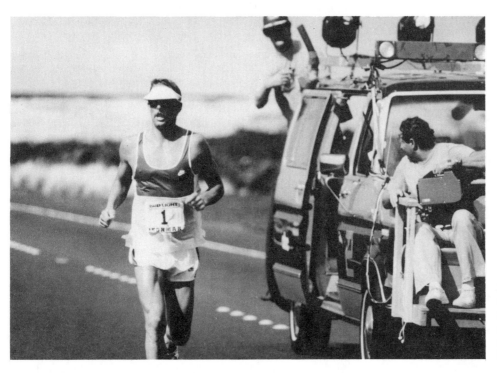

I like to pay attention to people around me, then turn my concentration back to the matter at hand—racing.

1 *After you cross the line, keep on moving.* Walk around for another three to five minutes. Gently shake your arms and legs. Do not go right to the massage table—you need that extra few minutes' cool-down to remove lactate.

2 *Drink lots of fluid.* Don't stop drinking just because the race is over. You have lost fluids during the race and now is the time to rehydrate.

3 *Eat something.* Even if you don't have much of an appetite, you should eat something very light to keep your blood sugar stable. Don't overdo it, though. A banana or a rice cake is just about right.

4 *If it's hot, get in the shade.* You have been in the sun all day—take a much-needed break from the heat and the glare.

5 *Stay warm.* When you stop exercising, your body temperature will start to drop, and you can easily get chilled. Put on a T-shirt or a light jacket to keep your torso warm.

6 *Do some easy stretches.* Very gently stretch your hips, legs, and lower back (see page 173).

7 *Get medical attention if you need it.* If you feel as though your body has basically shut down after a triathlon, or if you are dizzy or need support to stand, if you are nauseous and don't feel hungry or thirsty—you have probably depleted your glycogen stores, and you should allow the race doctor to determine whether you need an intravenous replenishment of glucose.

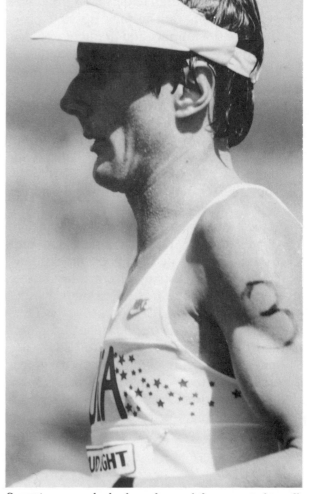

Sometimes your body shuts down while your mind is still on automatic pilot. (Pictured: Mark Allen, above; Patricia Puntous, opposite, left; myself, opposite right.)

After the 1984 Ironman, I spent about 15 minutes talking with reporters at the finish line. My wife Anna and my friend Pat Feeney were standing on each side of me for physical as well as moral support. After the impromptu press conference, I felt light-headed and a bit weak, so I chose to recuperate inside ABC's air-conditioned van. Thirty minutes—and almost that many rice cakes—later, I had recovered enough to get a post-race massage and socialize with my friends and family.

Fortunately, my level of aerobic and overall fitness allowed me to recover rapidly; I would not recommend that procedure for everyone. It is much safer—and easier—to let the race doctor advise and treat you if necessary.

WHEN SHOULD YOU DROP OUT OF A RACE?

For the average triathlete (if there is such a thing) the most basic goal of a race is to finish—that is understood. Nobody wants to

drop out early. But there are times when no other choice makes sense.

At the 1985 Nice Triathlon, I was bitterly disappointed when a flat tire put me out of commission. But the course was so steep and curvy that it wouldn't have been safe to put on a new tire that might have come unglued on a 50-mph downhill. As I told the television crew there, I value my life more than a race.

You have to weigh the risks at each race. It is unsportsmanslike to quit just because you are behind, but it is foolish to continue if doing so could harm your good health. I have had to drop out of a couple of races because of injuries that would have jeopardized the rest of my racing season.

Everybody wants to finish, but it is not worth ruining your health. If any of the follow-ing signs occur while you are racing, you should stop and seek medical attention:

1 You are no longer thirsty.
2 You stop sweating.
3 You get chills, or feel clammy.
4 Your performance falls off 20 percent or more.
5 You get disoriented or are unable to hear or focus clearly.

(Top-level athletes occasionally choose to keep going when symptoms such as the above occur, but they do so only because they know their recovery responses are especially rapid and their systems are trained to withstand those demands.)

9 YOU ARE WHAT YOU EAT: A CHAMPION'S DIET

I once ate a Zoo all by myself. A Zoo is an eight-and-a-half-pound mountain of ice cream covered by a half-gallon of caramel, butterscotch, pineapple, cherry, and hot fudge toppings, then topped with a half-quart of whipped cream and two cups of chopped nuts. In less than two hours, I consumed 9,867 sticky calories, 1,283 grams of carbohydrates, 1,492 grams of cholesterol, and 533 grams—more than a pound—of pure fat.

When I finally staggered out of the ice cream parlor—glassy-eyed and light-headed—I looked and felt as though I were drunk. It was a hard-fought victory, but I had proven

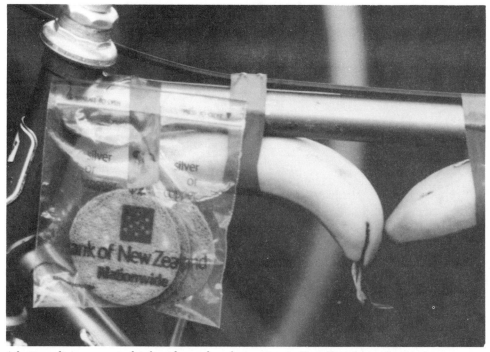

Adroit cyclists can eat, drink, ride, and soak up vitamin D—all at the same time!

that I could eat more ice cream than anyone on record at the University of California at Davis.

It may have been a dubious achievement, but it was not entirely without merit; the resulting stomach ache forced me to reevaluate my eating habits. Within a year, I went from an All-American diet of meat and potatoes and mom's apple pie to a meatless menu that was low-fat, low-sugar, and high in complex carbohydrates.

As an athlete, I had become interested in food as fuel. I found that eating red meat— mostly at dinner—gave me indigestion and restless nights. So I cut out red meat and fat. My passion for sugary foods such as pie and ice cream had led to dramatic fluctuations in performance; my energy sometimes dropped to the point where I needed afternoon naps. So I cut down on simple sugars. And finally, I found that I just didn't have as much endurance as I wanted, so I increased my intake of complex carbohydrates—the most immediate source of fuel.

Nutrition experts now agree that the most efficient fuel for athletic performance is also the best diet for good health. Eliminating excess fats and sugars lowers cholesterol and triglycerides, greatly decreasing the possibility of heart attacks or strokes. Cutting back on concentrated protein (red meat) improves digestion and decreases toxic by-products such as uric acid. And many foods that are rich in complex carbohydrates—such as whole grains—are rich in fiber as well, doubling the health benefit.

To compete at an optimal level, I have to provide my engine with optimal fuel. Athletes who adhere to the notion that all calories were created equal are really short-changing themselves. The quality of calories varies tremendously; if your calories are derived from an excessive amount of fat or protein, your overall capacity for endurance is going to suffer.

Some few top-level athletes perform well despite poor diets, but they are probably not performing to their own potential. Marathon

CALORIES BURNED PER MINUTE: CYCLING, RUNNING, SWIMMING*
(IN RELATION TO BODY WEIGHT)

	WEIGHT (POUNDS)							
	100	120	140	160	180	200	220	240
CYCLING								
10 MPH	5	7	8	9	10	11	12	13
15 MPH	8	9	10	12	13	14	16	17
20 MPH	13	14	16	17	18	19	21	22
25 MPH	18	19	20	21	22	23	24	25
30 MPH	23	24	25	26	27	28	30	33
RUNNING								
10 MIN/MILE	7	8	10	12	14	16	18	20
8 MIN/MILE	9	11	14	16	18	19	21	23
6 MIN/MILE	12	14	18	20	21	22	25	28
5 MIN/MILE	13	16	20	22	24	26	29	34
SWIMMING (CRAWL)								
30 MIN/MILE	6	7	9	10	11	12	13	14
22 MIN/MILE	13	14	15	16	19	20	21	22
17 MIN/MILE	16	17	19	20	21	24	25	28

*Use this chart to compute calorie expenditure based on the duration and the intensity of your workout, and your body weight. Each workout the caloric expenditure could be closely estimated.

runner Bill Rodgers, for example, is notorious for eating junk food. He has performed well, but never to the heights that his level of talent suggests he could have.

Jim Fixx was another runner who exercised religiously but ate lots of fats and sugars. His genetic predisposition to heart disease was fulfilled at an early age, due partially to an extremely high cholesterol intake, and he died of a heart attack.

Athletic ability and aerobic fitness alone do not guarantee optimum performance or even good health—you have to burn "clean" fuel.

FOOD BREAKDOWN: PROTEIN, FAT, CARBOHYDRATES

After I dropped red meat, simple sugars, and excess fats from my diet, I tried to find out what ratio of protein, fat, and carbohydrates I should eat. At that time, there were as many opinions as there were so-called experts. So I researched nutrition, and eventually developed an optimum diet for health as well as athletic performance.

One of the first things I discovered was that my performance was consistent when my weight and caloric intake were stable. Like most people, I had lost weight when I cut excess fat from my diet; fat contains 9 calories per gram, while protein and carbohydrates contain only 4. In order to maintain my caloric intake, I had to eat a lot more food in general, or eat foods that were richer in either protein or carbohydrates. Because eating too much protein has many negative side effects, I chose to increase my consumption of complex carbohydrates—whole grains, vegetables, fruits, legumes, etc.

PROTEIN

Almost every substance in your body—bones, muscles, hair, cell membranes, arteries, hormones, and enzymes—is made up of protein. You need a certain amount of protein for growth of body tissue, and it is also useful as a fuel after your fat and carbohydrate stores have been depleted.

But excess protein isn't good for you. It can be very dehydrating; it takes nearly eight times as much water to burn a calorie of protein as to burn a calorie of fat or carbohydrate. It can also put undue stress on your kidneys and liver.

HOW MUCH PROTEIN DO I NEED?   When doctors and nutritionists first learned that muscle mass was composed primarily of protein, they assumed that an increase in protein intake would result in an increase in muscle mass. Athletes, they figured, needed great amounts of protein in their diet to rebuild muscles that were torn down during physical activity.

That theory has now been proven false. Your body can only use a limited amount of protein per day—about four fifths of a gram (.8) per kilogram of body weight (1 pound = .4536 kilogram). I weigh about 73 kilograms; I need 58 to 60 grams—about 250 calories—of protein per day.

Another general rule of thumb is to eat around 10 percent of your total calories in protein. If you are working out a lot and eating more calories per day, your protein intake will increase somewhat.

CAN I LOSE MUSCLE MASS BY NOT EATING ENOUGH PROTEIN?   It is more a matter of not eating enough useful fuel—primarily carbohydrates. In a long race (more than four hours) or repeated workout days with high mileage and high intensity, muscle tissue will break down. If you eat too few calories or too much junk food, you won't store enough glycogen in your muscles and liver for fuel, so you will begin to use protein as a source of energy. If you start losing muscle mass, you might want to add four to eight grams of protein to your daily diet, in addition to an increase of complex carbohydrates. Just because your muscle diameter is decreasing, however, does not necessarily mean you are losing muscle mass. Increased training and proper diet displaces fat to muscle tissue, so you will be leaner, but no less muscular.

**WHAT HAPPENS WHEN I EAT TOO MUCH PRO-
TEIN?** If you eat too much of anything, you will gain weight and accumulate more body fat—that goes without saying. So if you load up on more protein than you can use, the excess will be stored as fat.

In the process, according to the late Nathan Pritikin, a leading nutrition expert, ". . . protein . . . has to rid itself of its ammonia molecules, which are left as waste products." Ammonia is toxic to the cells and difficult to eliminate— that's why Pritikin said that protein does not "burn clean."

The toxic waste products must be diluted with large amounts of water in order to be excreted through the urine without damaging the kidneys, which makes high-protein diets very dehydrating.

Eating a lot of protein before or during a race can therefore be very dangerous. In hot or humid weather, the problems are compounded because your body will not be able to cool itself.

Excess protein also tends to prevent mineral absorption, particularly absorption of calcium. For that reason, some physiologists believe that athletes who eat a lot of protein are subject to osteoporosis—brittle bones—caused by calcium deficiency. Vegetarians who do not eat dairy products as a protein source may be especially vulnerable to calcium deficiency, and should take calcium supplements. (See page 223.)

DO I HAVE TO EAT MEAT TO GET "COMPLETE PROTEINS?" Contrary to the sermons of many aging football coaches, you don't have to eat meat to be strong and healthy. While no single vegetable has all eight of the essential amino amids, you can easily combine nonmeat foods for complete protein. Peanut butter, for example, is high in protein, but low in one particular amino acid—methionine. Whole wheat bread has plenty of methionine, so when you combine the two in a sandwich, the protein is complete. If you drink a glass of nonfat milk with two peanut butter sandwiches, you will get nearly half of your daily protein require-

ment. (The nonfat milk provides 6 to 8 grams of protein, and is even higher in calcium than low-fat or whole milk.)

There is an almost endless variety of complete-protein combinations within a vegetarian diet, especially if you eat dairy foods. Do you like Italian food? Any kind of pasta with cheese is a complete protein. How about Mexican food? Tacos, burritos, enchiladas, and rice and beans all contain complete proteins. The list is limited only by your imagination.

FATS

Fats—or *lipids*—are a necessary part of your diet, because they are a source of stored energy. They enable you to absorb vitamins A, D, E, and K. But certain fats are bad for you, and too much of any fat can interfere with circulation, digestion, and vitamin and mineral absorption.

FATS

SATURATED FATS

ALL WHOLE MILK DAIRY PRODUCTS: MILK
     CHEESE, SOUR CREAM, BUTTER, CREAM

EGG YOLK

CHOCOLATE

MEAT (RED AND POULTRY, PORK)

VEGETABLE SHORTENING

COCONUT OIL

MONOUNSATURATED FATS

PEANUTS (PEANUT BUTTER AND PEANUT OIL)

OLIVES (OLIVE OIL)

AVOCADO

CASHEWS

POLYUNSATURATED FATS

CORN OIL

SAFFLOWER OIL

SOYBEAN OIL   }   VEGETABLE OILS

SUNFLOWER OIL

COD LIVER OIL

WALNUTS, ALMONDS, PECANS, FILBERTS

FISH

WHAT ARE FATS? Fats come in three forms: saturated, monounsaturated and polyunsaturated. Saturated fats are from animal sources (except coconut oil) and are usually hard at room temperature.

WHAT IS CHOLESTEROL? The word "cholesterol" comes from the Greek words *chole* (bile) and *sterol* (solid). It is a fatlike substance found mostly in digestive bile, and is produced primarily by your liver. Your body will produce all the cholesterol you need, whether you eat any or not.

Present in all blood serum, it is essential to your health. It aids hormone production and surrounds nerve fibers like a protective sheath, and helps assimilate fat via bile acids. But too much cholesterol can cause *coronary arteriosclerosis*—blockage of blood flow between the arteries and the heart. That disease kills more Americans annually than every other cause of death combined.

Several factors can contribute to arteriosclerosis: heredity, cigarette smoking, stress, hypertension or high blood pressure, poor diet, obesity, diabetes, and lack of exercise.

WHAT DOES EXERCISE HAVE TO DO WITH CHOLESTEROL? Cholesterol is transported through the bloodstream by three types of fat proteins—high-density lipoproteins (HDL), low-density lipoproteins (LDL), and very low density lipoproteins (VLDL). High-density lipoproteins are larger than the others, and tend to break cholesterol away from the artery wall, while low-density and very low density lipoproteins tend to cling to it. Aerobic exercise increases the amount of HDL in the bloodstream, thereby allowing cholesterol to break away from the artery walls and to be transported to the liver, where it is broken down. That is one of the benefits of becoming an aerobically fit endurance athlete.

Be careful, though: some studies suggest that athletes who forsake their exercise program and eat high-fat diets are more prone to heart attacks than people who were sedentary all along. Apparently, your body becomes dependent upon the aerobic exercise to properly dissipate the cholesterol, and is doubly taxed when the exercise stops.

HOW MUCH CHOLESTEROL SHOULD I EAT EACH DAY? Doctors know that each individual has a different capacity to metabolize cholesterol; most experts agree that heredity is a major factor. But medical studies indicate that you don't need to take in any cholesterol in your diet after early childhood. In fact, more than 250 milligrams (the amount in an average egg yolk) per day is deemed to be excessive by many cardiologists.

Don't fool yourself into thinking that a vegetarian diet automatically guarantees low cholesterol or low fat. If you eat too much cheese, eggs, and whole milk, you can take in as much fat and cholesterol as someone who eats meat.

WHAT HAPPENS TO THE FATS I EAT? Fats are also called triglycerides. *Tri* is three, *glycerides* are fatty acids. When you exercise, those three fatty acids which are stored in the muscles and in adipose (fatty tissue) break away from the adipose and diffuse into the bloodstream for use as fuel. Any fatty acids not used as fuel will be immediately redeposited in adipose. Obviously, if you overeat, the excess will increase your fatty tissue.

WHAT SHOULD MY FAT INTAKE BE? Keep your fat intake down to 10 to 15 percent of your total calories. If you eat an excessive amount of fat, the problems are more than cosmetic. Fat will bind with red blood cells, causing them to clump within the arteries, inhibiting circulation and ultimately decreasing the amount of oxygen carried to your working muscles. If the percentage of fat to carbohydrates is too high, you will not be able to sufficiently replace glycogen stores from day to day, and your endurance capacity will decrease significantly.

In addition to decreased athletic performance, a high fat intake has been linked to colon cancer, prostate cancer, heart disease, high blood pressure, and skin problems.

ARE THERE ANY ADVANTAGES TO BEING A LITTLE BIT FAT? A lot of swimmers think that a little fat gives them an advantage because it makes them more buoyant, adds a layer of insulation against the cold water, and is available for fuel in long-term exercise. But the advantages are greatly outweighed by the disadvantages in cycling and running. I have seen many full-bodied triathletes have a great swim, and a fairly good bike ride (if it's a flat course where they don't have to push their weight uphill), but they just can't compete in the run.

WHAT HAPPENS TO THE EXCESS CALORIES I EAT? Excess calories—whether they are from fat, protein, or carbohydrates—end up as fatty tissue. While the caloric density of fat is just about double that of protein and carbohydrates, a calorie in any form is still a calorie. If you take in more than you use, the surplus will be stored as fatty tissue—and it is much easier to put on than it is to take off. A pound of pure fat is about 3,500 calories; to lose just one pound in a week (7 days), you would have to cut back your daily intake by 500 calories. On the other hand, you could gain that pound in one day by eating a couple of pieces of bacon and a chocolate bar in addition to your stabilized daily maximum. If you eat mostly carbohydrates, you get twice as much food for your calories, so it is a little easier to control your weight.

SHOULD I EAT FATS BEFORE A RACE? Never eat excessive fats before a race. Because fat is digested very slowly, you can feel the cumulative effects of it in your bloodstream for 60 hours.

CARBOHYDRATES

Carbohydrates should be the most abundant food in your diet. Made of carbon, hydrogen, and oxygen molecules, they are the most readily available source of fuel. The principal carbohydrates are sugars, starches, and cellulose, but all carbohydrates must eventually be broken down to glucose to be used as a fuel.

Simple sugars (monosaccharides) are composed of a single sugar molecule—glucose, fructose, or galactose. They are easily digested, and are used by the brain and nervous system as well as the muscles. (When you get nervous or irritable, it is often due to low blood sugar.) However, these simple carbohydrates usually lack B vitamins, necessary for their conversion to energy, so you have to make sure you get a plentiful supply of those vitamins in your diet and/or supplements. Simple sugars may also cause your pancreas to produce excess insulin. (See "The Carbo-Loading Fallacy, page 216.")

Starches and double-sugars (disaccharides) require prolonged enzyme action in order to break down to glucose for use as a fuel. Disaccharides contain two sugar molecules; sucrose (table sugar) is a combination of glucose and fructose (fruit sugar), for example, and maltose (malt sugar) is a combination of two glucose molecules.

At the 1983 Ironman, I ate throughout the entire race, but my glycogen stores were so depleted that I stll had to have an IV at the finish line.

Cellulose, such as the skins of fruit and vegetables, is a polysaccharide—made up of many glucose molecules. It takes a very long time for cellulose to break down to glucose for fuel, so it is not useful as an immediate source of energy. However, cellulose does aid your digestive process by providing bulk (fiber) in your diet.

Sugar storage: Sugar is stored in the form of glucose in your bloodstream, and glycogen in your liver and muscles.

CARBOHYDRATES IN YOUR DIET

The optimum performance diet is above 70 percent carbohydrates. The biggest limiting factor in triathlons is the amount of carbohydrates available as a source of fuel. Studies at Ball State University in Indiana showed that a diet composed of 50 to 60 percent carbohydrates was not sufficient to replenish glycogen stores after a strenuous endurance activity of more than two hours. Try to eat at least 70 percent, if not more. This means if you eat 3,000 calories a day, for example, 2,100 of those calories should come from carbohydrates.

Try to avoid "simple" sugar. When you eat fruits, (rather than juice), vegetables, beans, and grains, you are getting bulk as well as sugar itself. That bulk slows the immediate release of sugar in your bloodstream, which helps subdue the secretion of insulin from your pancreas. You must maintain as stable a blood sugar balance as possible, to avoid spurts of energy followed by sudden lapses.

Insulin is a hormone secreted by your pancreas to carry sugar to the cells for energy and storage. When you eat sugar, insulin "clears" it from your bloodstream. If there is a sudden influx of sugar in your bloodstream, there will be a corresponding influx of insulin to remove it. An overabundance of insulin will remove too much sugar—glucose—and you will lose necessary fuel. People often crave more sugar in response to a drop in blood glucose, but eating more simple sugar will only compound the problem.

If you want some quick energy from a candy bar or a Coke, remember that the burst will only last 7 to 10 minutes, and no longer. The only time it will do you any good is at the end of a race, and even then I don't recommend it, because it can further dehydrate you. However, if you are light-headed or slightly dizzy, you may need the sugar to get through that final few minutes, but be sure you plan it carefully, because you are going to feel a sudden drop afterward.

Know how to read food labels. Many food products have excessive sugar, salt, and fat added to them, but that fact is often disguised in the wording. For example, many products are sweetened with fructose, because it is the sweetest of the sugars. Since it is so sweet, they use a little less of it and call the product "low-sugar." Fructose, sucrose, glucose, maltose, and galactose are all sugar. Other forms of sugar include corn syrup, dextrin, dextrose, and honey.

Getting a drink at an aid station can be a challenge for the volunteer as well as the cyclist.

Many people believe that honey is "good for you" because it is "natural" and contains a few more minerals than table sugar, but it isn't any more natural than fruit and it contains a high concentration of fructose.

Try taking bread or potatoes with you on long rides. You have to keep your glycogen stores replenished, but sucking on a lollipop isn't the best way to do it. I sometimes bring a piece of bread, or a half of a baked potato, when I go for a long bicycle ride so that I can keep slow-acting carbohydrates in my system.

COMPLEX CARBOHYDRATE FOOD GROUPS

WHOLE GRAIN BREADS AND CEREALS

FRUITS

BEANS

POTATOES

PASTA

ALL GRAINS

PRE-RACE DIET

Your diet should be consistent year-round; there should be no distinctions between your normal diet and your training diet, other than an overall decrease in caloric intake during your less active periods. I believe in maintaining a high-complex-carbohydrate diet all the way up to a race.

THE CARBO-LOADING FALLACY

The idea of "carbo-loading" is supposedly to load your muscles and liver with glycogen before an endurance event. Three or four days before the race, you are supposed to do your last intense workout, generally about two hours, to deplete your glycogen stores. Then you starve yourself of carbohydrates by reducing your intake to about 10 or 20 percent of your total calories, and eat mostly fat and protein. The day before the race, you stuff yourself on starches and sugars, which—in theory—fill your muscles and liver with glycogen. Very few top athletes undergo the carbo-loading regimen anymore, because it can cause several problems:

1 *To change your diet that drastically, particularly if you were accustomed to 70 percent carbohydrates, would be extremely unhealthy.* With nothing but fat and protein in your system, you would be literally "running on empty"; your nervous system would be so starved that you would be extremely irritable at best.

2 *You would probably have a water retention problem.* For every gram of carbohydrates you take in, you retain up to a gram or two of water. Following several days of physical inactivity, your muscles and joints are especially susceptible to stiffness and bloating. You can also feel some angina pain, due to water retained in your heart tissue as a result of eating excessive carbohydrates.

3 *Putting that much fat in your bloodstream before a race is a major mistake.* As we discussed earlier, the effects of excessive fat in your bloodstream can be felt for up to 60 hours. You would be at a disadvantage to enter a race with a sluggish oxygen delivery system, regardless of how much fuel you had supposedly stored in your liver.

What kind of food is this triathlete hiding in his skin suit?

HOW MUCH SHOULD I EAT BEFORE A RACE?

In the days just prior to the race, you should adjust your diet to suit your expenditure of energy. The important thing is to make sure that your calories eaten balance with your calories expended, and are composed mostly of complex carbohydrates. The last thing you want to do is gain weight before a race, and it is very easy to do when you are tapering.

I usually eat a regular meal—mostly carbohydrates—a couple of days before the race. The day prior to the race, I eat very lightly.

WHAT TO EAT DURING A RACE

During a race you should be extremely careful about what you eat, because fatigue is directly related to food intake. You have to take in enough calories or you'll "hit the wall" when your muscles are depleted of available fuel.

On the other hand, if you eat too much, your pancreas will release extra insulin and your blood sugar will elevate dramatically right after you eat, then drop sharply. You'll feel a sudden surge of energy for 10 minutes or so, then you'll feel even more tired than before. Overeating will also draw fluid from your working muscles into your gastrointestinal tract (for digestion), which will inhibit the flow of plasma and oxygen to your muscles.

HOW MUCH DO I NEED TO EAT?

The amount of food you need is relative to your level of aerobic fitness. Your main source of energy is glycogen, which combines with fatty acids to form fuel. As you become more conditioned to prolonged aerobic exercise, your body is able to use less glycogen in proportion to fatty acids, which enables you to run longer on less food (caloric intake).

Every physical activity burns calories—some more than others. The amount of time you spend engaged in an aerobic activity—not necessarily the intensity at which you do it—determines how many calories you burn. I burned about 8,400 calories in just over nine hours at the October 1982 Ironman. If it takes you 12 hours to finish the same race, you'll probably burn about 10,400 calories—more if your run is proportionately longer.

The amount of calories you have available for fuel is a function of your size. It doesn't change with increased fitness. However, your muscles will store more glycogen after being

aerobically trained. Also, you will have an increased ability to conserve those calories for later use. Someone my size—six feet tall, 160 pounds—has about 3,500 available calories in the form of glycogen, but nearly 50,000 calories in fatty acids. Obviously, if I am more fit and can use more fatty acid calories for fuel, I won't need to eat as much in order to replenish glycogen.

The only way to determine your optimal food intake is to find out at what point your system becomes depleted of glycogen. Obviously, you don't want to find that out at a race. Incorporate high-intensity mini-triathlons (or time trials) in your training. Keep track of how many calories you eat, how many you expend, and how you feel during and after the exercise. Also consider the previous day's caloric intake and expenditure. Keep cutting back your intake until you come close to "hitting the wall." Then you'll know your minimum intake at that time; don't forget that your ability to use fatty acids for fuel will increase as you become more aerobically fit. Keep experimenting.

WHAT TYPE OF FOOD SHOULD I EAT?

Whether you eat simple sugars (glucose and fructose) or complex sugars (sucrose), they generally appear in your bloodstream fairly rapidly. You'll feel the effect of a banana or fig as soon as a candy bar. Most people will feel a slight pickup within 5 or 10 minutes of eating. After three to four hours of intense effort, I have felt a surge of energy within a minute of eating a dried fig.

Sugar seems to be the quickest source of energy. But in order to avoid a sharp decline in energy following an initial sugar-induced surge, you should keep your glycogen stores replenished as you go along. Don't wait until you are depleted to pop a fig or a banana in your mouth. Keep your blood sugar level as stable as possible.

Mark Allen nourishes himself while he rides.

The sugar content of your drink during a race should be 2 to 3 percent. In carbonated drinks, the sugar content is 10 to 15 percent, in Gatorade and other electrolyte replacement drinks it is 6 to 8 percent, and in candy bars, it is as high as 50 percent. There are many suitable soft drinks on the market; read the labels to make sure the sugar content is 2 to 3 percent.

Most top triathletes eat fruit of some kind during a race. I prefer dried figs because they are calorically dense (35 to 50 calories per fig) and high in fructose. They are not as bulky as bananas or oranges—typical triathlon fare—so I can carry them easily in the pouch on my jersey.

Hopefully we will find a perfect liquid fuel that is isotonically balanced—moves in and out of a blood cell equally easily—so that we can have the benefit of food without the bulk.

VITAMINS AND MINERALS

Vitamins are essential organic compounds found in various foods. They have no caloric value, but they are necessary for good health and are especially important to athletes in that they help regulate your metabolism and aid in the conversion of fat and carbohydrates to energy.

Unlike other essential substances—such as hormones and cholesterol—your body does not manufacture any of its own vitamins and minerals. All of them must be eaten or taken in supplements (except vitamin D, which can be absorbed from sunlight).

Fat-soluble vitamins (A, D, E, and K) are stored in your body, while water-soluble vitamins (B and C) are easily lost through excretion. If you take in an excessive amount of vitamin B or C, you will pass the excess through your urine. A surplus of A, D, E, or K, however, is often stored in the liver and kidneys. Those vitamins may have a toxic effect if taken in too great an amount.

Minerals are inorganic compounds essential to good health. They are also found in various foods. Electrolytes—minerals which help transmit electrical impulses from your nerves to your muscles—include sodium, potassium, chromium, and calcium. Some of those electrolytes are water-soluble and can be lost by overcooking food or through perspiration when you exercise, but your body has a remarkable ability to conserve minerals.

There are two basic types of minerals: macrominerals (needed in large amounts each day) and microminerals (needed in trace amounts).

SHOULD I TAKE SUPPLEMENTS?

There is an ongoing controversy about vitamin and mineral supplements. Some people swear by vitamin pills; others contend they are merely a source of "expensive urine." It is true that you can get all—or most—of the vitamins you need in your diet, but only if you know the food sources of each vitamin and plan each day's diet carefully to include all the vitamins you need. Most people do not know how much of each vitamin they can get through each food source, and do not plan each meal so that no major vitamin or mineral is missing.

Eating more food, more calories, does not mean you are getting more vitamins. When you increase your food intake, you are probably eating more of the same types of foods, so you

TRIATHLETE'S RDA

VITAMIN A: 5,000 IU

VITAMIN B COMPLEX: 20 TO 50 MG

VITAMIN C: 200 TO 400 MG

VITAMIN D: 400 IU

VITAMIN E: 30 TO 60 IU

IRON: 20 TO 30 MG (MORE FOR MENSTRUATING WOMEN)

CALCIUM: 200 TO 600 MG (MORE FOR WOMEN)

MAGNESIUM: 350 MG

POTASSIUM: 200 TO 400 MG

PHOSPHORUS: 600 TO 1,000 MG

ZINC: 10 TO 30 MG

IODINE: 100 MG

are not increasing the variety of vitamins and minerals in your diet. Since most vitamins work together, it is crucial to include all of them (not just an overdose of one or two of them) each day. For that reason, I definitely recommend taking supplements.

A healthy daily dose of vitamins can supplement your diet and aid performance, but remember: No vitamin is a magic potion. If you want to swim, bike, and run farther or faster, you have to do it yourself.

TRIATHLETES' RECOMMENDED DAILY ALLOWANCE

The Food and Drug Administration has established a daily dosage (RDA) of vitamins and minerals for the average person, but triathletes need to increase some of those dosages to meet the demands of endurance training. In addition to a well-rounded diet, I recommend taking the following daily supplements:

VITAMIN A

This vitamin is fat-soluble, which means that excess amounts you ingest will be stored in your body, not excreted through your urine. Do not take a vitamin A supplement unless you know your diet is deficient—the excess can be toxic. If your skin color takes on a slightly yellow or orange tone, you may have a vitamin A toxicity.

WHAT IT DOES FOR YOU. Vitamin A maintains skin and mucous membranes, may lower blood cholesterol, and protects bladder, kidneys, and lungs. It helps build strong bones and maintains eyesight; it seems to particularly aid night vision. If you are running or riding in the evening, and you have trouble seeing in the dim light, you may have a vitamin A deficiency. This is particularly common in the winter, when food sources of vitamin A are limited.

RECOMMENDED DAILY ALLOWANCE (RDA). 5,000 IU

FOOD SOURCES. Yellow and orange fruits and vegetables (squash, carrots, cantaloupe, peaches, etc.), cod liver oil, tomatoes, dairy products, broccoli, Brussels sprouts, and green pepper (very high in vitamin A). The yellow and orange vegetables produce a chemical (hydrocarbon) called carotene in the formation of vitamin A. If you get too much carotene, your skin develops an orangish color, as mentioned above. ("Tanning" pills sold in drug stores use carotene to help produce the illusion of a suntan.) Carrots are particularly high in carotene.

THE B-VITAMIN COMPLEX

These vitamins and co-enzymes provide the body with energy by converting carbohydrates into glucose for use as a fuel. They also metabolize fat and protein, aid the neuromuscular system, and improve muscle tone. They work best when combined with vitamin C. B vitamins must be taken together, so it is best to take a B-complex supplement rather than trying to take each B vitamin separately.

VITAMIN B₁ (THIAMINE)

WHAT IT DOES FOR YOU. Thiamine breaks carbohydrates down into glucose, and helps improve muscle tone. If you are deficient in thiamine, you will accumulate lactic acid more rapidly. On a hilly course or in a race where you have to work near your anaerobic threshold most of the time, the last thing you want is for a vitamin deficiency to accelerate lactic acid build-up and cramps.

RDA. The RDA of vitamin B_1 is only 1.5 milligrams, but I suggest that you double that amount. If you are taking a supplement in the form of a B complex, the individual amounts of each B vitamin will be listed on the label.

FOOD SOURCES. Brown rice and potatoes are rich in B_1, along with brewer's yeast, wheat germ, blackstrap molasses, bran, soybeans, and some meats. I eat a phenomenal amount of rice cakes and potatoes, so I know I get plenty of these vitamins!

VITAMIN B₂ (RIBOFLAVIN)

WHAT IT DOES FOR YOU. Helps break down carbohydrates as well as fats and proteins. It also aids in respiration, clear vision, and maintenance of skin, nails, and hair.

RDA. 1.7 mg.

FOOD SOURCES. Brewer's yeast, eggs, green leafy vegetables, lima beans, peas, wheat germ.

VITAMIN B₃ (Niacin)

WHAT IT DOES FOR YOU. Aids in breakdown and utilization of carbohydrates, fats, and proteins. It also reduces blood cholesterol levels and improves circulation.

RDA. 20 mg.

FOOD SOURCES. Lean meat, poultry, fish, peanuts, brewer's yeast, wheat germ, soybeans.

VITAMIN B₆ (Pyridoxine)

WHAT IT DOES FOR YOU. Aids in breakdown and utilization of carbohydrates, fats, and proteins. It also maintains the balance of sodium and potassium, which promotes proper functioning of the nervous and musculoskeletal systems. Some people believe that B_6 helps prevent leg cramps, especially during the transitions, when circulation may be relatively poor.

RDA. 2 mg.

FOOD SOURCES. Fish, grains, soybeans, bananas, wheat germ, tofu, green leafy vegetables, pecans, brewer's yeast, some meats.

VITAMIN B₁₂ (Cobalamin)

WHAT IT DOES FOR YOU. Aids in fat, protein, and carbohydrate metabolism; forms red blood cells. Aids in proper functioning of nervous tissues (aids coordination).

RDA. 6 mcg.

FOOD SOURCES. Dairy products (cheese, milk, eggs), brewer's yeast, wheat germ, fish, some organ meats.

BIOTIN

WHAT IT DOES FOR YOU. Helps in making fatty acids and in oxidizing fatty acids and carbohydrates.

RDA. 0.3 mg.

FOOD SOURCES. Brewer's yeast, brown rice, soybeans, soy flour, egg yolk, fish, grains, oats, chicken.

PANTOTHENIC ACID

WHAT IT DOES FOR YOU. Aids in utilization of other vitamins, as well as the metabolism of fats, proteins, and carbohydrates. Stimulates the adrenal glands and aids nerves. If you are restless at night, or feel chronically fatigued, or lose your appetite even though you are exercising, you may have a pantothenic acid deficiency. If you have a considerable amount of stress on the job or in your personal life, you will need a greater amount of this co-enzyme to dissipate the stress.

RDA. 10 mg.

FOOD SOURCES. Organ meats, (but remember they are high in cholesterol), brewer's yeast, egg yolks, whole grain cereals, soybeans, sunflower seeds, peas, peanuts, peanut butter.

FOLIC ACID

WHAT IT DOES FOR YOU. Helps break down proteins, form red blood cells, form nucleic acid (for growth and reproduction of cells).

RDA. 1 mg.

FOOD SOURCES. Green leafy vegetables, asparagus, endive, turnips, potatoes, beans, peas, black-eyed peas, orange juice, brewer's yeast, liver.

PABA (Para Aminobenzoic Acid)

WHAT IT DOES FOR YOU. Helps break down and utilize protein, forms blood cells, prevents sunburn. You can take it internally or use it topically, as in a sunscreen cream on your skin. Since triathletes spend a great deal of time outdoors, I recommend eating plenty of foods rich in PABA.

RDA. Not established.

FOOD SOURCES. Yeast, wheat germ, eggs, grains, molasses.

VITAMIN C (Ascorbic Acid)

Because vitamin C seems to break down excess mucous, it has been used to "cure" everything from the common cold to urinary tract infections. Dr. Linus Pauling, the famous cancer researcher, claims that an abundance of vitamin C can aid in preventing many forms of cancer.

Vitamin C works hand in hand with the B vitamins and iron, which is important to vegetarian triathletes who may be slightly anemic. Supplementing your diet with additional vitamin C will enhance iron absorption from non-meat sources.

Proponents of vitamin C have said that it is impossible to take too much; since it is water-soluble, any excess will be excreted through your urine. But even though you may not develop vitamin C toxicity, there is evidence that you can get "too much of a good thing" in certain situations. Soviet medical researchers who studied pregnant women discovered a relationship between excessive levels of vitamin C and miscarriages within the first three months of pregnancy. If you are pregnant, you may want to avoid megadoses of this vitamin.

WHAT IT DOES FOR YOU. In addition to the benefits listed above, vitamin C aids the development of red blood cells, helps dissipate stress, maintains collagen (a protein necessary for developing strong connective tissue), fights bacterial infections, and promotes strong teeth and bones.

RDA. 200 to 400 mg.

FOOD SOURCES. Fresh fruits (especially citrus, cantaloupes, honeydew melons), tomatoes, broccoli, and green peppers (very high).

VITAMIN D

Most triathletes get all the vitamin D they need from their normal diet and exposure to natural sunlight, but if you are a vegetarian who does not eat any dairy products, you may want to take a supplement. Vitamin D helps absorb calcium and magnesium, which is vital to proper neuromuscular transmissions; a deficiency can cause muscle spasms (not common in the United States).

WHAT IT DOES FOR YOU. Enhances calcium absorption for strong teeth and bones, protects against muscle weakness, prevents nearsightedness.

RDA. 400 IU.

FOOD SOURCES. Egg yolks, fish, cod liver oil.

VITAMIN E

Before the 1984 Olympics in Los Angeles, scores of athletes came to Southern California to train—and acclimate—in the smog. Local newspapers warned runners that jogging 30 or 40 miles a week in the smog would have the same effect on their lungs as smoking 10 to 20 cigarettes a day. Vitamin E can prevent some of that effect because it is an antioxidant; it keeps the oxygen you inhale from combining with the pollutants.

WHAT IT DOES FOR YOU. In addition to being an anti-oxidant, vitamin E is an anticoagulant and an antithrombin. It keeps your blood "thinned" and flowing freely, and it dissolves clots. It may also lower blood cholesterol. For all those reasons, it is used in the prevention and treatment of heart disease. It is a treatment for skin abrasions and burns, and it prevents scarring. It may also relieve some of the symptoms of arthritis and bursitis.

RDA. 30 to 60 IU.

FOOD SOURCES. Most vegetable oils, wheat germ, soybean oil, safflower oil, all seeds, eggs, milk, peanuts, grains, wheat, rice, cabbage, asparagus.

VITAMIN K

WHAT IT DOES FOR YOU. It is essential in blood clotting, and has been used to treat hemorrhages, nosebleeds, and menstrual cramps. Some researchers believe it is useful in the treatment of cancer and that it can prevent cerebral palsy.

RDA. Not established

FOOD SOURCES. Green leafy vegetables, carrot tops, kale, pork, liver, safflower, fish, soybeans, potatoes, asparagus, cabbage, tomatoes.

CALCIUM

The old home remedy of a glass of warm milk has probably gotten more insomniacs through sleepless nights than all of the sleeping pills on the market combined. Milk is one of nature's richest sources of calcium, which calms your nerves, regulates a relaxed pulse, and allows you to rest. Triathletes need all of those attributes.

At least half of the mineral volume in your system is—or should be—calcium. Vitamin C aids calcium absorption, while phosphorus and fats hinder it. Most soft drinks are high in phosphorus and should be avoided, especially during a race.

WHAT IT DOES FOR YOU. Calcium aids in the prevention of osteoporosis (brittle bones), calms nerves, aids in insomnia, helps normal blood clotting, and maintains rhythmic heart action. It is said to prevent leg and feet cramps as well as menstrual cramps (and premenstrual tension).

RDA. 1,000 to 1,200 mg.

FOOD SOURCES. Skim milk is actually higher in calcium than whole or low-fat milk. Blackstrap molasses contains even more calcium than milk. Also yogurt, cheese, salmon, spinach, kale, broccoli, cottage cheese, oranges, collard greens, whole grains.

PHOSPHORUS

Phosphorus, magnesium, and calcium all work together, in the sense that you must have calcium in order to absorb the other two. The ratio of calcium to phosphorus should be about 2.5 to 1; too much phosphorus will deplete calcium stores.

WHAT IT DOES FOR YOU. Phosphorus helps utilize carbohydrates, stimulates muscle contraction, and assures proper kidney functioning, all of which are very important in triathlons.

RDA. 800 mg.

FOOD SOURCES. Meat, poultry, fish, eggs, seeds, whole grains, and nuts.

MAGNESIUM

One of the functions of magnesium is to regulate body temperature. I take a daily calcium/magnesium (combined) supplement, which has probably helped me withstand the extreme temperature conditions at the Hawaii Ironman.

WHAT IT DOES FOR YOU. In addition to regulating body temperature, magnesium helps in the absorption of calcium. (It is best to take a combined supplement, which will keep the ratio in proper balance.) It is necessary for carbohydrate and amino acid (protein) metabolism, and helps stimulate muscle contractions.

RDA. 35 mg.

FOOD SOURCES. Dark green vegetables, seeds, nuts, soybeans, whole grains, peas, dry beans.

POTASSIUM

Potassium should be 3 to 5 percent of your total mineral content. But it maintains the proper pH (alkalinity) balance in your body fluids and works with sodium to regulate your water balance. A potassium deficiency can result in dehydration, which you want to avoid at all costs, especially during a race.

Potassium is water-soluble and is easily lost through urine, so you have to consciously maintain your potassium levels at all times while training or racing. It takes several hours for potassium to dissipate in your bloodstream, so you should eat small amounts often.

WHAT IT DOES FOR YOU. In addition to regulating body fluids, potassium helps release energy from glucose, stimulates muscle contraction, aids in regular bowel functions, and helps regulate your heartbeat.

RDA. 2,500 mg.

FOOD SOURCES. Oranges, bananas, potatoes (especially the peels), dried fruit (I prefer figs), sunflower seeds (unsalted), whole grains, peanut butter, green leafy vegetables.

IRON

Caffeine interferes with iron absorption, so cutting back on coffee and tea will be to your advantage, especially if you are a vegetarian who may already be somewhat iron-deficient. In any case, you should never drink coffee or tea directly before or after meals if you want to absorb the iron you eat.

Cooking in iron pots or skillets is also helpful, especially with acidic foods, such as tomato sauce, that will absorb iron from the pot's surface.

WHAT IT DOES FOR YOU. Produces hemoglobin, therefore aiding in oxygen transport. This is critical to triathletes. It also increases resistance to stress and infection, and helps prevent fatigue.

RDA. I recommend 6 to 8 mg for every 1,000 calories you eat.

FOOD SOURCES. Eggs, whole grain breads, wheat germ, lean meat (especially liver), brewer's yeast.

COPPER

Copper works directly with iron. It is not water-soluble, so excess amounts are stored in your tissues. Because many water supplies are carried through copper-plated pipes, there is an increasing tendency to accumulate toxic levels.

WHAT IT DOES FOR YOU. Along with iron, it helps form red blood cells and aids in oxygen transport. This is obviously important to triathletes.

RDA. Not established.

FOOD SOURCES. Dry beans, oysters, whole grains, almonds, legumes.

SULFUR

WHAT IT DOES FOR YOU. Helps in forming complete proteins (bonding amino acids) and in insulin production and release.

RDA. Not established.
FOOD SOURCES. Legumes, wheat germ, all wheat products, peanut butter, clams, fish.

CHLORIDE

Chloride combines with sodium to help regulate body fluids. The amount you need is so small that there is no RDA and you do not need to worry about getting enough in your diet.

CHROMIUM

WHAT IT DOES FOR YOU. Aids in carbohydrate utilization, metabolizes glucose, synthesizes fatty acids and cholesterol. Helps regulate blood sugar levels.
RDA. Not established
FOOD SOURCES. Unsaturated fats (such as corn oil), clams, brewer's yeast, liver, whole grains, lean meat.

MANGANESE

WHAT IT DOES FOR YOU. Necessary for carbohydrate, fat, and protein metabolism, promotes healthy skeletal development, aids neuromuscular coordination and equilibrium.
RDA. 8 mg.
FOOD SOURCES. Egg yolks, sunflower seeds, wheat germ, whole grains, dried peas and beans, brewer's yeast.

SELENIUM

Selenium works with vitamin E in some of its metabolic processes. The RDA has not been established, but it is found in broccoli, onions, tomatoes, and tuna, as well as bran and wheat germ. Only trace amounts are required; you need not worry about a supplement.

IODINE

WHAT IT DOES FOR YOU. Promotes proper thyroid function. (The thyroid is an endocrine gland that regulates body metabolism.)
RDA. 140 mcg.
FOOD SOURCES. Iodized salt, kelp, saltwater fish.

ZINC

WHAT IT DOES FOR YOU. Aids in absorption of B vitamins and phosphorus, may help reduce blood cholesterol, aids fertility, and promotes normal growth.
RDA. 20 mg.
FOOD SOURCES. Whole grains, wheat germ, liver, eggs, brewer's yeast.

FLUORIDE

WHAT IT DOES FOR YOU. Builds strong teeth and bones.
RDA. Not established
FOOD SOURCES. Fluoridated water and seafood. If you drink bottled water, you may want to take a fluoride capsule as a supplement, but it is usually not necessary.

DO I NEED ELECTROLYTE REPLACEMENT FLUIDS?

In long, humid races like the Ironman, you are likely to lose a fair amount of minerals through perspiration. In those kinds of races, you should take in a small amount of electrolyte replacement fluid, but mostly water. Most of the fluids on the market are far too high in potassium and sugar; water is then drawn away from your working muscles to your gastrointestinal tract in order to break down the sugar.

ALCOHOL AND CAFFEINE

Caffeine and alcohol are drugs. Caffeine increases the utilization of fats and spares the release of carbohydrates. Some triathletes believe it helps their performance. Alcohol has a quite different effect, but some triathletes like it, too. Walt Stack, a 75-year-old Ironman, rode the 1981 race with a six-pack of beer in each pannier, and finished the triathlon 24 hours later with a grin on his face. Who's going to argue with him?

CAN CAFFEINE AID PERFORMANCE?

In another study at Ball State University, several athletes ingested coffee without knowing it and all of them found that their performance improved markedly. They were able to exercise for 7 percent longer than without the coffee.

Caffeine stimulates your central nervous system, which essentially speeds up your rate of fat metabolism and cuts down the amount of muscle glycogen you use for fuel. It also triggers the release of insulin into your bloodstream, which lowers your blood sugar level—when your available sugar declines, you have to resort to fats for fuel.

But there is a negative side to that situation: When your blood sugar level is inconsistent, so is your performance. Also, coffee contains a lot of acid, and nobody wants a painful case of heartburn during a race. Finally, caffeine is a diuretic—it stimulates excess urination and you lose water—which can severely compound dehydration in hot, humid climates like Hawaii. It can also make you nauseous, particularly on a relatively empty stomach.

If you do drink coffee, remember that the amount of caffeine varies with each type of coffee. Dark, European-roast coffees and espresso are much stronger in caffeine than their canned American counterparts. Also, the effect is delayed; it takes 15 to 20 minutes for the caffeine to circulate in your bloodstream, and at least 45 minures for the peak stimulation to occur. You should take it at least 40 minutes prior to the race.

Though it may be worth testing, I have never tried drinking coffee before a race. The known risks far outweigh the possible benefits.

MY OWN DIET

For some reason, my eating habits seem to fascinate people—especially reporters. *Sports Illustrated* once devoted a full page to an epic description of me eating an ordinary dinner.

"The scene looked like a model of the solar system," Dan Levin wrote. "Scott was the sun, and his plates were the planets."

Most magazine articles have portrayed me as an enigmatic cross between Euell Gibbons and Porky Pig—a fanatic vegetarian who rinses his low-fat cottage cheese, then eats 25 pounds of it.

I do like to eat, but I am certainly not an indiscriminate glutton. There is a qualitative difference between eating a dozen apples for a snack—which I have done—and downing the same number of candy bars. For one thing, there are nearly four times as many calories in the candy, and less than half the nutrients.

Very few people would quarrel with the idea that a piece of fruit is better for you than a piece of chocolate. But there are some "health food" myths that I personally discovered in my search for a perfect diet.

Take cheese, for instance. Most people believe—as I once did—that cheese is a wholesome, inculpable food. I thought I was doing myself a big favor by not eating meat; instead, I ate about two pounds of cheese every day. Then I found out that most cheese is about 50 percent fat. My fat intake and cholesterol level were probably higher than my next-door neighbor's, who was sitting down to a T-bone steak every night.

So I put a stop to my cheese binge in favor of nuts. That was going to be my new source of dense protein, I thought. I ate all kinds of nuts—walnuts, cashews, peanuts—until I found out that they, too, are full of fat. So long, nuts.

Left with few alternatives, I decided to forgo fats altogether. That is basically how the infamous Dave Scott almost-no-fat diet was born. Less than 5 percent of my total calories were fat. No wonder I ate so much—I was hungry all the time. If you don't eat any fat, you never have that full feeling in your stomach. It was a far cry from the nine-pound "Zoo" I had eaten just a couple of years before.

Now my diet is much more balanced. I eat cheese again, but not more than three or four ounces a couple of times a week. I use vegetable oils in cooking (in very small amounts), but I usually make my salad dressing from nonfat yogurt.

I drink nonfat milk, but I have cheerfully learned that a little bit of alcohol may lower blood cholesterol, so I have some "medicinal" beer or wine about twice a week.

I don't eat eggs, but I do eat turkey on Thanksgiving and Christmas—if I didn't, my family would disown me and my in-laws wouldn't understand me. I eat broiled fish occasionally (not at home). I never, ever eat anything fried—it is against my gastronomical religion!

BREAKFAST

A typical day for me begins with a breakfast of a couple of packages of shredded wheat cereal with about 3 tablespoons of plain nonfat yogurt, drowning in nonfat milk. Along with that I have a couple of bananas, a couple of pieces of dry whole wheat toast (no salt, no sugar, no butter). My second course is a half-dozen rice cakes and two or three apples. I like to eat a hearty breakfast!

LUNCH

I usually eat a light lunch. When I am training, I don't like to stop and sit around long enough for a big meal. For me, a good lunch consists of cottage cheese (rinsed) and tofu on a corn tortilla with tomatoes and salsa (hot sauce). I eat that with a couple of apples, and if I am especially hungry, I'll add a piece of whole wheat bread.

DINNER

For dinner, I usually steam vegetables and make soup—bean soup is a favorite. My staple is baked potatoes with cottage cheese or yogurt. (I eat cottage cheese and plain yogurt every day.) I also like tortillas stuffed with beans, onions, tomatoes, cottage cheese, tofu, and hot spices—the triathlete's burrito! With that I eat beans and rice, and I almost always eat three or four more apples. I round it out with a green salad, and maybe a fruit salad.

SNACKS

Throughout the day, I eat pieces of fruit and unsalted air-popped popcorn. Popcorn is high in fiber and low in calories, so I eat a lot of it.

WATER

I drink at least 8 to 10 glasses of water a day, along with eating a lot of fruit and vegetables that have a high water content.

It took me a long time, and a lot of empty calories, to develop a well-rounded diet that works for my health and eating pleasure as well as my athletic performance. The way I eat now is the way I hope to eat for the rest of my life.

10 HINDSIGHT

 imes have certainly changed since I first heard of the Ironman Triathlon. The known world of triathletes had an eccentric population of about 20, and the Ironman (then on the island of Oahu) was a tropical oddity, a spectacle that lured curious *Sports Illustrated* reporters nearly 6,000 miles from their desks in New York City to see what kind of daredevils would swim two-and-a-half miles in the ocean, then cycle more than a hundred miles, then run a marathon.

Now the novelty of ultra-distance races has been diminished by thousands of shorter races that take the average participant under three or four hours to complete; elite competitors

finish them in times comparable to world-class marathon times, or less. You don't have to train all day long to be good at those distances, so many people can participate.

In fact, demographers estimate more than a million triathletes in the United States, and thousands more in countries around the world. Triathlon is no longer a cult—it is a bona fide sport. Iron Curtain triathletes have competed side by side with Americans, and there are rumors that the young Soviet triathletes are absolutely fearsome. Federations in England, Ireland, the Netherlands, France, Germany, Belgium, Australia, New Zealand, Canada, and the United States are working to make triathlon (short-distance) an Olympic sport.

As the sport has grown, so have the stakes. There is more prize money, more marketing and advertising potential, more races, and certainly more organization. For the most part, races are shorter and safer than before.

Yet there remains a popular misconception that triathlons are survival contests for super-humans who train from sunup to sundown, seven days a week. The sports media still describe races as "grueling" and "brutal," and most reporters are shocked to learn that I often train less than 20 hours a week, and don't use any steroids or herbs or other substances to beef up my performance.

In fact, one of the most beneficial character-istics of endurance sports is that they rely on superb physical and mental conditioning, not just brute strength. Steroids and amphetamines and "blood doping" (infusing an extra quart of one's own stored blood before a race) have never proven to actually aid endurance; it takes a combination of fitness and fortitude to win a race.

I have been called a purist, but I still believe that the best triathlete is the healthiest triathlete. I hope you will use this book to prove that point.

My wife Anna congratulates me after the 1984 Ironman.
Sharing the victory makes it even more rewarding.

APPENDICES

A DAVE SCOTT'S TRIATHLON RECORD

1980

JANUARY: Winner
Ironman Triathlon World
   Championship
Oahu, Hawaii
2.4-mile swim, 112-mile bike,
   26.2-mile run
9:24:00

1982

FEBRUARY: 2d place
Ironman Triathlon World
   Championship
Kailua-Kona, Hawaii
2.4-mile swim, 112-mile bike,
   26.2-mile run
9:36:00

JUNE: Winner
United States Triathlon Series
San Diego, California
1.5-mile swim, 25-mile bike,
   9.4-mile run
2:18:10

AUGUST: Winner
United States Triathlon Series
1.2-mile swim, 25-mile bike,
   9.4-mile run
Portland, Oregon
2:12:48

AUGUST: Winner
United States Triathlon Series
Seattle, Washington
1.2-mile swim, 25-mile bike,
   9.4-mile run
2:15:48

SEPTEMBER: National Champion
United States Triathlon Series

SEPTEMBER: Winner
Mighty Hamptons Triathlon
Sag Harbor, New York
1.5-mile swim, 25-mile bike,
   10-mile run
2:26:09

OCTOBER: Winner
Ironman Triathlon World
   Championship
Kailua-Kona, Hawaii
2.4-mile swim, 112-mile bike,
   26.2-mile run
9:08:32

1983

MAY:
Winner
Gulf Coast Triathlon
Panama City Beach, Florida
1.2-mile swim, 62-mile bike,
  13.9-mile run
4:30:31

JULY:
2d place
United States Triathlon Series
San Francisco, California
1.2-mile swim, 25-mile bike,
  9.4-mile run
2:33:10

SEPTEMBER:
2d place
Nice International Triathlon
France
1.9-mile swim, 75-mile bike,
  18.4-mile run
6:08:00

OCTOBER:
Winner
Ironman Triathlon World
  Championship
Kailua-Kona, Hawaii
2.4-mile swim, 112-mile bike,
  26.2-mile run
9:05:57

1984

JANUARY:
3d place
Kauai Triathlon
Kauai, Hawaii
1.35-mile swim, 12.4-mile run,
  51.3-mile bike
3:58:21

SEPTEMBER:
2d place
Nice International Triathlon
France
6:08:00

OCTOBER:
Winner
Ironman Triathlon World
  Championship
Kailua-Kona, Hawaii
2.4-mile swim, 112-mile bike,
  26.2-mile run
8:54:20

1985

MAY:
Winner
United States Triathlon Series
Fort Lauderdale, Florida
1.2-mile swim, 25-mile bike,
  9.4-mile run
1:55:22

JUNE:
2d place
The President's Cup Triathlon
Dallas, Texas
1.2-mile swim, 41-mile bike,
  10-mile run
3:08:00

JUNE:
Winner
Ironman Triathlon
Japan
2.4-mile swim, 112-mile bike,
  26.2-mile run
8:39:00

B WHERE TO SWIM

UNITED STATES MASTERS SWIMMING

There are hundreds of United States Masters Swimming groups and teams across the country, managed by volunteers in 50 local associations within seven regions. A Masters association can tell you where to swim in your area, and can direct you to lap swimming, independent and team workouts.

To contact the USMS group nearest you, call or write:

U.S. Masters Swimming, Inc.
Dorothy Donnelly, Executive Secretary
Five Piggott Lane
Avon, CT 06001
(203) 677-9464

Telephone hours are 8:30 a.m. to 10:30 p.m., eastern time, seven days a week. When the secretary is not available, a voice-activated recorder will take your message. Please state what you are looking for, and leave your name and address (including zip code).

SWIMMING PUBLICATIONS

For the latest swim meet and triathlon calendars, as well as comprehensive lists of places to swim (including open water), *SWIM* magazine is a glossy, full-color national magazine published every other month, devoted entirely to adult fitness and competitive swimmers. The one-year subscription rate is $12.00 for six issues.

SWIM magazine
P.O. Box 2168
Simi Valley, CA 93062

The official USMS newsletter, *Swim Master*, is published nine times per year, with an annual subscription rate of $8.00.

Swim Master
2308 NE 19th Ave.
Fort Lauderdale, FL 33305

C TRIATHLON CLUBS AND ORGANIZATIONS

Triathlon clubs are a great resource for information, training partners, and news. If you are new to an area and want to find a good place to swim, or the best riding or running trails, contact the local club or association listed below for advice. If no club is listed in your area, contact Tri-Fed/USA, national clubs chairperson Paula Tocci, (212) 986-0722.

WESTERN REGION
(CALIFORNIA, NEVADA, HAWAII)

Bay Area Triathlon Club
P.O. Box 5344
San Francisco, CA 94101
Contact: Tim Callahan
          Mark Guglielmana

North Coast Triathlon Club
1370 Townview Dr., #101
Santa Rosa, CA 95404
Contact: Bob Stiles

Team Hawaii
P.O. Box N
Kailua-Kona, HI 96740
Contact: J. Curtis Tyler

Redding Triathlon Club
2635 Park Marina Dr.
Redding, CA 96049
Contact: Mike Jones

Chuck's Team Santa Barbara
428 Conejo Rd.
Santa Barbara, CA 93103
Contact: Lynelle Paulick

Carlsbad Triathlon Club
1200 Elm Ave.
Carlsbad, CA 92008
Contact: Carl Pope III

Las Vegas Triathlon Club
338 Banuelo Dr.
Henderson, NV 89015
Contact: Craig Roles

Kamuela Striders
P.O. Box 595
Kamuela, HI
Contact: Alvin Wayakama

Southern California Triathlon Club
P.O. Box 10033
Marina del Rey, CA 90291
Contact: Richard X. Reyes

*Triathletics West
P.O. Box 8040-128
Walnut Creek, CA 94596
Contact: Mark Evans

*Training information center (not a club per se).

NORTHWESTERN REGION
(WASHINGTON, OREGON, IDAHO, ALASKA)

Sumner Tritons
P.O. Box 365
Sumner, WA 98390
Contact: President

Sun Valley Triathlon Club
P.O. Box 178
Ketchum, ID 83340
Contact: Rob Rosso

Portland Triathlon Association
2125 S.E. 47
Hillsboro, OR 97123
Contact: Frank Gaulard

SOUTHWESTERN REGION
(COLORADO, ARIZONA, NEW MEXICO, UTAH, WYOMING, MONTANA)

Arizona Triathlon Association
P.O. Box 14168
Phoenix, AZ 85063-4168
Contact: Lex Anderson

Triathlon Club of Colorado
2625 E. 3rd Ave., Ste. 250
Denver, CO 80206
Contact: Steve Hegge

Triathletes, Inc., Arizona
P.O. Box 352
Peoria, AZ
Contact: W. Thomas Hickox
        Sabina Peters-Stern
        Lex Anderson

Salt Lake City Triathlon Club
1115 W. Putter Circle
Salt Lake City, UT 84123
Contact: Fred Scurti

MIDWESTERN REGION
(ILLINOIS, OHIO, MICHIGAN, INDIANA, MINNESOTA, WISCONSIN, MISSOURI, NEBRASKA, NORTH AND SOUTH DAKOTA, KANSAS, IOWA)

Indiana Triathlon Association
4510 Park Ave.
Indianapolis, IN 46205
Contact: Mike Sterling

Knox County Triathlon Club
Road #3 Millstone Lane
Mt. Vernon, OH 43050
Contact: President

Michigan Triathlon Association, Inc.
P.O. Box 356
Franklin, MI 48025
Contact: President

Illinois Triathletes in Training
URH 356 Weston
Champaign, IL 61820
Contact: Karl Wagner

Kansas City Triathletes
Gary Gribble's Olympic Village
8600 Ward Parkway
Kansas City, MO 64114
Contact: Gary Gribble

Indiana Triathlon Association
4510 N. Park Ave.
Indianapolis, IN 46205
Contact: Mark Sterling

Milwaukee Triathlon Club
8133 N. 107 St. #K
Milwaukee, WI 53224
Contact: Chuck Cahill

Mid-America Triathletes
P.O. Box 9162
St. Louis, MO 63117
Contact: Mike Zogmaier

Team Toledo Triathlon Club
7445 Airport Hwy. Advocate Bldg.
Holland, OH 43528
Contact: John Wagner

Minnesota Triathlon Association
1137 W. Montana Ave.
St. Paul, MN 55108
Contact: Morgan Nicol

Solbsports
8348 Wicklow Ave.
Cincinnati, OH 45236
Contact: Jeff Harris

Upper Midwest Triathlon Association
P.O. Box 16303
Minneapolis, MN 55616
Contact: Robert Mock

SOUTH
(TENNESSEE, ARKANSAS, LOUISIANA, MISSISSIPPI, ALABAMA, OKLAHOMA, KENTUCKY, TEXAS)

Music City Triathlon Club
524 American Dr.
Nashville, TN 37211
Contact: Ray Ashworth

New Orleans Triathlon Association
1500 Calhoun St.
New Orleans, LA 70118
Contact: Charlie Houlihan

Nautilus Triathlon Club
P.O. Box 7464
Paducah, KY 42001
Contact: Joe Shane

Stillwater Triathlon Association
220 South Main St.
Stillwater, OK 74074
Contact: Monte Roe

North Shore Athletics
Box 1751
Covington, LA 70434
Contact: Melinda La Bauve

Mississippi Triathlon Club
43 Sagewood Dr.
Brandon, MS 39042
Contact: Joanne Zadroga

Tulsa Wheelmen
P.O. Box 52242
Tulsa, OK 74152
Contact: Jim Carlson

Oklahoma Runner
P.O. Box 20798
Oklahoma City, OK 73156
Contact: Doug Thurston

Viaduct Vultures Triathlon Club
Oxford Realty
3499 Independence Ave.
Birmingham, AL 35213
Contact: Johnny Montgomery

Club Tri-Memphis
P.O. Box 396
La Grange, TN 38046
Contact: Peggy Hill

Bay Area Triathletes
1214 Saxony Lane
Houston, TX 77058
Contact: Ester Ellis

John Simmons
903 Ferris Ave.
Waxahachie, TX 75165
Contact: John Simmons

Texas Triathlon Club
280 Litchfield Lane
Houston, TX 77024
Contact: Jean Hoepful

New Orleans Triathlon Association
Crime Labs
3300 Metairie Rd.
Metairie, LA 70001
Contact: Joseph Warren

SOUTHEAST REGION
(WASHINGTON, D.C., WEST VIRGINIA, VIRGINIA, MARYLAND, NORTH AND SOUTH CAROLINA, GEORGIA, FLORIDA)

North Virginia Triathlon Association
P.O. Box 1715
Alexandria, VA 22313
Contact: Alton Young

Palmetto State Triathlon Association
1001 Woodrow St. #B
Columbia, SC 29205
Contact: Jim Schmid

Atlanta Tri-Train Club
1601 Brentwood Dr.
Tilburn, GA 30247
Contact: Terry Worley

Tidewater Triathlon Club
123 Pennsylvania Ave.
Virginia Beach, VA 23462
Contact: Bill Dempsey

Skyline Racquet & Health Club
5715 Leesburg Pike
Baileys Cross Roads, VA 22041
Contact: Mark Dreibelbus

Reston Triathlon Association
P.O. Box 2356
Reston, VA 22090
Contact: Jim Des Rosiers

Atlanta Triathlon Club
3518 Roswell Rd., N.W. B-12
Atlanta, GA 30305
Contact: Terry D. Kennedy

Race Pace Triathlon Shop
6600 C. Baltimore
Baltimore, MD 21228
Contact: Phil Howe

White Oak Triathletes
1162 Bonifant St.
Silver Spring, MD 20901
Contact: Paul Burlett

The Sporting Club
8250 Greensboro Dr.
McLean, VA 22102
Contact: Chip Hill

Washington Area Triathlon Association
P.O. Box 1715
Alexandria, VA 22313
Contact: Steve Young

Carolina Triathlon Club
UNC-G Dept. of Food & Nutrition
Greensboro, NC 27412
Contact: Dr. Terry Balgave

Spartanburg YMCA Studies
280 South Pine St.
Spartanburg, SC 29302
Contact: Mary Miles

Atlanta Triathlon Club
1267 Stillwood Dr.
Atlanta, GA 30306
Contact: Loretta Redd

Florida West Triathletes
2830 Mauna Loa
Sarasota, FL 34241
Contact: Chuck Erickson

American Triathletes/So. Fla.
P.O. Box 17554
Plantation, FL 33318
Contact: Paul Carter

Team Tampa Triathletes
1307 East Flora
Tampa, FL 33610
Contact: Mike Laughrey

Tampa Bay Triathletes
2609 Sunset Way
St. Pete Beach, FL 33076
Contact: Mark Van Gilder

North Florida Triathletes
6213 Anvil Rd.
Jacksonville, FL 32211
Contact: Pat Wagoner

Central Florida Triathletes
Rt. 2, Box 62
Clermont, FL 32711
Contact: Fred Sommer

J. Lynne Endurance Sports
1919 Pennsylvania Ave.
Washington, D.C. 20006
Contact: Jean-Mark Katzoff

West Fla. "Y" Runners Club
1005 So. Highland Ave.
Clearwater, FL 33546
Contact: Al James

The Dukes Triathlon Club
SAS Institute, Box 8000
Cary, NC 27511
Contact: Bob Hastings

Florida Gator Triathletes
P.O. Box 2635
Gainesville, FL 32604
Contact: Janet Wendle

Greater Miami Triathlon Club
10643A SW 113th Pl.
Miami, FL 33176
Contact: Scott Spages

MID-ATLANTIC REGION
(NEW YORK, PENNSYLVANIA, NEW JERSEY, DELAWARE)

Club "A"
Adam's Schwinn Cyclery
Larkfield Rd.
East Northport, NY

Triathlon Association of New Jersey
426 Dixon Ave.
Boonton, NJ 07005
Contact: Alex Turner

Big Apple Triathlon Club
301 E. 79th St., #30-D
New York, NY 10021
Contact: Dan Honig

Philadelphia Triathlon Club
950 Walnut St. #709
Philadelphia, PA 19107
Contact: Doug Hiller

North Buffalo Triathlon Club
180 University Ave.
Buffalo, NY 14214
Contact: Paul Tonovitz

National Association of Triathletes
2017 Walnut St.
Philadelphia, PA 19103

Team Red Line
700 Columbus Circle
New York, NY 10019
Contact: Doug Stern

Long Island Tri Club
14 Ft. Salonga Rd.
Centerport, NY 11721
Contact: Frank

Garden State Tri-Mates
c/o Nancy Link
451 Brookside Lane
Somerville, NJ 08876
Contact: Peter Mogendorf

Tri-State Triathletes
Caldwell Cycle & Fitness
336 Bloomfield Ave.
Caldwell, NJ 07006
Contact: John Kokes

Pocono NE Triathlon Association
71 N. Franklin St.
Wilkes-Barre, PA 18701
Contact: David Daris

NEW ENGLAND REGION
(MASSACHUSETTS, CONNECTICUT, RHODE ISLAND, MAINE, VERMONT, NEW HAMPSHIRE)

Cape Cod Triathlon Association
Box 1118
Hyannis, MA 02601

North Shore Triathlon Association
234 Essex St.
Lynn, MA 01902
Contact: Tom Carmody

New England Triathlon Association
420 Salem St.
Medford, MA
Contact: Dave McGillivray

East Coast Triathletes
176 Commonwealth Ave.
West Newton, MA
Contact: Phillip Tocciox

Springfield Triathlon Association
89 Perkins, St.
Springfield, MA 01118
Contact: Joe Dejna

Fairfield Bombers Tri Club
11 Belltown Rd. #3
Stamford, CT 06905
Contact: Mark Santella

Willimantic Athletic Club
Box 812
Willimantic, CT 06226
Contact: Peter Leeds

Green Mountain Triathlon Club
Indian Creek #7
911 Dorset St.
So. Burlington, VT 05401
Contact: Lisa Ruskin

Green Mountain Bicycle Club
260 Crescent Rd.
Burlington, VT 05401
Contact: Dale Critchlow

Providence Track Club
575 Grand Ave.
Pawtucket, RI 02861
Contact: Ed Poirier

Tri-Busters Triathlon Club
Threads & Treads
17 E. Putnam
Greenwich, CT 06830
Contact: Liz Cope

Connecticut Triathlon Association
262 Celia Dr.
Wolcott, CT 06705
Contact: Ed Gammon

Triathlon Team New Hampshire
P.O. Box 502
Durham, NH 03824
Contact: Peter Markos

Green Mountain Athletic Association
26 Chapman Rd.
No. Williston, VT 05495
Contact: Jeanette Perry

Vermont Masters Swim Team
151 Ledge Rd.
Burlington, VT 05401
Contact: Jack Sartore

INDEX

Abdominals and triceps (dumbbells), 158-9
Accelerations, in running workout, 135
Active rest
  explosive speed training, 105
  sprint race training, 106
Activities per day, training, 93
Adenosine diphosphate (ADP), 27
Adenosine triphosphate (ATP), 26–28
Aerobic exercise
  benefits, 28–29
  limitations, 29
  and oxygen, 24
Aid stations, cycling course, 192
Alcohol, 226
Allen, Mark, 71, 100, 200
Alternate leg rests, 65-66
Altitude training, 102
Amphetamines, 230
Anaerobic energy (ATP-CP), 27
Anaerobic glycolysis, 27
Anaerobic threshold, 27
  training, 26, 109-11
Ankle
  flexion, cycling, 64-65
  strength and flutter kick, swimming, 48
Antagonistic muscles, 21-22
Arms
  while cycling, 62
  while running, 78-80, 205
  while swimming, 198
Arteriosclerosis, 213
Ascorbic acid, 222
ATP-aerobic, 26, 28
ATP-CP, 26-27
ATP-lactic acid, 26, 27-28

Back exercises, with any alternate, 160
Bench press, 146-47
Bent-over rowing, 149
Biceps, 22
  curl, 156

Bicycle
  fitting, 56-59
  frame, 56-57
  handlebars, 59
  handlebar stem, 58-59
  repairs, 71-72
  seat height, 57-58
  see also Cycling
Bike-to-run transition, 195, 203-4
Biomechanics, 21
Biotin, 221
Blood doping, 230-31
Body position
  cycling, 60-63
  and kick, swimming, 48
  running, 77-83
Bones, and strength training, 139
Bounding, 135
Bow wave, freestyle stroke, 45-46
Brakes, using in cycling, 70
Brancazio, Peter J., 22, 24
Breakfast, 227
Breaking monotony, while running, 83
Breathing
  while cycling, 59, 201-2
  while running, 83-84
  while swimming, 44-47
  and weight training, 145-46
Bryant, Bill, 71
Bushong, Kim, 189-90

Cadence, cycling, 63-64
Caffeine, 226
Calcium, 223
Calf raises, and two-arm triceps presses, 161-63
Calf stretches, 66
Calories
  burned per minute while cycling, running, and
    swimming, 210
  burned while racing, 218
  excess, 214

Carbohydrates, in diet, 214-16
Carbo-loading fallacy, 216
Cardiac output, 23-24
Carotene, 220
Catch, freestyle stroke, 32, 37
Cellulose, 215
Checklist, racing transitions, 194
Chloride, 225
Cholesterol, 213
Chromium, 225
Circular strokes, cycling, 64
Clayton, Derek, 110
Cleated cycling shoes, 73
Clincher tires, 73
Clothing
    cycling, 59, 72-73, 134
    running, 87
    swimming, 52
    selection, 194
Cobalamin, 221
Collins, John, 15
Competitive season
    training, 120-21
    weight-training, 142-43
    workout schedule, 126-27
Competitors, comparing self to, 184
Cool-down, 116-17
    stretching, 173
    swimming workout, 133
Copper, 224
Cornering cycling course, 192
Coronary arteriosclerosis, 213
Costill, Dave, 107
Course
    preview of, 190-93
    using in bike race, 202
Crawl stroke. *See* Freestyle stroke
Creatine phosphate (CP), 27
Crossover flutter kick, two-beat, 49
Cross-training, benefits, 93-94
Cues to how well you're doing in freestyle swimming, 51
Curl, 22
    biceps, 156
    hamstring, 153
Cycling, 54-55
    ankle flexion, 64-65
    calories burned per minute, 210
    circular vs. elliptical strokes, 64
    clothing, 59, 72-73, 134
    course, preview of, 191-92
    elbows and arms, 62
    equipment, 55, 72-74
    foot position, 62-63
    hand position, 60-61
    hill climbing, 66-69
    paraphernalia, 74
    racing, 201-4
    relaxing feet and legs, 65-66
    repairs, 71-72
    riding in wind, 70
    riding position, 60-63
    shoes, cleated, 73
    sprint race training, 107
    strokes, cyclists vs. triathletes, 63-66

    tires, 73
    training pace, 103
    upper body, 62
    using brakes, 70
    workout schedule, 123
    workout tips, 134
    see also Bicycle
Cyclists vs. triathletes, cycling strokes, 63-66

Deltoid, 35, 41
Diaphragm, 84
Diet, 208-10
    alcohol, 226
    caffeine, 226
    carbohydrates, 214-16
    fat, 212-14
    pre-race, 196, 216-17
    protein, 211-12
    Scott, 226-28
    vitamins and minerals, 219-25
    see also Fluids; Food
Dinner, 227
Disaccharides, 214
Distance per stroke, 33
Distance training, 111-12
Dorsi flex, 199
Double-sugars, 214
Downward press, freestyle stroke, 32, 37
Drafting, swimming race, 199
Drills, to improve feel for water, 50
Dropping out of race, 206-7
Dry land drills, to improve feel for water, 50

Eating
    after race, 206
    during race, 216, 217-19
    see also Diet; Fluids; Food
Ego, keeping under control, 184-85
Elbows
    in cycling, 62
    flexion, freestyle stroke, 33
Electrolyte replacement fluids, 225
Elliptical strokes, cycling, 64
Energy systems, for training, 113
Entry
    drills to correct problems, 36
    freestyle stroke, 32, 33-35
Equipment
    cycling, 55, 72-74
    running, 87
    swimming, 52-53
Ernst, Joanne, 94
Exercise
    abdominals, 159
    aerobic, 24, 28-29
    back, 160
    bench press, 146-47
    biceps curl, 156
    calf raises, 163
    hamstring curl, 153
    latissimus pull-down, 151
    leg extensions, 157
    military press, 150
    pre-race warm-up, 196-97

quadriceps extension, 152
rowing, 148-49
triceps (dumbbells), 158
triceps extension, 154-55
triceps presses, two arm, 161-62
weight training, 145-46
Explosive speed training, 104-5

Face, relaxing while running, 78
Fartlek training, 135
Fast-twitch muscle fibers, 25-26
Fat, in diet, 212-14
Feeney, Pat, 55, 184, 206
Feet
  while cycling, 62-63, 65-66
  while running, 80-83
  while swimming, 47-49
Fiber, usage for training, 113
Fingers, wiggling while running, 205
Finish, freestyle stroke, 32, 40
Finish line
  race, 205-6
  swim course, 191
Fins, swimming, 52
Fixx, Jim, 210
Flexibility, 174, 175
Flexors, 77
Fluids
  for distance training, 112
  electrolyte replacement, 225
  fuel efficiency, 100
  after race, 206
  and swim workout, 133
  and thermoregulation, 101
  see also Diet; Food
Fluoride, 225
Flutter kicks, 48-49
Folic acid, 222
Food
  carbohydrates in, 214-16
  for distance training, 112
  fuel efficiency, 99-100
  labels, 215
  protein, 211-12
  for racing transitions, 194
  and thermoregulation, 101
  see also Diet; Fluids
Food and Drug Administration, 220
Foot position. See Feet
Form, running, 205
Form drag, 32
Frame, bicycle, 56-57
Freestyle stroke
  basic technique, 32-33
  catch, 37
  downward press, 37
  entry, 32, 33-36
  after entry, before catch, 35
  finish, 40
  getting ready for finish, 40
  problems, correcting, 36, 44
  pull, 38-39
  reason for, 31-32
  recovery, 40-43

shoulder rotation, 35
Fructose, 214
Fuel
  efficiency, food and fluids, 99-100
  how body produces and uses, 26-28

Gadgets, cycling, 74
Galactose, 214
Game plan, establishing, 187-88
Gastroenemus, 63
Gear
  bike race, 68-69, 201, 203
  for transitions, 195
Gloves, padded, for cycling, 73
Glucose, 214
Gluteals, 58
Glycerol, 28
Glycogen, 27, 28
Goals, setting, 186-87
Goggles, swimming, 52

Hamstring curl
  and leg extensions, 157
  and quadriceps extension, 152-53
Hamstrings, 76
Handlebars, bicycle, 59
Handlebar stem, bicycle, 58-59
Hand paddles, swimming, 53
Hands
  feeling in water, 51
  position, cycling, 60-61
  using while running, 78-80
Hard/easy theory, training, 92
Hawaii Ironman Triathlon, 94, 100, 183
Head-up swimming, 199
Heart, 23-24
  rate, 23
Heat, coping with, 100-102
Helmet, hard-shell, for cycling, 59, 73
Hemoglobin, 25
High-density lipoproteins (HDL), 213
Hill
  climbing, in bike race, 66-69
  running, 84-85
  topping off, in bike race, 202
Hinault, Bernard, 58
Hindsight, 229-31
Hosing down, and thermoregulation, 101
Howard, John, 60, 72
Hyperthermia, 100-102
Hypoxic training, 132

Injuries, training, 92-93
Insulin, 215
Intensity, training, 94-95
In-water drills, to improve feel for water, 50
Iodine, 225
Iron, 224
Ironman Triathlon, 15-17, 44, 51, 65, 70, 71, 72, 77, 134,
    182, 183, 184, 186-87, 200, 206, 226, 229
Isokinetic strength, 141
Isokinetic workout, 171
Isometric strength, 140-41
Isotonic strength, 141

Japan Ironman Triathlon, 73, 112
Joints, mobility, and strength training, 139

Kauai Triathlon, 119
Kick
    freestyle stroke, 47-49
    swimming race, 198
Kickboards, swimming, 52
Kinesthetic awareness, swimming, 50-51

Lactic acid, 27-28
    and training, 98-99
La Lanne, Jack, 136
Laminar flow, 32
Landmarks, cycling course, 191-92
Latissimus dorsi, 35
Latissimus pull-down and military press, 150-51
Leg(s)
    while cycling, 65-66
    extensions, and hamstring curl, 157
    while running, 80-83
    while swimming, 47-49
LeMond, Greg, 57, 67
Length, stride, 80-81
Levin, Dan, 226
Ligaments, and strength training, 139
Line
    cycling course, 192
    running course, 193
Lipids, 212
Lipolytic system, 28
Lipoproteins, 213
Long-term goals, training, 90
Low-density lipoproteins (LDL), 213
Lunch, 227

Magnesium, 224
Malibu Triathlon, 71
Maltose, 214
Manganese, 225
Markers
    cycling course, 192
    swim course, 191
Massage, pre-race, 197
Maximum heart rate, 23
Measurement of training intensity, 94-95
Medical attention, after race, 206
Mid-stroke leg rest, cycling, 66
Mileage
    markers, cycling course, 192
    training, 92
Military press, and latissimus pull-down, 150-51
Minerals, and vitamins, in diet, 219-25
Mini-triathlon, 16-17, 118, 119, 121
Mini-ups, 159
Mitochondria, 24
Molina, Scott, 57-58, 71, 92, 100, 107, 112
Monosaccharides, 214
Monotony while running, breaking, 83
Monounsaturated fats, 212
Motor neuron, 25
Motor units, 139

Muscles, 24-25
    antagonistic, 21-22
    biceps, 22
    deltoids, 35, 41
    fiber, 24-26
    flexors, 77
    gastroenemus, 63
    gluteals, 58
    hamstrings, 76
    latissimus dorsi, 35
    quadriceps, 47, 63, 74-75
    soleus, 63
    spindles, 25
    sternocleidomastoids, 78
    stretching, 181
    trapezius, 41, 47, 78
    triceps, 22
    vastus lateralis, 58
    vastus medialis, 62-63, 63
    and weight training, 138, 145

Neck, relaxing while running, 78
Nerves, and strength, 139-40
Nervous system, and weight training, 138
Neuromuscular junction, 25
Newman, Chuck, 17
Niacin, 221
Nice Triathlon, 71, 182, 184, 207
Norton, Mike, 16

Obstacles, cycling course, 191-92
Odometer, for cycling, 74
Osteoporosis, 139
Oxidative, 25
Oxygen, delivery route, 24

PABA, 222
Pain, while racing, 188
Pantothenic acid, 221-22
Para aminobenzoic acid (PABA), 222
Paraphernalia, cycling, 74
Partner stretches, 175
Passive stretching, 173
Patellar tendon, 63
Pedaling, bike race, 202
Personal time trial
    pace chart, 97
    record, 96
    training, 95-96
Phosphorus, 223
Physiological makeup, and training, 90-91
Plantar flexion, 48
Polysaccharides, 215
Polyunsaturated fats, 212
Position, bike race, 201
Post-competitive season
    training, 121
    weight training, 142-43
    workout schedule, 127-28
Potassium, 224
Pre-competitive season
    training, 119-20
    weight training, 142-43
    workout schedule, 125-26

Pre-race
    diet, 196, 216-17
    warm-up, 196-97
Pre-season
    training, 117-118
    weight training, 142-43
    workout schedule, 124-25
Preview, of race course, 190-93
Pritikin, Nathan, 212
Pritikin Institute, 107
Progressive sets, 116
Protein, in diet, 211-12
Psychology, race, 186-89
Pull, freestyle stroke, 32, 38-39
Pull buoys, swimming, 53
Pulse, 23
Pump, for cycling, 74
Pyramid training, 135
Pyridoxine, 221

Quadriceps, 47, 63, 74-75
    extension, and hamstring curl, 152-53

Racing
    activity before, 190-95
    attitude toward, 185-86
    breaks in, 182-83
    cycling, 201-4
    dropping out, 206-7
    eating during, 216, 217-19
    finish line, 205-6
    getting organized, 193
    judging success, 184-85
    morning before, 195-97
    psychology, 186-89
    reasons for, 183-85
    running, 204-5
    at starting line, 197
    swimming, 198-201
    tapering, 189-90
    transitions, 194-95
Recovery, freestyle stroke, 32, 40-43
Recovery response
    anaerobic threshold training, 110
    explosive speed training, 105
    sprint race training, 106
    VO$_2$ max training, 108-9
Rehabilitation, 174, 175
Relaxing, bike race, 201
Repairs, cycling, 71-72
Repetitions, sprint race training, 106-7
Rest, and training, 92, 96
Resting pulse, 23
Reverse sit-ups, 159
Riboflavin, 221
Riding
    position, cycling, 60-63
    in wind, 70
Risk taking, 188
Rodgers, Bill, 210
Rowing
    and bench press, 146-49
    bent-over, 149
    upright, 148

Running, 75-76
    body position, 77-83
    breathing while, 83-84
    calories burned per minute, 210
    equipment, 87
    hill, 84-85
    keeping in stride, 80-83
    monotony, breaking, 83
    relaxing face, neck, and shoulders, 78
    sprint race training, 107
    and stretching, 85-86
    training pace, 104
    using arms and hands, 78-80
    workout schedule, 124
    workout tips, 134-35

Saturated fats, 212
"The Scientific Approach to Distance Running" (Costill),
        107
Scott, Anna, 206
Scott, Patti, 13-15
Seasonal goals, training, 90
Seat height, bicycle, 57-58
Selenium, 225
Sets
    progressive, 116
    workout, 116
Shirt, selection, 194
Shoes
    cleated cycling, 73
    running, 87
    selection, 194
Shorts
    cycling, 73
    selection, 194
Short-term goals, training, 90
Shoulders
    relaxing while running, 78
    rotation, freestyle stroke, 35
Side kick, 199
Simple sugars, 214
Sit-ups, reverse, 159
Six-beat flutter kick, 49
Skeletal muscles, 24
Skin suits, lycra, 134
Slow-twitch muscle fibers, 25-26
Snacks, 228
Soleus, 63
Sore muscles, and weight training, 145
Spinal cord, 24
Sportscience (Brancazio), 22
Sports Illustrated, 226, 229
Sprint race training, 105-7
Stack, Walt, 226
Standing up, when hill climbing on bicycle, 67
Starches, 214
Starting line, race, 197
Static stretching, 173
Sternocleidomastoids, 78
Steroids, 230
Strength
    types, 140-41
    and weight training, 139-40

Strengths
  capitalizing on, 188-89
  using in bike race, 202
Stretching, 173
  in bike race, 203
  muscles, 181
  pre-race, 197
  after race, 206
  and running, 85-86
Stretch reflex, 173
Stride, running, 80-83, 135, 204
Stroke
  cycling, 63-64
  swimming race, 198
  volume, 23
Success, judging, 184-85
Sucrose, 214
Sugar
  double, 214
  simple, 214
  storage, 215
Suit, swimming, 52
Sulfur, 224-25
Sunglasses, for cycling, 73
Supplements, vitamins and minerals, 219-20
Sweating, and thermoregulation, 101-2
Swim bench workout, 171
Swimming, 30-31
  breathing, 44-47
  calories burned per minute, 210
  equipment, 52-53
  feel for water, 50-51
  freestyle stroke, 31-44
  kicking, 47-49
  learning own cues, 51-52
  organizations and publications, 237
  preview of course, 190-91
  racing, 198-201
  tethered, 105
  training pace, 103
  workout, pre-season to post-competitive season, 131-32
  workout schedule, 123
  workout tips, 132-33
Swim-to-bike transition, 195, 200
System checks, swimming race, 199

Tapering, 189-90
Tendons, 24
  and strength training, 139
Tethered swimming, 105
Thermoregulation, and training, 100-102
Thiamine, 221
Time, and training program, 91
Time trial, percentage of maximum effort for training, 112
Tinley, Scott, 51, 107, 183-84, 188
Tips
  cycling, 134
  running, 134-35
  swimming, 132-33
Tires, bicycle, 73
  flat, 71-72
Top tube length, bicycle, 57
Training, year-round
  altitude, 102

anaerobic threshold, 109-11
basics, 92-93
competitive season, 120-21
cross-training benefits, 93-94
distance, 111-12
explosive speed, 104-5
fuel efficiency of food and fluids, 99-100
intensity, 94-95
and lactic acid, 98-99
month off, 121
parameters, 90-91
personal time trial, 95-96
post-competitive season, 121
pre-competitive season, 119-20
pre-season, 117-18
rest and recovery, 96-98
sprint race, 105-7
and thermoregulation, 100-102
types, 102-4
VO_2 max, 107-9
workout format, 116-17
workout schedules, 122-35
year-round, 88-90
Training types
  energy system used for each, 113
  fiber usage for each, 113
  intensity spectrum for each, 113
  percentage of maximum time trail effort for each, 112
  work/rest ratio for each, 114-15
Transition
  bike-to-run, 195, 203-4
  racing, 194-95
  swim-to-bike, 200
Trapezius, 41, 47, 78
Triathlete
  vs. cyclist, cycling strokes, 63-66
  recommended daily allowance of vitamins and minerals, 220-25
Triathlon
  clubs and organizations, 238-45
  Scott record, 235-36
  training, 13-20
Triceps, 22
  and abdominals, 158-59
  extension, 154-55
  presses, two-arm, and calf raises, 161-63
Triglycerides, 213
Tubular (sew-up) tires, 73
Turns
  cycling course, 192
  running course, 193
  swim course, 191
Twitch, muscle fiber, 25-26
Two-arm triceps presses, and calf raises, 161-63
Two-beat crossover flutter kick, 49
Two-beat flutter kick, 49

U.S. Cycling Federation (USCF), 59, 73
U.S. Triathlon Series, 184
Upper body, cycling, 62
Upright rowing, 148

Vastus lateralis, 58
Vastus medialis, 62-63

Very low density lipoproteins (VLDL), 213
Visor, and thermoregulation, 101
Vitamins
    A, 220
    B_1, 221
    B_2, 221
    B_3, 221
    B_6, 221
    B_{12}, 221
    B complex, 220-21
    C, 222
    D, 222-23
    E, 223
    K, 223
    and minerals in diet, 219-25
VO_2 max (maximum oxygen intake), 24
    training, 107-9

Waikiki Rough Water Swim, 15
Wake, 32
Wake-up time, pre-race, 195-96
Warm-up, 116
    pre-race, 196-97
    stretching, 173
    swimming, 133
Warren, Tom, 16
Water
    for beating heat, 101
    bottle and holder, for cycling, 74
    feel for, 50
    retention, and carbohydrates, 216
    in Scott diet, 228
Weaknesses of opponents, capitalizing on, 189
Weight loss, in heat, 102
Weight training, 136-38
    back exercises with any alternate, 160
    bench press and rowing, 146-49
    determining own program, 138
    exercises, 145-46
    flexibility, 174
    how to get best results, 144-45

isokinetic workout, 171
    leg extensions and hamstring curl, 157
    military press and latissimus pull-down, 150-51
    partner stretches, 175
    quadriceps extension and hamstring curl, 152-53
    rehabilitation, 174
    seasons, 142-43
    and strength, 139-40
    stretching, 173-75
    triceps (dumbbells) and abdominals, 158-59
    triceps extension and biceps curl, 154-56
    two-arm triceps presses and calf raises, 161-71
Whip kick, 199
Wind, cycling in, 70
Wind-load simulators, 134
Windy areas, cycling course, 192
Women
    flexibility, 174
    thermoregulation, 101-2
Workout
    anaerobic threshold training, 110
    cool-down, 116-17
    isokinetic, 171
    progressive sets, 116
    schedules, 122-35
    sets, 116, 128-30
    spring race training, 107
    swim bench, 171
    swimming, year-round, 131-32
    VO_2 max training, 109
    warm-up, 116
Work/rest ratio
    anaerobic threshold training, 110
    explosive speed training, 105
    sprint race training, 106
    for training types, 114-15
    VO_2 max training, 108
World's Toughest Triathlon, 57

Zinc, 225